'This important book brings together key figures in contemporary trans academia, activism and art, to explore the notion of "trans" in all its complexity. It is essential reading for anyone who wants to learn, from those who really know, about trans identities and trans lives. Its key message is one of hope, and at a time when trans people face a renewed backlash against their very existence, this text will nourish them and their allies for the struggle. This fascinating, multidimensional project is a model for the kind of thinking and politics we all need today.'

Alison Phipps, Professor of Gender Studies, University of Sussex, UK

'*The Emergence of Trans* is a much-needed and multi-faceted exploration of how the meaning of trans has taken shape. A range of brilliant essays and artwork plot the breakaway of trans from a history of discourses that position trans as degenerate and pathological to become a term that reflects a myriad of identities and experiences today. It also looks towards the future, to the potential that trans holds to change the world for everyone.'

Jay Stewart, CEO, Gendered Intelligence, UK

'*The Emergence of Trans: Cultures, Politics and Everyday Lives* is a must read for anyone who wants to gain a better understanding of trans life, history, culture and politics. I would recommend it to every healthcare provider's reading list.'

Asa Radix, Director of Research and Education,
Callen-Lorde Community Health Centre, New York, USA

'*The Emergence of Trans* is a compelling read. I was drawn into each chapter and eager to read each author's contribution. The book makes for an insightful and thought-provoking read for all interested in the exploration of identities. With the flowering of trans identities this discussion has never been more relevant than now. This book reflects much of the work we see at cliniQ with people exploring their identity in our therapeutic service, and brings the discussion of what it means to be trans into focus.'

Michelle Ross, Director of cliniQ sexual health and well-being service, London, UK

'Brilliant – captivating razor-sharp theory without pretence or obfuscation, this collection embraces the creative, playful, exploratory dimensions of scholastic enquiry. A vital and cohesive contribution to Transgender Studies within Social Sciences.'

Ben Vincent, Research Fellow, The Open University, UK

The Emergence of Trans

This book represents the vanguard of new work in the rapidly growing arena of Trans Studies. Thematically organised, it brings together studies from an international, cross-disciplinary range of contributors to address a range of questions pertinent to the emergence of trans lives and discourses. Examining the ways in which the emergence of trans challenges, develops and extends understandings of gender and reconfigures everyday lives, it asks how trans lives and discourses articulate and contest with issues of rights, education and popular common-sense. With attention to the question of how trans has shaped and been shaped by new modes of social action and networking, *The Emergence of Trans* also explores what the proliferation of trans representation across multiple media forms and public discourse suggests about the wider cultural moment, and considers the challenges presented for health care, social policy, gender and sexuality theory, and everyday articulations of identity. As such, it will appeal to scholars and students of gender and sexuality studies, as well as activists, professionals and individuals interested in trans lives and discourses.

Ruth Pearce is Research Fellow in the School of Sociology and Social Policy at the University of Leeds, UK. Her research explores issues of inequality, marginalisation, power and political struggle from a trans feminist perspective. She is also the author of *Understanding Trans Health: Discourse, Power and Possibility*.

Igi Moon is Associate Fellow in Sociology at the University of Warwick, UK. They have written on therapy, sexuality and gender in *Feeling Queer: Queer Feelings: Radical Approaches to Counselling Sex, Sexuality and Gender* and are editor of *Counselling Ideologies: Queer Challenges to Heteronormativity*. They represent the British Psychological Society as Chair of the Coalition Against Conversion Therapy.

Kat Gupta is Lecturer in English Language and Linguistics at the University of Roehampton, UK. Their research uses corpus linguistics and critical discourse analysis to explore representation, marginalisation and power, with a particular focus on LGBT, queer and gender issues.

Deborah Lynn Steinberg was Professor of Gender, Culture and Popular Media in the Department of Sociology at the University of Warwick, UK. She wrote widely on gender and sexuality politics, with books including *Border Patrols: Policing the Boundaries of Heterosexuality* (with D. Epstein and R. Johnson) and *Bodies in Glass: Genetics, Eugenics, Embryo Ethics* as well as on politics and public mourning in *Mourning Diana: Nation, Culture and the Performance of Grief* (with A. Kear) and *Blairism and the War of Persuasion* (with R. Johnson). She was also the author of *Genes and the Bio-imaginary*.

Gender, Bodies and Transformation

Series editor: Meredith Jones

University of Technology, Sydney, Australia

This series explores the intersection of two key themes in relation to scholarship on bodies: gender and transformation. Bodies are gendered via biology, culture, medicine and society, such that gender, so deeply and intimately connected to identity, is a crucial part of any thorough analysis of the body. At the same time, bodies are – and have always been – sites of transformation, whether through 'natural' processes such as pregnancy, illness and ageing, or the more eye-catching, 'unnatural' transformations of cosmetic surgery, violence, extreme bodybuilding or dieting, cross-species transplantation, elective amputation or tattooing.

Interdisciplinary in scope and welcoming work from a range of approaches, including cultural and media studies, sociology, gender studies, feminist theory, phenomenology, queer studies and ethnography, Gender, Bodies and Transformation publishes scholarly examinations of contemporary cultural changes that are relevant to both gender and the transformation of bodies, whether in single bodies or between bodies.

Also in the series:

Fat Sex
New Directions in Theory and Activism
Edited by Helen Hester and Caroline Walters

Transgender Architectonics
The Shape of Change in Modernist Space
Lucas Crawford

Out Online
Trans Self-Representation and Community Building on YouTube
Tobias Raun

The Emergence of Trans
Cultures, Politics and Everyday Lives
Edited by Ruth Pearce, Igi Moon, Kat Gupta and Deborah Lynn Steinberg

For more information about this series, please visit: www.routledge.com/ Gender-Bodies-and-Transformation/book-series/ASHSER1393

The Emergence of Trans

Cultures, Politics and Everyday Lives

Edited by Ruth Pearce,
Igi Moon, Kat Gupta and
Deborah Lynn Steinberg

Routledge
Taylor & Francis Group

LONDON AND NEW YORK

First published 2020
by Routledge
2 Park Square, Milton Park, Abingdon, Oxon OX14 4RN

and by Routledge
52 Vanderbilt Avenue, New York, NY 10017

Routledge is an imprint of the Taylor & Francis Group, an informa business

© 2020 selection and editorial matter, Ruth Pearce, Igi Moon, Kat Gupta
and Deborah Lynn Steinberg; individual chapters, the contributors

British Library Cataloguing-in-Publication Data
A catalogue record for this book is available from the British Library

Library of Congress Cataloging-in-Publication Data
Names: Pearce, Ruth (Of University of Leeds. School of Sociology and
    Social Policy) | Moon, Igi, 1959– editor. | Gupta, Kat, 1984– editor.
Title: The emergence of trans : cultures, politics and everyday lives / edited
    by Ruth Pearce, Igi Moon, Kat Gupta and Deborah Lynn Steinberg.
Description: 1 Edition. | New York : Routledge, 2019. | Series: Gender,
    bodies and transformation | Includes bibliographical references and index.
Identifiers: LCCN 2019015154 (print) | LCCN 2019017296 (ebook) |
    ISBN 9781315145815 (ebk) | ISBN 9781138504097 (hbk) |
    ISBN 9781138504103 (pbk)
Subjects: LCSH: Transgender people—Identity. | Transgender people—
    Social aspects. | Interpersonal relations.
Classification: LCC HQ77.9 (ebook) | LCC HQ77.9 .E574 2019 (print) |
    DDC 306.76/8—dc23
LC record available at https://lccn.loc.gov/2019015154

ISBN: 978-1-138-50409-7 (hbk)
ISBN: 978-1-138-50410-3 (pbk)
ISBN: 978-1-315-14581-5 (ebk)

Typeset in Bembo
by Apex CoVantage, LLC

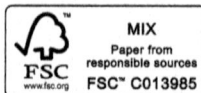

MIX
Paper from
responsible sources
FSC
www.fsc.org   FSC™ C013985

Printed in the United Kingdom
by Henry Ling Limited

To all who struggle to emerge

Contents

Contributor biographies

Clare Bartholomaeus is Research Associate in the College of Education, Psychology and Social Work at Flinders University. Her research interests include gender, diversity and children/young people. She is co-author of the book *Transgender People and Education* with Damien W. Riggs (Palgrave Macmillan, 2017).

Clare Beckett-Wrighton is Senior Lecturer in the faculty of Social Sciences at the University of Bradford. Her research interests consider the lived experience of processes of change in identity within heteronormative society. She is also a member of the Board of Trustees for the Bradford LGBT Strategic Partnership.

Mijke van der Drift is Associate Lecturer at Goldsmiths, University of London, and Tutor at the Royal Academy of Art, The Hague, and Sandberg Institute, Amsterdam. Mijke studied Philosophy and Cultural Studies in Amsterdam, Berlin and London, and obtained a PhD from Goldsmiths, University of London. Mijke works internationally on Radical Transfeminism, Ethics, Philosophy, Gender Studies and Art.

Bróna Nic Giolla Easpaig is a Research Fellow with NHMRC Centre for Research Excellence in Implementation Science in Oncology, where she designs and leads the qualitative studies in health services research.

Rachael Fox is Senior Lecturer at Charles Sturt University, NSW Australia. She is a Member of the Australian Psychological Society (MAPS); an Academic Member of the College of Community Psychology and Board Member of the College; a Chartered Member (CPsychol) of the British Psychological Society; a Member of the European Community Psychology Association (ECPA); and a Member of the Society for Community Research and Action (SCRA) (Division 27 of the American Psychological Association). Originally from the UK, Rachael completed her studies at the University of Stirling (BSc[Hons], PhD in Community Psychology). Her work involves young people and social exclusion, engaging in qualitative research involving: migrant children and families; young LGBTIQ people; young carers; evaluating health and mental health service provision; and student experiences of higher education. She works in methodologies around critical theory, ethnography, discursive approaches and participatory action research.

Kat Gupta is a lecturer in English Language and Linguistics at the University of Roehampton. Their research interests include corpus linguistics, critical discourse analysis, digital humanities, gender, queer theory and issues of ideology and power. Kat's recent monograph, *Representation of the British Suffrage Movement* (2016, Bloomsbury) examines the media representation of the suffrage movement in *The Times* 1908–1914, with particular focus on the ideologically convenient conflation of distinct suffrage identities. Their current research focuses on desire, sex and bodies in online erotica.

Julian Honkasalo is a Kone Foundation postdoctoral researcher in gender studies at the University of Helsinki. He holds a PhD in gender studies (University of Helsinki) and an MA in political science (The New School for Social Research). Honkasalo's current research project focuses on the historical connection between eugenics and trans sterilization legislation.

Rhi Humphrey would describe themselves as an activist before describing themselves an academic. They have been involved in LGBT/I, queer, trans, disability and student activism for more than 10 years. Rhi is currently attempting to be an activist academic while a student at the University of Glasgow because research changes the world. Their research addresses trans and intersex activism and activist relationships in the UK, Malta and Australia. Their research interests include activism, gender studies, trans studies, intersex studies, queer theory and sexuality. They have published on queer methodologies for community-based research; barriers to education faced by trans students; gender-based harassment in online gaming communities; and the ways trans media representation affects trans audiences.

Natacha Kennedy is a lecturer in education at Goldsmiths College, University of London. She has known she was trans since she was about 5 years old and has engaged in activism to improve the position of trans people on local as well as international levels. A former contributor to *The Guardian* newspaper on trans issues, her main academic interest is cisgenderism and learning processes with reference to trans people.

Ellen Lamont is Assistant Professor of Sociology at Appalachian State University. Her current research examines how gender and sexuality shape people's hook-up, dating, and relationship behaviors and narratives. She has published articles in *Gender & Society*, *Men & Masculinities*, and *Sociological Forum*. She has a forthcoming book on gender and courtship titled *The Mating Game: How Gender Still Shapes How We Date* (University of California Press).

Kirsty Lohman is Leverhulme Early Career Fellow at the University of Surrey. Her research interests include musical/cultural participation, gender, feminism and political engagement. Her PhD thesis was an ethnography of the punk scene in the Netherlands, focusing particularly on political and lifestyle choices of participants as they negotiate ageing as a punk. She plays in the Midlands-based punk bands Not Right, Die Wrecked and Fear & Slothing, and helps to run Coventry's punk night Revolt.

Igi Moon's work focuses on psychotherapy, gender, sexuality and emotion. It is an interesting combination! They have published two edited books before this one, *Counselling Ideologies: Queer Challenges to Heteronormativity* (Routledge, 2010) and *Feeling Queer or Queer Feelings: Radical Approaches to Counselling Sex, Sexualities and Gender* (Routledge, 2007). They are presently working on developing a trans-therapeutic approach to working with trans and non-binary people and establishing a therapy clinic at Roehampton University. Igi is a Chartered Psychologist and Fellow of the British Psychological Society (BPS). They represent the BPS on a number of committees and they are presently involved with extending the Memorandum of Understanding against Conversion Therapies to protect trans and non-binary people. They are also an Associate Fellow at Warwick University in the Department of Sociology. Most of all they like playing with ideas. And the cat!

Ruth Pearce is Research Fellow in the School of Sociology and Social Policy at the University of Leeds. Her research explores issues of inequality, marginalisation, power and political struggle from a trans feminist perspective. Ruth's monograph, *Understanding Trans Health: Discourse, Power and Possibility*, was published by Policy Press in 2018. She was bassist, vocalist and lyricist in the trans punk band Not Right, and currently performs in Dispute Settlement Mechanism. Ruth writes about her work and interests at http://ruthpearce.net.

Eric Plemons is Associate Professor in the School of Anthropology at the University of Arizona, USA. As a medical anthropologist, Dr. Plemons's research focuses on the politics and practice of transgender medicine and surgery. His first book, *The Look of a Woman: Facial Feminization Surgery and the Aims of Trans- Medicine* (Duke University Press, 2017) was awarded the 2017 Ruth Benedict Prize for outstanding monograph by the Association for Queer Anthropology. His current research examines the ways that US institutions are responding to a growing demand for transgender healthcare.

Damien W. Riggs is Professor in social work at Flinders University, and an Australian Research Council Future Fellow. He is the author of more than 200 publications in the fields of gender, family and mental health, including *Working with Transgender Young People and their Families: A Critical Developmental Approach* (Palgrave, 2019). Damien also works as a psychotherapist in private practice, specialising in working with transgender children.

stef m. shuster is Assistant Professor in Lyman Briggs College and the Department of Sociology at Michigan State University. Their research examines the social construction of 'evidence' in three domains, including medicine, social movements and the construction of knowledge. Their research has recently appeared in the *Journal of Health and Social Behavior, Gender & Society* and the *Social Psychology Quarterly*.

Deborah Lynn Steinberg was Professor of Gender, Culture and Media Studies in the Department of Sociology at the University of Warwick, UK. Her research interests included: cultures of science; gender and sexuality studies; media and cultural theory; and mourning and politics. Her most recent book, *Genes and the Bioimaginary: Science, Spectacle, Culture*, was published by Ashgate in 2015. Previous books include: *Bodies in Glass: Genetics, Eugenics, Embryo Ethics* (1997); *Made to Order: The Myth of Reproductive and Genetic Progress* (1987); *Border Patrols: Policing the Boundaries of Heterosexuality* (1989); *Mourning Diana: Nation, Culture and the Performance of Grief* (1999); and *Blairism and the War of Persuasion: Labour's Passive Revolution* (2004).

Rev. Elena Rose Vera, a.k.a. "Little Light," is a Filipina-Ashkenazi trans woman originally from rural Oregon. A founding member of the Speak! Radical Women of Color Media Collective, trustee of San Francisco's historic Church for the Fellowship of All Peoples, longtime co-curator of the Girl Talk: A Trans and Cis Woman Dialogue performance series, and co-editor of the acclaimed anthology *Queer and Trans Artists of Color Volume 2*, she has distinguished herself as a political and theological writer with a focus on the intersections between colonial history, race, gender, and queer liberation. Elena currently serves as Executive Director of Trans Lifeline (www.translifeline.org).

Rami Yasir is a poet, illustrator and workshop facilitator of Palestinian-Jordanian and Sudanese descent. Their work explores home, race, gender, sexuality and exploring oneself through art. Follow them on Twitter @YasirRami for general information, or @RealLifeLombax for poetry.

Acknowledgements

The editors thank the Economic and Social Research Council (ESRC) for funding the seminar series that inspired this book. We are also enormously grateful to the authors and artists who contributed their work to this book, the scholars who provided anonymous peer review, and the trans and queer creators, activists, writers and possibility models who continue to inspire us.

Introduction

The many-voiced monster: collective determination and the emergence of trans

Ruth Pearce, Kat Gupta and Igi Moon

> What I say may be in a language incomprehensible, but there is a time for that, and it is right now, because this is a monster's creed.
>
> – Elena Rose

This book is intended as a statement of hope, and of possibility. It is about the context and consequences of trans emergence. It is about how 'trans' becomes, and how we 'become' trans. It is about how trans people are changed by the experience of emergence, and how trans emergence might change our worlds.

The authors who have contributed to this book explore notions of trans emergence from many different angles, encompassing medical discourse and practice, art and music, popular media, research praxis, interpersonal relationships and nonnormative ethics. These are all stories about how trans becomes *possible*, and how, to echo Laverne Cox (2017), we might create trans *possibility models*: examples of liveable trans lives in all their complexity and myriad forms. As editors, we are particularly interested in the consequences of 'transgender' and latterly, the stand-alone 'trans': concepts which cannot easily be conceptualised, categories that defy the categorical.

Sex and gender diversity exists and has always existed across human societies (Feinberg, 1997; Snorton, 2017; Chiang, Henry and Leung, 2018). However, over the past three centuries the 'great' white men of Western medicine have engaged in two interrelated tasks: to clearly define sex (and latterly, gender) along binary lines, and to account for humanity's failure to conform to these categories by pathologising deviation as disorder, through processes of differential categorisation and diagnosis (Stryker, 2008; Tosh, 2016). None of the resulting sexological and psychiatric models for gender difference have truly passed the test of time, for the languages of androgyny, gynandry, defemination, uranismus, inversion, transvestism, transsexualism, gender identity disorder, gender dysphoria and gender incongruence (to name but a few) all fail to capture the complications, the fuzzy boundaries and open borders of gendered experience and socio-political affiliation.[1]

'Trans', like 'queer', embraces this incomprehensibility, reconfiguring notions of community, body, origin, outcome. It is a difficult concept, and activists, support groups and service providers all continue to grapple with the practical consequences and radical productive potential of this difficulty. What 'trans' offers is an overarching but open-ended means to describe bodies, identities and experiences that defy normative notions of sexual possibility, encompassing (potentially) all individuals whose gender identity and/or physical body differs in any way from that they were assigned at birth.

Visibility and vulnerability

Normative discourses of gender in many societies hold that there are two and only two sexes, that these two sexes exist in binary opposition, that certain ('gendered') expectations relating to dress, behaviour and social role align with these sexes, and that there is no room for movement within or between sexes or gendered expectations. Notions of trans or transgender possibility stand in opposition to these discourses. Therefore, while being or becoming trans is a matter of self-emergence or self-creation in a repudiation of social norms, there is also something very important that is shared between people. While trans bodies, identities and experiences vary enormously, the very existence of trans discourses, stories of *possibility* and trans ways of being provide a sense of collective belonging as well as a site of continual co-creation. To return to Cox's notion of a possibility *model*: through encountering discourses of trans possibility, through seeing other trans people exist and move through the world, an individual might come to understand that this might indeed be a way to make sense of their own experiences. Trans self-creation is therefore something that almost inevitably happens in community: through the more closely bound environs of local support groups or internet discussion sites, and through the wider 'imagined community' of trans being (Whittle, 1998; Stryker, 2006).

We write this introduction at a time in which trans people have been both hyper-visible and hyper-vulnerable in many parts of the world; as Nat Raha (2017: 633) observes, this is a moment in which 'the position of transgender people is marked by extreme contradiction'. The 2010s have been heralded as a time of unprecedented social progress for trans people in many Anglophone media outlets, with American magazine *Time* famously declaring a 'trans tipping point' in 2014. However, this obscures a longer history of trans people as subjects of spectacular media interest: for example, Christine Jorgensen's transition was an international sensation in 1952, April Ashley was outed by the *Sunday People* in 1964 and an image of Thomas Beatie's pregnancy received similar mass attention in 2008 (as 'the pregnant man'). Nevertheless, the last few years have seen an enormous *increase* in the number of trans public figures: actors, politicians, writers, journalists, musicians, YouTube stars, religious leaders and so on. This change reflects both a dramatic (albeit predictable) rise in the visible trans population, and a growing public acknowledgement of trans possibility, as seen, for example, in the increasing everyday use of terminology such as 'trans', 'non-binary' and 'cis'. Such visibility arguably creates a greater range of trans possibility models, thereby turbo-charging the emergence of trans as more people come out or publicly disclose their trans status (which in turn creates a wider range of possibility models).

At the same time, trans people are more visible to those who feel threatened by our emergence, and those who might wish us harm. Consequently, the 2010s have also seen the spread of anti-trans ideologies coached in the language of religious conservatism and/or radical feminism, along with the drafting of laws that would ban trans people from public spaces associated with our gender, such as toilets and changing rooms (Aizura, 2017). In the resulting public debates that proliferate across mainstream and social media platforms, university classrooms and public meetings, trans people are frequently portrayed as *monstrous*: a freakish threat to children, to lesbians, to women, to the very notion of womanhood and/or to the fixity of sex itself. Trans women and girls in particular are portrayed as potential sexual predators, or otherwise as some kind of Trojan Horse whose access to women's spaces will enable predatory men to similarly enter these spaces by claiming that they are women. Trans men and boys are more typically regarded as damaged or mutilated individuals who have rejected 'natural' 'female' bodies at the cost of their reproductive capacity. Non-binary people are often portrayed as fantasists seeking to reject the very 'reality' of binary sex and gender. As Anthony Clair Wagner (2015: 341–342) observes in their account of abjected bodies, '[t]he reaction that is provoked by this fear-mongering is one of violent aggression – monsters can be beaten, abused, cast out, and even killed with impunity'.

These arguments have a long history. They are often associated to 'trans-exclusionary' strands of radical feminism dating back to the 1970s, exemplified by works such as Janice Raymond's 1997 book, *The Transsexual Empire: The Making of the She-Male*, and Mary Daly's 1978 book section, 'Boundary Violation and the Transsexual Phenomenon' (in *Gyn/ecology*), which 'characterizes transsexuals as the agents of a "necrophilic invasion" of female space' (Stryker, 1994: 238). However, they are also part of a wider pattern in which queer and coloured bodies are othered within binaristic white European and colonial societies, as Christan Williams (2016) recounts in her account of black and gay bathroom panics in the United States, and Nigel Patel (2017) observes in their analysis of sexual and racial segregation in South Africa and Western Europe from the seventeenth century to the present day.

What has changed is the aforementioned fact that specifically *trans* lives and bodies are exceptionally visible in white Western and colonial societies at this moment in history. This is the context in which US President Donald Trump has proposed to strip trans people of all legal recognition through eliminating references to gender, creating a legal definition of sex that incorporates only female and male categories and cannot be changed from the sex assigned at birth. Similarly, Brazilian President Jair Bolsonaro signed an executive order removing LGBTQ rights from the agenda of the Human Rights ministry. 'Girls will be princesses and boys will be princes', incoming Human Rights Minister Damares Alves explained, 'there will be no more ideological indoctrination of children and teenagers in Brazil' (Walker, 2019).

Visibility, therefore, can have significant drawbacks. The emergence of 'trans' as language of possibility and mode of organising has also worked to create a trans-aware culture against which a backlash might emerge, an issue explored by Natacha Kennedy in Chapter 3. Rather than simply having negative repercussions, the moment of visibility itself can also be negative: this topic is examined by Kat Gupta in Chapter 9, with the example of how a trans woman was represented in the UK media both before and after her untimely death. However, it is also important to acknowledge that some trans people are more visible than others, *and* that different trans people have benefited differently (or not at all) from the growth in trans awareness. In his introduction to a recent special section on 'trans recognition' in the journal *South Atlantic Quarterly*, Aren Aizura (2017: 607) argues that recognition does not entail justice: for example, 'trans-inclusive' jails do not end incarceration, and the inclusion of trans people in the US military 'literally deploys trans and gender nonconforming people in the service of "counterterrorist" colonial wars'. Raha (2017: 633) expands on these arguments, noting that the fresh push for trans legal rights following the 2014 'tipping point' fails to address the ongoing 'stratification of livable trans and gender-nonconforming lives along the lines of race, class, gender, dis/ability, nationality, and migration status'. Liberal approaches to trans 'equality' are therefore insufficient, as they fail to account for the wider socio-economic structures which result in some trans people being made (considerably) more vulnerable (more monstrous?) than others, *especially* at a time of heightened visibility.

If trans lives are only barely liveable, what possibilities might be offered through alternatives to mainstream media discourses of 'visibility' and a liberal politics focused on abstract freedoms and legal rights? In recent years, we have been inspired by numerous responses to this question from trans communities and activists, which range from an emergent *radical transfeminism* identified by Raha (2017), to the creation of new services run by trans people, for trans people (prominent examples include the transgender health program at New York's Callen-Lorde Community Health Centre, and UK trans sexual health services cliniQ and Clinic T). These are, importantly, material interventions that aim to address the deep and systemic inequalities faced by trans people, especially trans women of colour and others who experience multiple intersecting forms of marginalisation. However, we believe that it is important also to attend to the psychic and the spiritual, and it is in this spirit that we turn also to the *possibilities* of trans monstrosity.

Monstrosity

If trans people are to be monsters – our lives and bodies a source of disgust and shame, our difference the cause of fear and anger – then maybe we can reclaim this monstrosity as a source of possibility and determination. Turning shame to strength is an alchemy of the marginalised. We can admire and find pride in our lives and bodies, embracing our very aberration as a source of bravery and love. This is a matter of *transfiguring* values as we transform monstrosity: holding on joyously and stubbornly to the power that comes with strangeness and difference.

It is not just those who fear or hate trans people who exploit the language of monstrosity; so, too, have many trans writers and theorists before us. In her essay *My Words to Victor Frankenstein Above the Village of Chamounix*, Susan Stryker observes that this represents something more than reclamation, speaking to the radical context and possibilities of trans emergence:

> 'Monster' is derived from the Latin noun *monstrum*, 'divine portent', itself formed from the root of the verb *monere*, 'to warn'. It came to refer to living things of anomalous shape or structure, or to fabulous creatures like the sphinx who were composed of strikingly incongruous parts, because the ancients considered the appearance of such things to be a sign of some impending supernatural event. Monsters, like angels, functioned as messengers and heralds of the extraordinary. They served to announce impending revelation, saying, in effect, 'Pay attention: something of profound importance is happening'.
>
> (Stryker, 1994: 240)

This is not a straightforward task. Anson Koch-Rein draws our attention to the risks that attend discourses of monstrosity:

> In a world where the monster is circulating as metaphoric violence against trans★ people, reclaiming such a figure faces the difficulty of formulating resistance in the same metaphorical language as the transphobic attack. Moreover, a figure of difference, the monster appears in racist, ableist, homophobic, and sexist discourses, making its use especially fraught.
>
> (Koch-Rein, 2014: 134–135)

Nevertheless, Koch-Rein (2014: 135) ultimately echoes Stryker's attachment to the ambiguous power implicated in open monstrosity: 'It is precisely the monster's ambivalent ability to speak to oppression and negative affect that appeals to trans★people reclaiming the monster for their own voices'. Hence, monstrosity is always lurking just around the corner within the growing world of trans arts and culture.

In their *Dance with the Dead Cock* series, Anthony Clair Wagner exhibits the bold, androgynous 'hybrid' trans body of a youth standing nude in a misty meadow, one that openly challenges the viewer through simultaneous vulnerability and provocation, manifesting the artist's 'allegiance with nature' (Wagner, 2015: 342). Cat Fitzpatrick and Casey Plett (2017) feature numerous stories of monstrosity in their trans science fiction and fantasy compilation *Meanwhile, Elsewhere*. Depictions range from the peacefully communal, agendered and highly sexualised terraforming bioconstruct Inri in M Téllez's (2017) parable 'Heat Death of Western Human Arrogance', to the undead Beryl of Bridget

Liang's (2017) slashfest 'Delicate Bodies', who violently exacts vengeance on those who always viewed her fat, brown trans body as debased even before she contracted a zombie virus. Trans artist and philosopher Natalie Wynn frequently refers to herself as a 'degenerate' on her YouTube channel *Contrapoints*, utilising unnatural lighting and increasingly dramatic costumes and characters to powerful effect in videos that by turns explore trans culture, interrogate left-wing politics and challenge the ideology and aesthetics of the alt-right. In 'Pronouns', Wynn (2018) introduces her discussion in the devilish form of Lenora LaVey, a drag queen dressed entirely in red and black. Wynn *knows* that she is abject, and that her complex analysis of debates around trans people's gendered identities and respectful pronoun use will be portrayed as monstrous regardless (even because) of the nuance of her argument; she plays knowingly with this knowledge. As the outrageous LaVey, a caprine skull sits atop her head amidst dramatic feathers; tall candles pierce the darkness behind her. 'Death!' she announces as the video begins. 'Death, death, death, death. It's the only thing that everyone fears, and the only thing that gets me off'.

This multiplicity of voices is important, for we do not have to be the same monster; while many of us may find ways to embrace our strangeness and aberration, monsters come in different shapes with different configurations of skin and teeth. Rather than remaining alone, set apart from society and forced into living cruel, estranged lives, our challenge is to identify and treasure both our commonalities and differences: to become one of many. In doing so, we can imagine different modes of being, different ways to live, different routes and pathways, different spaces in which to thrive. In the monstrous, we create space; our territory is an expanse of possibility. We are at our *most* powerful as a community of monsters, speaking collectively in many voices. As isolated individuals, we may be mocked or shunned, abused or beaten for our embodied transgressions. Together, we have the strength to queer categories, break binaries, create entirely new discursive and material realities: a point aptly illustrated in Rami Yasir's visual allegory 'Make Yourself' (Chapter 11). We have uncanny abilities: to shapeshift, to disappear and reappear, to travel eccentrically through time (Barker and Scheele, 2019), to appear as simultaneously young and old, to dance on linearities until they shatter.

Medical models for the management of trans bodies and lives have historically attempted to remove our fangs, containing and constraining our monstrosity. As Julian Honkasalo describes in Chapter 1, 'the twentieth-century discourse on medical treatment [centred] a stabilizing of the binary gender system as well as aesthetic ideals of the psyche and body'. Yet we are at our most powerful when we embrace our very differences and revel in our queerness. Reclaiming monstrosity as strength and courage and resilience and joy is a challenge for us and our communities, a demand to make of ourselves. This also challenges others: it demands that they recognise us as powerful, self-realised, creative, independent beings. As monsters, we can snarl in the face of pity, laugh a sharp-fanged laugh in the face of those who would see us as tragic figures trying desperately to ape the shape of a cisgender life.

Affect is central to the genealogy of monsters. To recognise trans as monstrous is to recognise the complex interplay of feelings: not simply the fear we may inspire in others, the shame and confusion this may bring ourselves, but also the hatred and joy of becoming, the ferocity and tenderness of community care and collective movement. The trans movement, the trans moment, is a movement and moment of feeling, of *trans-emotionality*, in which conversations across difference ensure that the interiority of affect is no longer tied to normative frameworks for how 'girls' and 'boys', 'women' and 'men' are *supposed* to feel (Green, 2017; Moon, 2019). Trans feelings are monstrous because they have so often and for so long existed beyond the capacity of language and identifiable emotion, in a context where there is no acceptable way to make sense of them. With the emergence of trans, we are also seeing the emergence of a more articulate monster, the monster who speaks back. Through the languages of inversion and transvestism and transsexualism and transgender and trans and genderqueer and non-binary we have gradually expanded the scope of possibility, feeling our way towards being able to better account for our relation to the internal and external alike.

What is being demanded in this utterance? Trans people are asked to account for feelings that simply cannot be described through the language of cis emotionality. Phrases such as 'wrong body', 'gender identity' and 'brain gender' have perhaps represented a step forward, but remain woefully inadequate (Lester, 2017). Terms such as 'cis' and even 'non-binary' help us to account for relations of relative power and (in)equality between those who have a particular range of 'trans' experiences and those who do not, but also retain an investment in binary thinking and absolute categories (Enke, 2012). With the emergence of trans, we have an opportunity to move beyond the 'argh', the monstrous snarl of warning or wail of inarticulate pain, and instead forge an epistemology of monsters, a way of knowing and talking that fundamentally shifts our understanding of human experience. The epigram that opens this chapter cites Elena Rose's underground classic *the seam of skin and scales*, reproduced in Chapter 4. Rose's work was a key influence on our thinking here, particularly her call to 'look the monstrous in the eye [...] to say that we are beautiful in our fierceness, and that we are our own'.

What happens when a monster begins to speak for itself? The potential impact on politics, culture, media, health care and the production of knowledge itself is immeasurable. If trans ideas and trans people's experiences challenge understandings of what is and might be, they threaten the current order of things as much as they promise the possibility of renewal and change. If trans languages challenge our fundamental understandings of sex and gender, how then might we account for both patriarchal structures and feminist resistance in a society built on the principle of binary segregation from birth? If trans patients challenge the logic of pathologisation, what consequences might there be for a medical system that rewards particular forms of diagnostic expertise with financial gain and prestige? It is no wonder that we face an enormous backlash from those who would see us silenced, those who wish to halt or reverse the profound changes in understanding and possibility heralded by the emergence of trans.

This book speaks in many voices. It is itself a many-headed, many-voiced monster, bringing the disciplines of anthropology, linguistics, gender studies, history, medicine, philosophy, psychology and sociology into conversation, speaking to and from artistic and activist perspectives as well as academic. In turn, it is one among many, a small part of the rapidly growing field of transgender studies, which is itself a cause and effect of the emergence of trans. These voices, multiple and powerful and inspiring as they are, cannot contain the scope of trans possibility; but they offer important food for thought.

Nourishment

This book developed out of a need to feel seen, understood and recognised, within and beyond the academy where we work. As trans people, we were (are – will be?) often starved of connection and company: lone monsters, surviving in sometimes hostile environments. We found nourishment in community.

For us, nourishment is physical, mental, social, spiritual. It crosses the bodily boundaries and the categorical distinctions of inside/outside, helping us to embrace the healing, care and learning that are vital for our continued (collective) existence. At the first, experimental seminars we collaboratively organised at the University of Warwick – *Spotlight on: Asexuality* (2011, with Mark Carrigan) and *Spotlight on: Genderqueer* (2013, with Robin Gurney) – we very literally found nourishment in a shared lunch. In the absence of formal grant funding for these events, we welcomed people's generosity in bringing and sharing food, carefully labelled with ingredients and allergens so that no attendee would go hungry or suffer the effects of food hostile to their body.[2] This felt important at events which sought to utilise the resources of the academy (in terms of space, time, technology) to open up conversations that were inclusive of asexual, genderqueer and trans people from all walks of life. In both instances the space we co-created sustained our bodies as it fed our minds, and gave succour to our hunger for community.

The first of these events informed the writing of a successful funding bid for the 2012–2014 ESRC-sponsored seminar series, *Retheorising Gender and Sexuality: The Emergence of Trans*, held once again at the University of Warwick. Across four events the seminar series offered a site for nuance and complexity, a vital and enriching space that enabled us to reach beyond 'trans 101' discussions to examine deeper questions about gender, sex and sexuality, therapy, media, art, culture. Again, this was a matter of nourishment, a sharing of delectable ideas, experiences and research findings among activists, artists, health-care practitioners and therapists as well as academics. At these events, we recognised the importance of drawing links between the discursive and the material, a praxis which extended beyond our theoretical analyses and into our organising. Trans people face enormous economic inequalities (Government Equalities Office, 2018), so we spent the grant money on food and speaker costs, and provided free places at the event. We also livestreamed some of the sessions, and with the help of Alex Drummond filmed many of the talks so those who could not attend were still able to follow the event.[3] You can read more about some of the ideas and questions that emerged in the closing chapter of this book, 'A genealogy of genealogies'.

For the final event, our late colleague Deborah Lynn Steinberg – who played a key role in shaping the funding bid and was a co-editor of this volume – decided that we should host a two-day residential conference. We provided free accommodation as well as meals for all attendees, and travel bursaries for trans people who might otherwise have been unable to attend. This was a redistribution of academic wealth in the service of trans community. We have fond memories of deep conversations stretching into the night, our minds and bodies well nourished after a long day, but our souls still hungry for connection.

Writing this book, too, has an embodied act of nourishment – *transfiguring* discourse at a time of frustration, fear and despair. At times we could not see hope around us, and so we wrote our own hope and sought to support contributors who offered to do the same. Through this creativity and community the contributors to this book have created a communion of monsters to sustain us during difficult times. This was a communion that grew out of the seminar series, with numerous authors revisiting or building on ideas discussed at those events, and others joining us in response to a new call for papers.

It is therefore fitting that this introduction in turn grew out of a day of nourishment, of ideas bounced around by Igi, Ruth and Kat in a kitchen in south-west London. As the smell of frying onion, garlic and ginger wafted into the air, we began to excitedly explore the importance of feeding both mind and body, how to meet our physical and intellectual needs, and our social need for togetherness. With Kat cooking a delicious vegetable curry our hunger and anticipation grew, and we began to think (with a nod to Margrit Shildrick, 1997) about leaky bodies, bodies without clear edges; not simply through salivating over appetising ideas and foods, but also in terms of the porousness of thoughts in thinking and writing together. Here was embodied togetherness in collective nourishment, our voices melding and merging into the emergence of this piece of writing. There is porousness too in writing together/apart: this sentence is written by Ruth, working with aromatic notes from that sumptuous kitchen, itself a leaky space as smells and tastes lingered in the living room next door and again many days later, in the fragrance of our excited annotations. Then here and there, a choice phrase from Igi, a sentence distinctly from Kat; and other paragraphs whose origins can only ever be attributed to the collective voice of the many-headed monster.

In that kitchen and at that moment of heightened affect, Ruth was reminded too of the deeply embodied experience of writing with Deborah. Our memories of the *Emergence of Trans* seminar series come with a bittersweet flavour, for it was then too that Deborah received a cancer diagnosis. By the last event she was clearly weakened and had to leave early on the second day, although not before sharing some wise words and a deeply felt hug. The illness took a terrible toll on Deborah's body, but her mind reminded razor sharp until her final days. In July, August, September of 2016, as the summer drew to a close and the chill of autumn crept into the air, Ruth visited Deborah's house in Birmingham to draft the proposal for this book. By this time, Deborah was betrayed by her hands, too rigid and painful to type. So she dictated, fluent theory flying from her lips as Ruth sat at the computer, frantically fighting to keep up, before responding with new thoughts and formulations. In these moments, we were each other's voices. Speaking together.

Of course, these visits were also an occasion for eating, a sharing of food at one with the sharing of ideas. On one occasion in the garden, sat with lunch after a writing session with our loyal sentinel, Lola the chihuahua, Deborah explored her own gender deviance. Of this book's editorial team, Deborah did not consider herself trans; but nor too did she necessarily consider herself cis, describing herself instead as embodying a 'lesbian gender'. Within trans spaces this kind of position is often perceived and portrayed as a denial of privilege, but perhaps something more profound is going on. For all its fluid boundaries and monstrous possibility, even the stand-alone 'trans', as a linguistic technology of the here and now, cannot necessarily provide succour for all gender outlaws. To truly escape binary thinking and embrace the possibility of the monstrous, we must remember that trans language is but an ingredient in the recipe of gender liberation, not a requirement that calls for adherence to necessary identity categories.

As Deborah was dying in the months that followed, she explained that her body felt monstrous in a different way, aching and estranged on the brink of departure. She kept a blog, reflecting on her feelings and fears until she could write no more. She passed away in February 2017, just days after we were offered the contract for this book. We are still mourning her loss, but her contributions, the generosity of ideas and deeds, remain and continue to nourish us.

Whatever happens to the body of a person or text, the contribution to thinking and the expansion of human possibility remain. Like Deborah, we are absolutely determined to leave thoughts that others might continue to work with, meanings and perspectives that may continue to grow and evolve into beautiful, monstrous new forms with time. The body of knowledge mutates beyond the corporeal. The material body may perish but the ideas carry on. Trans goes beyond itself: while Deborah herself did not identify as trans, she was without a doubt a part of our community.

Collective determination

When we speak as the many-headed monster, we do so collectively even if it is in multiple voices, tones and registers. This is not a matter of necessarily being in perfect harmony with one another, but rather a matter of desire in getting to the root of things, an interest in the radical potential of the emergence of trans.

This book was not a single enterprise: rather, its emergence is both the sum of numerous individual projects and one part a wider mutable form, a project that has mutated. *The Emergence of Trans* has shifted shape from seminar series to journal special issue to book, with multiple points of origin and a shifting cast of participants and contributors.

It has been a long, complex journey, fraught with difficulty and loss, but one we are grateful to have set out on. We are delighted to share this book with the world as the latest (final?) iteration of a project begun many years ago, and we hope that it will help to nourish you in turn for many years to come.

Notes

1   The failure of clinical science to account for trans experience is powerfully illustrated in Zowie Davy and Michael Toze's systematic review of literature on the DSM-5 diagnosis 'gender dysphoria'. The authors conclude that approaches to employing 'gender dysphoria' are highly inconsistent: 'Frequent changes of terminology, and crossover between medicalized and identity terms, appear to have contributed to conflation and confusion to the extent that GD is sometimes referred to as a specific diagnosis; sometimes as a phenomenological experience of distress; and sometimes as a personal characteristic within individuals' (Davy and Toze, 2018: 168).
2   Several people did, however, bemoan the absence of hummus, normally a favourite at queer events in the UK. Numerous attendees explained that they had considered bringing hummus along, but decided not to on the assumption that everyone else would be bringing it instead.
3   Many of these videos are available through our website: http://transseminars.com.

References

Aizura, A.Z. (2017) 'Unrecognizable: On trans recognition in 2017', *South Atlantic Quarterly*, 116(3): 606–611.

Barker, M.-J. & Scheele, J. (2019) *Gender: A Graphic Guide*. London: Icon Books.

Chiang, H., Henry, T.A. & Leung, H.H.-S. (2018) 'Trans-in-Asia, Asia-in-Trans: An Introduction', *TSQ: Transgender Studies Quarterly*, 5(3): 298–310.

Cox, L. (2017) 'Laverne's Story...,' web page, *Laverne Cox*. Available at: https://lavernecox.com/about/ [Accessed 18/01/19].

Davy, Z. & Toze, M. (2018) 'What is gender dysphoria? A critical systematic narrative review', *Transgender Health*, 3(1): 159–169.

Enke, A.F. (2012) 'The education of little cis: Cisgender and the discipline of opposing bodies', in Enke, A.F. (ed) *Transfeminist Perspectives in and Beyond Transgender and Gender Studies*. Philadelphia: Temple University Press, pp. 60–77.

Feinberg, L. (1997) *Transgender Warriors: Making History from Joan of Arc to Dennis Rodman*. Boston: Beacon Press.

Fitzpatrick, C. & Plett, C. (2017) *Meanwhile, Elsewhere: Science Fiction and Fantasy from Transgender Writers*. New York: Topside Press.

Green, K.M. (2017) 'Trans* movement/trans* moment: An afterword', *International Journal of Qualitative Studies in Education*, 30(3): 320–321.

Government Equalities Office. (2018) *National LGBT Survey: Research Report*. London: Government Equalities Office.

Koch-Rein, A. (2014) 'Monster', *TSQ: Transgender Studies Quarterly*, 1(1): 134–135.

Lester, C. (2017) *Trans Like Me: A Journey for All of Us*. London: Virago.

Liang, B. (2017) 'Delicate bodies', in Fitzpatrick, C. & Plett, C. (eds) *Meanwhile, Elsewhere: Science Fiction and Fantasy from Transgender Writers*. New York: Topside Press, pp. 9–29.

Moon, I. (2019) '"Boying" the boy and "girling" the girl: From affective interpellation to trans-emotionality', *Sexualities*, 1–2(22): 65–79.

Patel, N. (2017) 'Violent cistems: Trans experiences of bathroom space', *Agenda*, 31(1): 51–63.

Raha, N. (2017) 'Transfeminine brokenness, radical transfeminism', *South Atlantic Quarterly*, 116(3): 632–646.

Shildrick, M. (1997) *Leaky Bodies and Boundaries: Feminism, Postmodernism and (Bio)Ethics.* London: Routledge.

Snorton. (2017) *Black on Both Sides: A Racial History of Trans Identity.* Minneapolis: University of Minnesota Press.

Stryker, S. (1994) 'My words to Victor Frankenstein above the village of Chamounix: Performing transgender rage', *GLQ: A Journal of Lesbian and Gay Studies*, 1(3): 237–254.

Stryker, S. (2006) '(De)subjugated knowledges: An introduction to transgender studies', in Stryker, S. & Whittle, S. (eds) *The Transgender Studies Reader.* New York: Routledge, pp. 1–17.

Stryker, S. (2008) *Transgender History.* Berkeley: Seal Press.

Téllez, M. (2017) 'Heat death of western human arrogance', in Fitzpatrick, C. & Plett, C. (eds) *Meanwhile, Elsewhere: Science Fiction and Fantasy from Transgender Writers.* New York: Topside Press, pp. 253–259.

Tosh, J. (2016) *Psychology and Gender Dysphoria: Feminist and Transgender Perspectives.* London: Routledge.

Wagner, A.C. (2015) 'Artist statement: Visible monstrosity as empowerment', *TSQ: Transgender Studies Quarterly*, 2(2): 341–344.

Walker, H. (2019) 'Brazilian president Bolsonaro's assault on LGBTQ rights has begun', *Out Magazine*. Available at: www.out.com/news-opinion/2019/1/03/brazilian-president-bol sonaros-assault-lgbtq-rights-has-begun [Accessed 18/01/19].

Whittle, S. (1998) 'The trans-cyberian mail way', *Social Legal Studies*, 7(3): 389–408.

Williams, C. (2016) 'The politics of transphobia: Bathroom bills and the dialectic of oppression', blog post, *The Transadvocate*. Available at: www.transadvocate.com/the-politics-of-transphobia_n_18825.htm.

Wynn. (2018) 'Pronouns,' video recording, *YouTube*. Available at: www.youtube.com/watch?v=9bbINLWtMKI&t=1720s [Accessed 18/01/19].

Part I

Trans genealogies

Foreword

This book explores the consequences, characteristics and contestations of trans emergence from numerous perspectives. No examination of 'emergence' would be complete without a look at how contemporary understandings of trans identities and experiences have come to be in the Western context in which we write.

It is beyond the scope of this book to provide a broad history of trans discourse, language or politics.[1] What the contributors to this section of the book offer is a spotlight on several key arenas in which trans has 'emerged'. They explore the intersections of patient experience and professional practice in trans therapeutics, 'pathways of care' surrounding medical interventions and the management of trans bodies, and how changing understandings and experiences of trans becoming reflect (and feed into) wider shifts in the discursive landscape of gendered possibility. Across the first four chapters, we shift from the macro to the micro while remaining attentive to the interplay of individual circumstance and social context: from the broad sweep of eugenic history, to the evolution of specific forms of trans medicine, to personal epiphanies and trans becoming. As we editors have previously argued, '[t]o describe a genealogy is to look beyond linear narratives of causation' (Pearce, Moon and Steinberg, 2019). Similarly, Kadji Amin (2018: 602) observes that the truth of the present cannot be found in a singular historical origin point; he therefore highlights the importance of recognising 'not one but multiple ramifying but often contradictory origins' in conducting trans genealogies. Consequently, we sought contributions to this section that look deep into the complexities inherent in the negotiation of meaning over time, which together form a multifaceted account of trans becoming.

We begin with Julian Honkasalo's genealogy of state-enforced sterilisation requirements for trans people. These have a long history in Europe, and are still a condition of legal gender recognition in many countries. In Chapter 1, Honkasalo links trans sterilisation to the wider history of eugenics in the white Western world, teasing out the threads of racism, anti-Semitism and homophobia which have played an inherent part in the biopolitical administration of gender. He concludes by reflecting on contemporary debates over trans reproductive rights, illustrating how these follow from the continued influence of eugenic logics.

In Chapter 2, Eric Plemons draws on ethnographical fieldwork to explore how changing conceptualisations of sex, gender and trans possibility play a role in the increasing popularity of facial feminisation surgeries among trans women. He observes that the initial focus on genital reassignment surgeries in twentieth-century trans medicine reflected widespread contemporaneous understandings of sex as a property of individual bodies that follows from genital anatomy, whereas a stated desire for facial feminisation surgeries seems to have become more common as understandings of sex and gender as intersubjective and performative have proliferated more recently. In making this argument, Plemons highlights the importance of taking trans patient narratives seriously, while observing the instability and multiplicity of categories.

While trans has emerged (and continues to emerge) through the wider interplay of culture, biopolitics and medicine, in Chapter 3 Natacha Kennedy provides us tools with which to examine the genealogy of *individual* identity emergence. Through an employment of social activity method (SAM), she captures the interplay of internal experience, social interactions and the wider historical context of trans erasure and delegitimisation in trans people's experiences of personal epiphany. In this way, we might come to understand the multiplicity of trans becoming, recognising that processes of change vary within trans communities while also reflecting wider mechanisms of identity formation.

A more intimate account of individual emergence is provided in Chapter 4 by Elena Rose, who links trans identity and experience back to a far deeper and more troubling history. 'the seam of skin and scales' is a genealogy of monsters, an account of promise in the present and the primordial, the mythical and the material, as emergent within the trans body, within trans lives. This poem was originally published on Rose's blog *Taking Steps* in 2007. We include it both as an important contribution to thinking, and as an example of how trans theory and trans histories alike owe at least as much to everyday trans cultures and cultural production (the theme of the following section of this book) as they do to the realms of science, medicine and scholarship.

Note

1 Readers seeking to explore these matters are advised to consult important existing histories such as Susan Stryker's (2008) excellent *Transgender History* and Christine Burns' (2018) *Trans Britain*, as well as more critical works such as C Riley Snorton's (2017) important book, *Black on Both Sides*, Henry Rubin's (2003) *Self-made Men* and Joanne Meyerowitz's (2002) *How Sex Changed*, as well as the 2018 Transgender Studies Quarterly special issue on *Trans*historicities*.

References

Amin, K. (2018) 'Glands, Eugenics, and Rejuvenation in *Man into Woman*: A Biopolitical Genealogy of Transsexuality,' *TSQ: Transgender Studies Quarterly*, 5(4): 589–605.

Burns, C. (2018) *Trans Britain: Our Journey From The Shadows.* London: Unbound.

Meyerowitz, J. (2002) *How Sex Changed: A History of Transsexuality in the United States.* Cambridge, MA: Harvard University Press.

Pearce, R., Moon, I. & Steinberg, D.L. (2019) 'Introduction: The Emergence of "Trans"', *Sexualities,* 22(1): 3–12.

Rubin, H. (2003) *Self-made Men: Identity and Embodiment Among Transsexual Men.* Nashville: Vanderbilt University Press.

Snorton, C.R. (2017) *Black on Both Sides: A Racial History of Trans Identity.* Minneapolis: University of Minnesota Press.

Stryker, S. (2008) *Transgender History.* Berkeley: Seal Press.

1 In the shadow of eugenics

Transgender sterilisation legislation and the struggle for self-determination

Julian Honkasalo

Introduction

This chapter draws on the history of eugenics to examine the rationale behind infertility requirements for transgender persons undergoing legal and/or medical gender reassignment. Since state-enforced sterilisation is usually theorised in relation to reproductive heterosexuality, and understood as a past historical practice that targeted the assumed hereditary degeneracy of heterosexual populations, the practice of present-day, state-enforced transgender sterilisation has not caught enough scholarly attention in the tradition of critical research on eugenics or in the fields of queer and transgender studies. Similarly, transgender reproductive justice and health remain marginal issues in mainstream lesbian and gay rights and equality movements. Understanding this history is important for an account of how transgender persons have navigated the complex and intersectional terrain of discrimination in their plight for social justice and the right to self-determination.

The chapter is structured in three parts. I first examine the moral, medical and political legitimation of the nineteenth-century invention of eugenic sterilisation. I then analyze the ways in which the eugenics movement gave rise to 'male effeminacy' and 'femininity' as legitimate criteria for positioning certain groups of people, such as Jewish and homosexual men, as hereditary degenerates, and furthermore show how the eugenic pathologisation of femininity set forth medical models for governing black women, lesbians and transgender men. Finally, I argue that the rise of 'sex change' and 'sex reassignment' legislation for 'transsexuals' has created a double-bind, decriminalising physical transition and ratifying legal recognition, whilst at the same time continuing the biopolitical administering of transgender lives and bodies. I also discuss contemporary emerging debates concerning trans reproductive justice.[1] My genealogical analysis seeks to answer the following questions: how do certain forms of transgender embodiment and gender expression come to be viewed as legitimately subject to sterilisation by the state? Furthermore, what do various moral, psychiatric, juridical and political techniques approaches to gender nonconformity and transgender reproduction reveal about Western notions of citizenship?

The invention of eugenic sterilisation

Although Francis Galton first made human eugenics famous in his 1883 *Inquiries Into Human Faculty and Its Development*, the practice of eugenic sterilisation has its origins in the medical experiments of American prison doctors. Whereas castration had previously been used for punitive ends, Indiana doctors Harry C. Sharp and AJ Oschner regarded sterilisation as curative. Sharp's attempts to stop prisoners from masturbating led him to expand his practice of curative vasectomy to the sterilisation of 'degenerates', 'defects' and 'deviants' in general. During his position as a doctor of the Indiana Reformatory, he performed vasectomies on more than 400 men. Sharp also encouraged the state of Indiana to create the world's first sterilisation laws in 1907 (Largent, 2011: 29–30). The Chicago-based urologist and criminal anthropologist, G. Frank Lydston, wrote in 1905 that resistance to sterilisation was unjustified since vasectomy or resection of the fallopian tubes was quick and safe, and caused no disfigurement (Ordover, 2003: 74–77). British sexologist Havelock Ellis published a similar argument in a fall 1907 issue of *The Eugenics Review*.

By 1910, Charles Davenport had established The Eugenic Records Office, which was responsible for collecting hereditary information about the American population. By 1930, more than 30 American states had enacted sterilisation laws, and anti-miscegenation laws were ratified by nearly all states. During this period, eugenics societies and scientific research institutes were established all over the world, such as the British *Eugenics Education Society* in 1905, the German *Internationale Gesellschaft für Rassenhygiene* in 1907, the Brazilian *Sociedade Eugênica de São Paolo* in 1918 and the Swedish *Statens Institut för Rasbiologi* in 1922.

Early American and European eugenicists included biologists, penologists, social workers, educators and even first-wave feminists. Since crime and poverty were widely perceived as biological, hereditary problems, rather than socioeconomic and political questions, supporters of eugenic sterilisation argued that it was more humane to prevent degenerates such as 'the poor' or the 'feebleminded' from reproducing, than to have society institutionalise or imprison their supposedly poorly raised offspring (Stern, 2015). Although individual supporters of eugenics differed in their methods and goals, the international eugenics movement shared the moral task of so called racial responsibility, that is, promoting the life and reproduction of desired populations, whilst preventing the reproduction of degenerate populations (Spade and Rohls, 2016: 7).

Eugenics quickly became a highly respected science that aimed to save civilisation from degeneration. For instance, all Scandinavian welfare states – the Swedish *folkhem* (people's home) in particular – were based on this ideal. Sterilisation of the 'feebleminded' was the first step towards humane treatment in care homes and mental hospitals. Usually a patient's genetic background was examined by tracking (or speculating about) signs of degeneration in three generations. Sterilisations were conducted in state-controlled public institutions, such as hospitals, prisons, reform schools and care homes. Official records show that between the years 1935–1975, nearly 63,000 Swedes underwent state-mandated sterilisation, a number higher than any other European country except for Germany, and nearly as high as the total number of recorded sterilisations in all American states throughout the entire twentieth century.

Moreover, 'positive eugenics' – that is, increased reproduction by 'healthy' and 'fit', heterosexual persons – was strongly encouraged through various state-funded programs to ensure the improvement of the nation's hereditary pool (Broberg and Roll-Hansen, 2005). For example, in 1914, London-based educational pioneer Alice Ravenhill published a booklet entitled, *Eugenic Education for Women and Girls*, which argued for the significance of women's domestic care work for a healthy family and hygienic society. The booklet also set forth ideological guidelines for the eugenic responsibility of motherhood.

Theorising the logics of nationalism and ableism inherent in the eugenics movement, Snyder and Mitchell (2005) and Ordover (2003) argue that eugenics functioned by enforcing *aesthetic* ideals by means of quantitative methods. The isolation, institutionalisation and incarceration of undesirable groups, such as immigrants, disabled persons and poor or working-class people, were based on simple techniques of statistical standardisation through which all human beings could be defined as either 'normal' (fit to breed) or 'defective' (unfit to breed) (Snyder and Mitchell 2005: 77–79). As Snyder and Mitchell show, eugenics was not simply an ideology inherent to the nation state or the welfare state. American and European governments and eugenics societies collaborated and shared information and population records in their transatlantic task of creating a 'healthy' hereditary gene pool. Hence, eugenics was an American-European, transatlantic apparatus of power. The aesthetic ideals of the eugenics movement therefore raise the question of what discourses made it possible for educators, medical practitioners, politicians and social workers to define transgression and resistance towards binary gender norms as a transatlantic marker of psychopathology.

Effeminacy as a sign of degeneracy

Galton's studies on hereditary fitness, talent and character triggered speculations in Europe about whiteness as a sign of genetic superiority. However, as Sander Gilman argues in *The Jew's Body* (1991), in contrast to colonial, imperialist theorisations about skin color and racial fitness, Galton thought that European Jews hid their presumed inner pathologies and were capable of passing as 'normal'. Based on such presumptions, early European anti-Semitist scientists invented a physiognomy, (a specified range of quantifiable physical and visible markers) that characterised the 'Jewish type', so that Jews could be recognised. Physiognomic practices included measurements of the pitch of the voice, the posture of the body and the size of body parts, including genitalia (Gilman, 1991: 64–69, 96–97, 178).

A key feature of nineteenth-century anti-Semitic science was the conception of Jewish men as fundamentally effeminate. Effeminacy was not simply a symbolic means of administering masculinity, manhood and race. Instead, Jewish 'male effeminacy' was thought to be an external sign of pathology. Hence, femininity came to signify racial degeneration and disease. The anti-Semitic invention of supposed physical markers for the 'Jewish type' – such as shape and size of the feet, legs and nose, skin complexion and circumcision – were then interpreted as visible symptoms of sexually transmitted diseases such as syphilis (Gilman, 1991: 96, 123–127).

The stereotypical 'monstrosity' of 'the Jew' was based on another stereotype about Jewish male gender and sexuality. Gilman argues that Marcel Proust, for instance, used the anti-Semitic conception of 'the Jewish type' as a model for his portrait of the 'invert' or 'sodomite' in *In Search of Lost Time*, because sexual ambiguity and gender inversion were central to Proust's portrayal of the *race* of homosexuals. According to Gilman, this is no accident. '"Homosexuality" is a scientific label for a new "disease" coined by Karoly Benkert in 1869 at the very moment in history that the new "scientific" term for Jew-hating, "anti-Semitism" was created by Wilhelm Marr' (Gilman, 1991: 126).

In conjunction with Galton's research on hereditary fitness, new norms regulating masculinity and manhood emerged in rising industrial, capitalist societies. Whereas manhood was traditionally defined in relation to boyhood, masculinity was now understood as the opposite of femininity. The concern about the racial decline of civilisation was fueled by concerns about masculinity and virility both in Europe and overseas. In France, fertility theorists speculated about reproductive labor and the possibility that elderly and unmasculine men produced female offspring, whereas young men and masculine men were capable of generating boys. From the nineteenth century, self-help books and guides to human generation became popular among heterosexual couples. The purpose of these books was to help increase the racial fitness of the population (Nye, 1998: 86–87).

Nineteenth-century European cities, such as Berlin, Vienna, London, Copenhagen and Stockholm, also witnessed a new phenomenon of sex work conducted by 'fairies', 'cross-dressers' and 'female-impersonating' youth and adults (Kaye, 2003; Rydström and Mustola, 2007). Even soldiers engaged in sex work, which made their moral fitness as citizens questionable in the eyes of Queen Victoria's British Empire. Concerns over moral and physical fitness to serve the country were prevalent also in German notions of Aryan masculinity and opposition to Jewish men as 'effeminate' and incapable of military service, and thus undeserving of full citizenship rights (Gilman, 1991: 38–59).

In 1885, Britain amended its criminal law with the Labouchere Amendment which in its eleventh clause criminalised 'gross indecency', that is, both homosexual conduct and attempts to conduct.[2] Male sex work also gave rise to sexological speculations about how real 'invertism' (effeminacy) might compare to mere 'perversion' (homosexual acts, without gender inversion). In his major work, *Psychopathia Sexualis*, which set the paradigm for the rise of Western sexology, Richard von Krafft-Ebing (1886) defined invertism as a sign of mental and physical degeneration. Others, such as Magnus Hirschfeld (1868–1935) reformulated and further developed Krafft-Ebing's ideas, distinguishing same-sex desire from what he called 'transvestism', or the need to cross-dress.

Eugenic targeting of cis women and trans men

Nearly 70 years before Galton's studies, Georges Cuvier, widely known as the 'father' of modern biology and comparative anatomy, published a paper describing the post-mortem dissected brain and genitalia of Saartjie Baartman (1789–1815). Cuvier's aim was to establish a race-biological theory of what he perceived to be the evolutionary continuity between the human female and the quasi-Orangutan 'Hottentot woman'. Racist and ableist presumptions drove this research, influenced by earlier zoologists such as Swedish botanist Carl Linnaeus, who had classified the Khoisan – a hunter-gatherer people from the southern tip of Africa – as a human subspecies and the missing evolutionary link between the ape and the human. Similar evolutionary theories circulated also about cognitively disabled persons as a missing evolutionary link (Clare, 2015: 85–103). Baartman, a Khoisan woman, was used as a circus and freak show attraction, alongside numerous other black African women in late nineteenth-century France and Britain. Audience members could touch their chained, stripped bodies for a fee. These public displays objectified, sexualised and bestialised black women such as Baartman, reducing them to their body parts. This biological and physiological obsession with Khoisan women's labia set the tone for theorising women's sexuality more generally in the nineteenth century (Washington, 2006: 75–100; Gilman, 1985: 216).

Another important discourse contributing to the control, regulation and pathologisation of femininity was psychoanalysis. Eighteenth- and nineteenth-century psychiatric nosology classified hysteria as a mental illness associated with the female body. Many of the women sterilised as part of the eugenics movement were diagnosed with hysteria. Consequently, they were considered as unfit for the hereditary and moral duties of motherhood.

In addition to the eugenic regulation of disabled, racialised and hysteric women, as well as feminine boys and men, historical texts on early penological and psychiatric attempts to correct masculinity and gender nonconformity in poor and working-class girls and women show a pattern where female-to-male gender transgression is viewed as pathological – that is, as a possible sign of a pre-criminal, aggressive or anti-social personality. According to Nancy Ordover's extensive study on eugenics and queer anatomy, women accused of masturbation, 'nymphomania', cross-dressing or sexual acts with other women were often treated with punitive and invasive surgeries in nineteenth-century Europe and the US. These surgeries could involve the removal of organs such as the ovaries, the uterus or the clitoris (Ordover, 2003).

Ordover records numerous medical cases from Germany, Switzerland and the US in which masculine persons were accused of being perverted, promiscuous or psychopathic women, then arrested and condemned to mental asylums, where, in some cases, various types of invasive surgeries were performed

(Ordover, 2003: 90–95). Yet, Ordover theorises all cases exclusively as early examples of the pathologisation of 'gender-transgressing lesbians' and 'butch' lesbians. There is no mentioning or reflection on the possibility that some of these persons may have been living as men.[3]

The study of historical periods in which terms such as 'transgender' and 'transsexual' did not yet exist poses challenges. It is neither appropriate nor historically accurate to simply assume or project a transgender *identity* onto any gender nonnormative person who appears in historical documents such as medical texts, prison or hospital records. Nevertheless, transhistory and political genealogy cannot be written without examining the possibility that some persons appearing in documents that precede the invention of terms such as 'transsexual' and 'transgender', and who have been interpreted by gay and lesbian scholars to be (cis) homosexual or (cis) lesbian, may in fact have been persons belonging under the umbrella term 'trans'. As Gossett et al. (2017), Snorton (2017) and Clare (2015) argue, *erasure* is important to address because it conceals cis-sexist, racialised, gendered and ableist configurations of political, juridical and medical power that render various bodies as differentially and disproportionately vulnerable to discrimination, violence and exploitation. While recognising that 'trans', 'transgender' and 'transsexual' mean different things in different historical, political, geographical and sub-cultural contexts, and that these terms originate in western, colonial and sexological discourse, it might still be possible, through additional biographical or autobiographical accounts, to differentiate between the gendered practices of persons who may have transgressed gender norms to conceal same-sex practices or relationships and those persons who may have presented a gender different than their assigned sex for other reasons (Beemyn, 2014).

Bearing in mind the history of eugenic sterilisation and eugenic gender policing that I have outlined in the foregoing, I next examine the late twentieth-century state-mandated sterilisation requirements of transgender persons.

Steps towards gender self-determination: the invention of 'sex change surgery'

Several historical accounts have been written about the emergence of the so-called transsexual subject. Hausman (1995) and Gilman (1999), among others, have argued that since the invention of modern plastic surgery and anesthesia enabled the medical treatment of 'sex change' patients, it also enabled 'transsexuality' to become a legitimate identity category. Meyerowitz (2002) emphasises that the early twentieth-century German movement for sexual emancipation, characterised by the work of Hirschfeld and others, was a precondition for the American 'transsexual' movement. Repo (2015), following Hausman's argumentative framework, regards the 'transsexual subject' and gender identity as products of biopolitical 'gender discourse', while Valentine (2007) sees 'transgender' subjectivity as partly produced by American 'neo-liberalist and capitalist modes of production and consumption' (Valentine, 2007: 36).

These historical accounts shed light on some aspects of the clinical history of 'transsexuality'. However, shifting the perspective to the question of social justice and gender self-determination provides a much richer understanding of trans identity and community-building (Wickman, 2001; Stryker, 2017; Pearce, 2018). As I have argued previously, perceived gender nonconformity or gender transgression, as a detectable and quantifiable phenomenon that required penological and medical attention, had already emerged in the nineteenth-century eugenic matrix of criminology, medicine, psychiatry and anthropology. As the prison, the reform school and the mental institution have been perceived as sites of deviant sexuality and perversion for the past two centuries, these institutions functioned as research warehouses for quantifying sexual behavior, gender inversion and disability both in children and adults.

The attempt to find a treatment for persons suffering from dysphoria developed at first in conjunction with the criminological question of what to do with 'degenerates', such as 'sex offenders', 'moral perverts', 'cross-dressers', 'masturbators' and those with an 'unnaturally oriented sex drive'. Paradoxically, it was an offshoot of the eugenic, medico-juridical tradition that enabled legal justifications for the first hormonal treatments and gender-affirming surgeries on human test subjects. For instance, Hirschfield's Institut für Sexualwissenschaft appealed to eugenic science to legitimise human genitoplasties under the Weimar Republic's Criminal Code §175, which criminalised deviant forms of sexuality (Timm, 2010: 88–89).

This was often also the case elsewhere in Europe. Under the 1935 Danish Sterilization and Castration Act, only sex offenders and mentally disabled persons could be castrated, either voluntarily or by request of a guardian (Holm, 2017, 202–205, 242). Doctors often did not take trans patients seriously, or refused treatment altogether. David O. Cauldwell, for instance, conceived 'transsexualism' as a condition related to poor hereditary factors and unfavorable childhood conditions. He regarded the removal of healthy reproductive tissue as a violation of the US mayhem law, and thus refused to operate on a patient (Cauldwell, 2006 [1949]). As physicians, psychiatrists, sexologists and endocrinologists disagreed about the etiology and ontogenesis of 'transsexualism', they also disagreed over what to do about persons requesting gender-affirming surgeries. Since such patients were frequently diagnosed as 'sexual psychopaths' or 'schitzophrenics' during the nineteenth and twentieth centuries, institutionalisation often followed. Some were also subjected to dangerous experimental 'treatments', such as prefrontal lobotomy, electroshock, insulin shock or high dosages of psychotropic drugs (Honkasalo, 2016).

When the London-based doctor Sir Harold Gilles performed the world's first phalloplasty on a trans man in 1946, he diagnosed his patient, Michael Dillon, with hypospadias to portray the treatment as medically necessary and conceal the fact that he was performing a series of gender reassignment surgeries. Gilles had previously conducted reconstructive operations only on World War II soldiers who had suffered genital blast injuries (Kennedy, 2007: 63–64). In 1952, Christian Hamburger appealed to the Danish Castration Act to have his patient,

Christine Jorgensen, undergo a series of gender-affirming surgeries. Similarly, the American sexologist John Money, who popularised the use of the word 'gender' to distinguish social differences from perceived biological differences of physical sex, explored the hormonal reduction of male testosterone with the permission of existing sterilisation legislation for criminals. In 1966, Money experimented with the use of medroxyprogesterone on a 'bisexual, transvestite sex offender' at Johns Hopkins University (Money, 1970).[4] Although synthetic hormones were available, in many instances appealing to criminal law was the only way for both doctors and patients to justify hormonal therapy and gender reassignment surgeries on humans. In 1966, Harry Benjamin published *The Transsexual Phenomenon*, which became the groundwork for active promotion of the legalisation of 'sex change' operations as well as the legal recognition of 'transsexuals'. Yet, throughout the 1970s, American psychoanalysts, medical doctors and trans-exclusionary feminists debated the benefits and dangers of hormonal and surgical treatment. By the 1970s and '80s, many university-based gender identity clinics and private practices had closed. Transgender health care was never protected by the US Supreme Court (Stryker, 2017: 117).[5]

It was not until 1972 that the Swedish parliament passed the world's first law to regulate specific and detailed psychological, medical and legal measures for ratifying the 'sex' of what was then termed 'somatic intersexuals' (*somatiskt intersexuella*) and 'non-somatic intersexuals' (*icke-somatiskt intersexuella*), or 'transsexuals' (*transsexuella*) (SFS, 1972: 119: 28; Alm, 2006; Garland, 2015). Gender reassignment, including hormonal treatment and surgical procedures, was hence legalised and supervised by the state's National Board of Health and Welfare. The long legislation process of 1966–72 determined a set of conditions for changing juridical sex as well as for undergoing physical transitioning. The applicant was required to enter a psychiatric evaluation process, in which they had to show evidence that they had felt and behaved like the 'opposite sex' for a long time and would continue to do so permanently. An important part of this process was the 'real life test' which tested under psychiatric observation (sometimes including periods of hospitalisation) the fitness of the patient to function in the role of the 'opposite sex'. In addition, childhood history, personality, IQ, family history, masculinity/femininity as well as anatomical characteristics were examined (Honkasalo, 2019). The next step was to receive new legal identity documents which were conditioned upon a certificate showing that the applicant was at least 18 years old, a Swedish citizen and unmarried, and had undergone sterilisation or was for other reasons infertile (SOU, 1968: 28). The Swedish expert board also originally regarded gender-specific body measurements, such as for height as well as the size of hands and feet, as criteria for applicants.[6] Because the criteria for establishing the authenticity of the patient's 'transsexuality' were set against the legal status of intersex persons, there had to be strong evidence that the 'transsexual' (i.e. the 'non-somatic intersex') had a condition that was as severe, and medically clear, as the 'somatic intersex' (Alm, 2006). Another important factor was to ensure that the applicant was not in fact a homosexual or transvestite (SOU, 1968: 28; YK2185 I-II; E1A, 1971).

The 'sex change' was to be a singular, irreversible act and a realistic option only for a few, serious cases of 'transsexualism'. Anything regarded by the expert team as a failure to meet the diagnostic criteria could lead to a rejection of the application. The underlying heteronormative and binary framework was influenced by John Money's and Harry Benjamin's sexological studies from the 1950s and 1960s. However, various draft versions of the Swedish expert report that functioned as the basis for the law included suggestions that the applicant should not be a parent to children (either biological or adopted) and should not be allowed to adopt after transitioning.[7] The American sexological and legal discourse was by contrast not as strict concerning adoption. Some medical professionals held that trans persons should be supported to establish a (heterosexual) family and adopt children (Smith, 1971). The Swedish diagnostic model was shaped under strict bureaucratic state control, at a time when the eugenic sterilisation program was still in effect, whereas Benjamin's diagnostic was crafted in private practices or privatised university hospitals with some trans patients themselves participating in the formulation of diagnosis and care.

The Swedish law was regarded as progressive at the time, since it made gender reassignment and change of the gender marker on national ID documents not only legal, but also regulated through the public sector of the welfare state (Hoenig, 1977). The Swedish law served as a model for other European nations, with Norway setting up a service for the treatment of 'transsexuals' in 1979, and Germany ratifying a similar 'Transsexuellengesetz' ('transsexual act') in 1980. Italy followed in 1982, Austria in 1983 and the Netherlands in 1985. In addition to the infertility requirement, but in contrast to Sweden, all five countries also required partial or complete 'sex change' surgery that varied from penectomy, orchiectomy and vaginoplasty for persons assigned male at birth, and bilateral mastectomy, hysterectomy and ovarectomy for persons assigned female at birth (Amnesty, 2014; Rappole, 2015). Until the passage of the UK's Gender Recognition Act in 2004, all European countries required infertility as a condition for legal recognition (Dunne, 2017).

While it is beyond the scope of this chapter to explicate the specific histories and legal procedures of gender reassignment regulation in each European country, these laws are not simply old, outdated texts from the past that need to be updated.[8] Some countries did not provide legal recognition and health care to transgender persons at all before the twenty-first century, and some still do not do so. Other countries recognise only binary 'transsexualism' as a condition to be covered by public health care, whereas non-binary trans persons who do not fit into strict, normative categories are commonly denied access to hormonal therapy and gender reassignment surgeries. In Finland, for instance, the 'Act on the Confirmation of the Gender of a Transsexual' did not come into effect until 2003.[9] The Finnish law followed the 1972 Swedish model with requirements for a long-term psychiatric evaluation, as well as documents proving age, citizenship, infertility or sterilisation and (single) marital status. As of 2019, the sterilisation law is still in effect. Belgium passed a similar law in 2007.

In 1999, Sweden publicly apologised for the nation's 1935–75 eugenic sterilisation program and launched a compensation process for victims of coerced sterilisation. The official investigation into the state's eugenic practices did not consider Swedish trans persons as an intelligible category for the investigation. Instead, 'sex change' was held to be a voluntary process, which inevitably led to infertility (Tydén, 2002). Sixteen years after the *Steriliseringsutredning*, following decades of activist work, the law mandating the sterilisation of persons requesting change of juridical sex was ruled unconstitutional by the Stockholm Administrative Court of Appeal. In November 2017, the Swedish government published a nearly 1000-page official report on trans people's living conditions, titled *Stronger Status and Improved Living Conditions for Trans People* (SOU, 2017: 92). This report maps living conditions in relation to factors such as housing, health care, employment, recreational activities and the rights of asylum-seekers. One area that the investigation examined in detail was discrimination and violations in health care. The report states: 'We have noted specific challenges for trans men and non-binary people who are pregnant, relating to both the need for specific supports and technical difficulties with the medical records system' (SOU, 2017: 92, 50–51).

To this day, many European nations still require psychiatric treatment and evidence of infertility as a condition for obtaining full legal recognition (TGEU, 2018). In the United States, no federal law exists for the regulation of gender reassignment, but several states still require the removal of reproductive organs as a condition for changing the gender marker on a birth certificate (Rappole, 2015).

From ending sterilisation to fighting for reproductive justice

Despite the extensive legal and bureaucratic measures that states have taken to govern and administer transgender persons for more than 100 years, there is still a lack of laws and policies to protect and support fertility preservation, family-building and parenthood for this group. There is also a significant research gap on transgender reproductive health issues. This lack is connected to the systemic prejudice, stigma and overall discrimination that transgender persons suffer. In a paper on the ethics of reproductive assistance for transgender men and women, Murphy (2010), for instance, ponders whether persons with a GID mental illness diagnosis understand the consequences of pregnancy and are suitable for parenthood, and what the ethical consequences of transgender parenthood might be for their children.

There is a common belief that transgender persons do not wish to reproduce (Dunne, 2017). The first major clinical study on reproductive desire in transgender men was not published until 2011. This Belgian study showed that a majority of transgender men do wish to preserve their fertility, have children and establish a family in the future (Wierckx, 2011). Nixon (2013) cites an online survey from 2002 on reproductive desire in European transgender women and states that the results were similar (Nixon, 2013: 95). Nevertheless, the authors of the Belgian study list several 'ethical questions' that rise in conjunction with the desire of transgender men to preserve the possibility of becoming pregnant, or to conduct embryo or oocyte cryopreservation, for instance. One of these is the lack of research on the suitability of transgender persons to take on the responsibility of parenting as well as the lack of longitudinal studies on the possible harm caused to children born into such a family setting (Wierckx, 2011). A 2014 Dutch study on medically assisted reproduction for LGBT persons similarly speculates on the possibility that children of transgender parents may experience 'stigma, exclusion, bullying, etc.' but nevertheless concludes that '[f]ertility preservation should be offered to transsexual people considering sex reassignment' (De Wert et al., 2014).

The attitude among health-care professionals has been more relaxed and positive in the United States. In 2015, the American College of Obstetricians and Gynecologists published a study on 41 transgender men and concluded that transgender men not only wish to preserve their fertility, but also are fully capable of becoming pregnant and should receive equal access to reproductive health care. According to the study, the most important obstacle faced by transgender persons is social prejudice and stigma (Obedin-Maliver and Makaron, 2016). Another publication, also from 2015, by the Ethics Committee of the American Society of Reproductive Medicine concluded similarly that no justification exists for the denial of fertility treatment to transgender persons. The report stated that while existing data are scarce, there is no evidence to support the notion that children are harmed by having transgender parents (ASRM, 2015).

The debate over the reproductive rights of transgender persons is thus framed as a debate concerning the medical ethics of reproductive assistance to non-heterosexual, nonnormative and/or disabled persons, with additional issues concerning the right of the child (Leibetseder, 2016; Dunne, 2017; Honkasalo, 2018). Even as these studies provide an account of the reproductive desire in transgender persons, they do not examine the ethical problem of active state involvement in regulating trans reproduction and parenthood, instead discussing infertility simply as a natural, possible consequence of medical transitioning. Sometimes the lack of formal complaints or reported pregnancies from transitioned men is used as evidence for the argument that sterilisation laws are simply a formality without any real impact, and that infertility is a consequence of ongoing hormonal treatment and/or genital surgery, desired by the patients themselves. After all, 'transsexual' patients have historically applied for voluntary castration by appeal to existing castration laws. Although it is evident that many transgender persons need transition-related medical care, and should be granted a right to this care, these arguments ignore the question of what constitutes 'voluntary' treatment, considering the incentives at stake (such as new identity documents) and the extremely costly and often unavailable fertility preservation options. Furthermore, the argument that transgender sterilisation is voluntary dismisses the active role of the state in potentially legally demanding that some citizens provide medical proof of infertility. If sterilisation/infertility is no big deal, then why has no country formulated the law to include sterilisation as a reproductive right regarding permanent contraception, an option available to those patients who desire it but not mandatory?

While queer-feminist disability theorists such as Alison Kafer (2013) have written in detail about eugenics and the reproductive discrimination against disabled lesbian persons, they typically do not touch upon the sterilisation legislation framework that regulates transgender lives (Kafer, 2013: 28–34, 76–85). The opportunity to theorise intersections between able-nationalism, eugenic targeting of disabled persons and transgender citizenship is missing also in the extensive history of eugenics and queer anatomy by Ordover (2003) and on eugenics and disability by Snyder and Mitchell (2005) as well as in Jasbir Puar's theorisation of the intersections among race, nationality, disability and trans (Puar, 2017). The history of eugenic regulation of transgender populations is not examined by Spade and Rohls (2016) either. The topic of enforced sterilisation, compromised citizenship and reproductive justice is curiously absent even in the medical, cisnormative histories conducted by Hausman (1995), Gilman (1999), Meyerowitz (2002) and Repo (2015).[10] Legal scholars on the other hand, such as Karaian (2013) and Dunne (2017), theorise the negative attitude towards transgender assisted reproduction as a form of repronormativity, while Nixon (2013) regards it as a form of 'passive eugenics'.

Transgender activist communities and their allies have attempted to bring reproductive justice issues into the public view in various ways. In addition to European governments slowly beginning to repeal their transgender sterilisation laws, the plight of reproductive justice has increasingly received wide media attention from 2008 when Thomas Beatie was widely (albeit inaccurately) reported to be the first legally male person to give birth (Currah, 2008). Beatie also participated in the Swedish movement to end the enforced sterilisation of transgender persons. Nevertheless, as Obedin-Maliver and Makaron (2016) report: '[m]any of the news reports on pregnancies of transgender men having children sensationalise what for trans men, as for all parents having children, should be a personal and intimate experience' (Obedin-Maliver and Makaron, 7).

Conclusion

The rationale for perceiving the transgression of binary gender normativity as a severe form of psychopathology was present already in the early years of the American eugenics movement. By the twentieth century, a whole apparatus of scientific techniques had been developed, tested, distributed and deployed for the management and governance of nonnormative bodies. Characteristic to the invention of eugenic sterilisation is a shift from the criminological and punitive interventions of the earlier century, to the twentieth-century discourse on medical treatment centring a stabilising of the binary gender system as well as aesthetic ideals of the psyche and body. The American-European medical, psychiatric and juridical history of the past 130 years shows an active role for the state in the regulation and policing of gender and health. On one hand, individuals who sought to medically transition before 'sex change surgery' was legalised were often turned away, because of their presumed pathological desire to 'self-immolate' or to become 'mutilated'. On the other hand, states actively imposed compulsory psychiatric evaluation and surgeries as a condition for legal recognition, once legal recognition became possible. This double-bind gave rise to the current situation in which trans persons must compromise fundamental human rights and citizenship rights for the sake of self-determination and bodily integrity. Although individual transgender persons and important single-issue campaigns have received broad media visibility over the past years, the fight for self-determination and universal health care, including fertility preservation, remain fundamental issues of social justice that need to be taken seriously by health-care professionals, litigators, academics and the mainstream lesbian and gay rights movement.

Notes

1 Reproductive justice is a concept originally invented and coined in 1994 by black, American feminists inspired by The Combahee River Collective, in their statement "Black Women on Universal Health Care Reform", published in *The Washington Post*. Loretta J. Ross, one of the original writers of the statement, defines the meaning of reproductive justice as follows: 'Reproductive justice is based on three interconnected sets of human rights: (1) the right to have a child under the conditions of one's choosing; (2) the right not to have a child using birth control, abortion, or abstinence; and (3) the right to parent children in safe and healthy environments free from violence by individuals or the state. Reproductive justice was never meant to replace the reproductive health (service provision) or reproductive rights (legal advocacy) frameworks. Instead it was an amplifying organizing concept to shed light on the intersectional forms of oppression that threaten Black women's bodily integrity. It rapidly propelled a growing movement of women of color activists from many social locations to fight for reproductive dignity. [. . .] Not only biologically defined women experience reproductive oppression. By highlighting the distinction between biological sex and socially constructed gender, our analysis includes transmen, transwomen, and gender-nonconforming individuals.' (Ross, 2017: 290–291).

2 The law was most famously invoked to convict Oscar Wilde (1854–1900) and Alan Turing (1912–1954), among others. It was repealed in 1967.

3 This type of a bias is common in gay and lesbian history (Beemyn, 2014).

4 The impact of estrogen and testosterone on sex drive and gender expression had already been explored in the 1930s. In 1934, Erik Lundberg published a paper on hormonal injection experiments to reverse homosexuality in Swedish male prisoners (see Lundberg's letter to the 1941–51 committee preparing the legislation on sexual crimes and homosexuality, YK 1822, Vol F6A:1 and Lundberg, 1934). Ten years after Lundberg's publication, the Danish physician Carl Waernet conducted similar experiments at the Buchenwald concentration camp. See Tamagne, 2006, Appendix VI, for details on Waernet's experiments under Heinrich Himmler's appointment.

5 While homosexuality was removed from the American Psychiatric Association's second DSM manual in 1973, the new categories of 'gender identity disorder' (GID) and 'gender identity disorder of childhood' (GIDC) were added to the DSM-III in 1980. GID was added to The World Health Organization Tenth International Classification

of Diseases, under the category of personality and behavioral disorders. Hence, GID became recognised as a condition requiring medical attention. The mental illness classification was finally removed in the 2018 renewed ICD-11.

6 In a letter from N. O. Ericsson to the expert committee, dated 11 March 1968, there is even a suggestion of compulsory genital surgery, to prevent anyone from seeing the genitals of an intersex or trans person in an emergency room, or a boat or train sleeper cabin (YK2185 II).

7 The policy that 'transsexual' persons must be sterilised before receiving legal confirmation appears for the first time in the notes and memos to the drafts of the expert committee report during February and March 1967. During January and February, the expert committee discussed legal issues related to marriage, adoption and parenthood of persons seeking change in their legally assigned sex. The committee also discussed the possibility of a situation in which a juridical male would menstruate or give birth (YK 2185 I; see also Alm, 2006: 98)

8 For country-specific legislations in the context of Europe, Asia (including Australia and New Zealand), the US and Argentina, see Scherpe, ed. (2015). For a detailed perspective on trans sterilization in Europe, see Dunne (2017). For the diagnostic history in Scandinavian countries, see Pimenoff (2006), Parhi (2018) and Honkasalo (2018) for the country specific context of Finland. See Holm (2017) for Denmark. For the legal history in Sweden, see Alm (2006), Garland (2015) and Honkasalo (2019).

9 Up until 2002, Finnish trans patients had to apply for voluntary castration as a prerequisite for gender reassignment. This is because no legal framework existed, except for the 1970 law enabling the voluntary castration of sex offenders and persons with sexual habits that caused distress or harm to self and others (Pimenoff, 2006).

10 My use of the term *cisnormative* is context-sensitive and describes readings that do not engage with (or refer to) the work of trans scholars, trans theorists or transhistorians but examine instead 'sex change' as an intriguing research topic in the history of medicine and society. In such readings, trans experiences, activism and community are missing and trans lives are often reduced to the object of medical studies. The epistemic authority and narrative voice in such texts originates with (non-trans) doctors, psychiatrists, endocrinologists and surgeons, that is, 'the experts'. For an alternative method of conducting history that acknowledges trans and intersex experiences, see Holm, 2017 and for an alternative method of conducting research on trans health care, see Pearce, 2018.

References

Unpublished archival material

Riksarkivet, Stockholm (Swedish National Archives): YK 2185, Vol I-II.
Riksarkivet, Stockholm, Justitiedepartementets arkiv (Archives of the Ministry of Justice): E1A, 1971, Dec 3, B:2.
Riksarkivet Stockholm, Justitiedepartementets arkiv (Archives of the Ministry of Justice): YK 1822, Vol F6A:1.

Published material

Alm E (2006) *"Ett emballage för inälvor och emotioner". Föreställningar om kroppen i statliga utredningar från 1960- & 1970-talen.* Doctoral dissertation. Gothenburg: Gothenburg University.
Amnesty International Ltd (2014) *The State Decides Who I Am. Lack of Recognition for Transgender People.* London: Amnesty International.

ASRM (2015) Access to fertility services by transgender persons: An ethics committee opinion. Ethics Committee of the American society for reproductive medicine. *Fertility and Sterility*, 104(5): 1111–1115.

Beemyn G (2014) Transgender history in the United States. in Erickson-Schroth L (ed.) *Trans Bodies, Trans Selves*. Oxford: Oxford University Press.

Broberg G & Roll-Hansen N (2005) *Eugenics and the Welfare State: Norway, Sweden, Denmark and Finland* (2nd edition). East Lansing: Michigan State University Press.

Cauldwell D O (2006 [1949]) Psychopathia transsexualis. in Stryker S & Whittle S (eds.) *The Transgender Studies Reader*. New York: Routledge, pp. 40–44.

Clare E (2015) *Exile and Pride: Disability, Queerness, and Liberation*. Durham: Duke University Press.

Currah P (2008) Expecting bodies: The pregnant man and transgender exclusion from the employment non-discrimination act. *WGS: Women's Studies Quarterly*, 36(3&4): 330–336.

De Wert et al (2014) ESHRE task force on ethics and law 23: Medically assisted reproduction in singles, lesbian and gay couples, and transsexual people. *Human Reproduction*, 29(9): 1859–1865.

Dunne P (2017) Transgender sterilization requirements in Europe. *Medical Law Review*, 25(4): 554–581.

Garland J (2015) Sweden. in Scherpe J M (ed.) *The Legal Status of Transsexual and Transgender Persons*. Cambridge: Insertia, pp. 281–312.

Gilman S (1985) Black bodies, white bodies: Toward an iconography of female sexuality in late Nineteenth-Century art, medicine, and literature. *Critical Inquiry*, 12(1): 204–242.

Gilman S (1991) *The Jew's Body*. London and New York: Routledge.

Gilman S (1999) *Making the Body Beautiful: A Cultural History of Aesthetic Surgery*. Princeton: Princeton University Press.

Gossett R, Stanley E A and Burton J (eds.) (2017) *Trap Door – Trans Cultural Production and the Politics of Visibility*. Cambridge: MIT Press.

Hausman B (1995) *Changing Sex: Transsexualism, Technology and the Idea of Gender*. Durham: Duke University Press.

Hoenig J (1977) The legal position of the transsexual: Mostly unsatisfactory outside Sweden. *CMA Journal*, 5(116): 319–323.

Holm M-L (2017) *Reimagining Intersexed and Trans Embodied Lives through (Auto)biographical Accounts of the Past*. Doctoral dissertation. Linköping: Linköping University.

Honkasalo J (2016) When boys will not be boys: American eugenics and the pathologization of gender nonconformity. *NORMA International Journal for Masculinity Studies*, 11(4).

Honkasalo J (2018) Unfit for parenthood? Compulsory sterilization and transgender reproductive justice in Finland. *Journal of International Women's Studies*, 4(20): 40–52.

Honkasalo J (2019) The intimate labour of non-normative bodies: Transgender patients in early Swedish medical research. in Griffin G & Leibetseder D (eds.) *Bodily Interventions and Intimate Labour: Understanding Bioprecarity*. Manchester: Manchester University Press.

Kafer A (2013) *Feminist, Queer, Crip*. Bloomington: Indiana University Press.

Karaian L (2013) Pregnant men: Repronormativity, critical trans theory and the re(conceiving) of sex and pregnancy in law. *Social & Legal Studies*, 22(2): 211–230.

Kaye K (2003) Male prostitution in the Twentieth Century. *Journal of Homosexuality*, 40(1/2): 1–77.

Kennedy P (2007) *The First Man-made Man: The Story of Two Sex Changes, One Love Affair, and A Twentieth-century Medical Revolution*. New York: Bloomsbury.

Krafft-Ebing, R von (1886) *Psychopathia Sexualis – Eine Klinisch-Forensische Studie*. Stuttgart: Verlag von Ferdinand Enke.

Largent M A (2011) *Breeding Contempt: The History of Coerced Sterilization in the United States.* New Brunswick: Rutgers University Press.

Leibetseder D (2016) Reproductive ethics: An example of an allied dis/ability-queer-feminist justice. in Bee Scherer (ed.) *Queering Paradigms VI: Interventions, Ethics and Glocalities.* Oxford: Peter Lang, pp. 131–146.

Lundberg E (1934) Follikulinbelastning av homosexuella män. *Hygieia: Medicinsk Tidskrift,* 96(16).

Meyerowitz J (2002) *How Sex Changed: A history of Transsexuality in the United States.* Cambridge: Harvard University Press.

Money J (1970) Use of an androgen-depleting hormone in the treatment of male sex offenders. *The Journal of Sex-Research,* 6(3): 165–172.

Murphy T F (2010) The ethics of helping transgender men and women have children. *Perspectives in Biology and Medicine,* 53(1): 46–60.

Nixon M (2013) The right to (trans)parent: A reproductive justice approach to reproductive rights, fertility, and family-building issues facing transgender people. *William & Mary Journal of Women and the Law,* 73: 73–103.

Nye R A (1998) *Masculinity and Male Codes of Honor in Modern France.* Berkeley: University of California Press.

Obedin-Maliver J & Makadon H (2016) Transgender men and pregnancy. *Obstetric Medicine,* 9(1): 4–8.

Ordover N (2003) *American Eugenics: Race, Queer Anatomy, and the Science of Nationalism.* Minneapolis: University of Minnesota Press.

Parhi K (2018) Boyish mannerisms and womanly coquetry: patients with the diagnosis of *transvestitismus* in the Helsinki psychiatric clinic in Finland, 1954–68. *Medical History,* 1(62): 55–66.

Pearce R (2018) *Understanding Trans Health: Discourse, Power and Possibility.* Bristol: Policy Press.

Pimenoff V (2006) On the care of transsexuals in Finland. *International Journal of Transgenderism,* 9(2): 23–33.

Puar J K (2017) *The Right to Maim. Debility, Capacity, Disability.* Durham: Duke University Press.

Rappole A (2015) Trans people and legal recognition: What the U.S. federal government can learn from foreign nations. *Maryland Journal of International Law,* 30(1): 191–216.

Repo J (2015) *The Biopolitics of Gender.* Oxford: Oxford University Press.

Ross, L J (2017) Reproductive justice as intersectional feminist activism. *Souls* 19(3): 286–314.

Rydström J & Mustola K (eds.) (2007) *Criminally Queer. Homosexuality and Criminal Law in Scandinavia 1842–1999.* Amsterdam: Aksant.

Scherpe J M (ed.) (2015) *The Legal Status of Transsexual and Transgender Persons.* Cambridge: Insertia.

SFS: (1972:119) Lag om Fastställande av Könstillhörighet i vissa fall.

Smith D K (1971) Transsexualism, sex reassignment surgery and the law. *Cornell Law Review,* 56(6): 963–1009.

Snorton C R (2017) *Black on Both Sides: A Racial History of Trans Identity.* Minnesota: University of Minnesota Press.

Snyder S & Mitchell D (2005) *Cultural Locations of Disability.* Chicago: Chicago University Press.

SOU: (1968:28) Statens offentliga utredning. *Intersexuellas Könstillhörighet: Förslag till lag om fastställande av könstillhörighet i vissa fall.* Stockholm: Esselte.

SOU: (2017:92) Statens offentliga utredning. *Transpersoner i Sverige. Förslag till förstärkt ställning och bättre levnadsvilkor.* Stockholm: Esselte.

Spade D & Rofhls R (2016) Legal equality, gay numbers, and the (after?)math of eugenics. *The Scholar & Feminist Online*, 13(2): 1–25.

Stern A (2015) *Eugenic Nation. Faults and Frontiers of Better Breeding in Modern America.* Berkeley: University of California Press.

Stryker S (2017) *Transgender History.* Berkeley: Seal Press.

Tamagne F (2006) *A History of European Homosexuality. Volume I-II.* New York: Algora.

Timm, A F (2010) *The Politics of Fertility in Twentieth-Century Berlin.* Cambridge: Cambridge University Press.

Transgender Europe (2018) Trans Rights Europe Map & Index 2018. TGEU Website 14.5.2018. https://tgeu.org/trans-rights-map-2018/ Accessed 15 May 2018.

Tydén M (2002) *Från Politik till Praktik: De Svenska Steriliseringsutredningarna 1935–1975.* Stockholm: Almkwist & Wiksell.

Valentine D (2007) *Imagining Transgender – An Ethnography of A Category.* Durham: Duke University Press.

Washington H A (2006) *Medical Apartheid – The Dark History of Medical Experimentation on Black Americans from Colonial Times to the Present.* New York: Anchor Books.

Wickman J (2001) *Transgender Politics. The Construction and Deconstruction of Binary Gender in the Finnish Transgender Community.* Åbo: Åbo Akademis förlag.

Wierckx K (2011) Reproductive wish in transsexual men. *Human Reproduction*, 27(2): 483–487.

2   Reconceiving the body

A surgical genealogy of trans- therapeutics

Eric Plemons

Compiling a collection of essays on 'trans genealogies' is no small feat. *Trans* is a word that has been so chronically resistant to definition that it has even become challenging to write. *Trans, trans-* and *trans** are orthographic variations that not only name diverse groups of people, forms of life and conceptual apparatuses, but they also signal writers' different political orientations and intellectual projects.[1] With terms and concepts contested and shifting every day, there is little certainty in *trans-* beyond the connotation of movement itself. Still, despite – and in large measure because of – this constitutive movement, *trans-* does a lot of work.

My aim in this chapter is to cut a small path through the genealogical landscape, to consider the kinds of work *trans-* (and its many precursors and doubles – *transsexual, transgender, gender identity disorder, gender dysphoria, gender incongruence* and more) has done in the space of the surgical clinic. What kinds of surgical responses have a patient's claim to trans- medicine enabled and on what kinds of therapeutic logics does such a claim depend? Put otherwise, what kinds of surgical interventions have been legible as 'good' trans- medicine and what can attending to their practice tell us about the changing status of *trans-* as a claim to which surgery is a good response?

My argument is a simple one: as ideas shift about the kinds of things sex and gender are, so do the interventions required to 'change' them (see Plemons, 2017). If 'transition' names a movement from man to woman or vice versa, or if it names a meaningful departure from one or both of those terms without necessarily implicating an arrival at another one of them, what kinds of things are 'man' and woman', and what role can surgery play in their creation/rejection? In the earliest moments of transsexual medicine, to be a woman – the ostensive goal of the many early trans- patients, most of whom were trans- women – was to possess female genital anatomy (Benjamin, 1954).[2] Therefore, surgeries that aimed to 'change sex' were focused on the reconstruction of genital forms. Increasingly, however, the simple anatomical and especially genital definition of *woman* has been challenged by a different understanding of *woman*, of sex and gender in general and, by extension, a different aim of trans- medicine. According to this new claim – often described as a 'performative' model of sex/gender – to be a 'woman' is not to be a member of a given category by possessing a particular genital anatomy. Rather, one is counted in the category 'woman' when one is recognised by others as such (Butler, 1990, 1993). There are many forms by which this kind of productive recognition can take place.

While we might name this model as the theory of 'performativity' (see Berger, 2013), here I am less interested in the named theory than in how the recognition-based claims to sex/gender that it names have increasingly acquired the status of common sense. It is recognition as a member of a sex/gender group – not possession of the genital forms once thought to define that group – that has made the use of public restrooms a much publicised site of contestation. So, too, admission to single-gender colleges and universities or single-gender public gatherings. Inclusion in such spaces affords a form of public and social recognition, affirming that the body in the bathroom or the dorm room or the festival is one that belongs to the named group in question. In conferring admission, one confers recognition and we increasingly understand sex/gender to be produced in these moments, regardless of what kinds of genital forms any given person may possess. I'll show that the move towards recognition-based understandings of sex/gender is also being enacted in surgical clinics, where more and more trans- women are undergoing facial feminisation surgery, a form of surgical sex reassignment that makes an explicit claim to 'woman' as a product of recognition.

My genealogy of *trans-* as a surgical object is one that takes trans- surgical patients seriously and asks what it means when both genital sex reassignment surgery and facial feminisation surgery are seen as effective surgical responses to trans- women's desire to transition – that both of them count as 'good trans-medicine,' and both are claimed as forms of 'sex reassignment'. I juxtapose claims to the efficacy of these two distinct modes of surgical sex reassignment articulated in two different moments. The first emphasises the sex reassignment efficacy of genital reconstructive surgery. This claim is one that theorises 'sex' as a property of individual bodies and locates sexed characteristics in structures of genital anatomy. Genital sex reassignment surgery (GSRS) animated the very earliest forms of American trans- medicine, and a whole psychological and policy apparatus was developed to determine who could access such a procedure and under what forms of reasoning the desire to access it could be legitimised.[3] Once considered to define the project of surgical sex reassignment, genital surgery remains important to many trans- women, but it has been demoted from the role of constituting 'sex reassignment surgery' to but one of its possible iterations. The second claim is that surgical sex reassignment can be accomplished through reconstruction of the face. First considered complimentary to GSRS – in that genital surgery was considered to have changed sex and facial feminisation surgery (FFS) was an auxiliary procedure that made the patient appear more congruously feminine – over the past two decades, surgeons who perform FFS and the patients who undergo it have articulated the claim that through acts of social recognition FFS also changes sex.

While FFS could be interpreted as a newer means of enacting the trans-woman's end goal of 'woman' that was first articulated in and through GSRS,

it is my contention that FFS and GSRS aim to enact fundamentally different kinds of 'woman'. In making this claim, I show the genealogy of trans-
medicine as tracing and helping to inform shifting ideas about what sex and
gender are as material and conceptual properties and, therefore, through which
means they can be surgically enacted.

Naming the object of inquiry

It is difficult to write about trans- medicine because there are no stable categories or central vocabularies that hold disparate diagnostic or medical practices
together. Procedures are called by a variety of names, and sometimes names that
are used in common denote very different procedures in practice. As a result
of shifting categories, vocabularies and policies, by the time formal research
questions about trans- medicine are formulated, investigated and presented in
publications, the terms of the questions have changed, rendering that research
irrelevant as soon as it appears (Jones, Podolsky and Greene, 2012). Formal
diagnostic categories are updated or replaced, reflecting new ideas about
nomenclature and classification; health-care policies and delivery infrastruc-
tures require particular interventions in particular orders; political shifts make
identity terms irrelevant or unpopular; new professional best practice standards
are adopted that render old practices retrograde. Still another challenge is that
what may count as trans- medicine in one place can vary wildly from forms of
trans- medicine practiced elsewhere.

On account of this ever-changing landscape, I limit my inquiry here by
focusing on practices in the United States. In the US context, trans- medicine
has been shaped by a market-based system of health-care delivery that is mediated by public and private insurance companies, whose power to determine
which interventions are 'medically necessary' for which qualifying diagnoses
has a significant impact on doctors' and patients' medical decision-making
(Dolgin, 2015). Ongoing debates over the 'medical necessity' of trans- medicine have been reflected in the gymnastics of DSM categorisation and also
account for the repeated assertions of 'medical necessity' in recent editions of
the professional *Standards of Care* (SOC) produced by the World Professional
Association for Transgender Health (an overwhelmingly American organisation
[Matte et al., 2009]) (WPATH, 2007).

Since the 1990s, American trans- medicine has largely been a patient-driven
affair. Lacking a coherent treatment policy or schedule, individual patients
advocate for the interventions they want to undergo. Access to some of these
are dictated by the SOC; others are not. Indeed, which interventions are controlled by 'best practice' models of trans- health are themselves indicative of
how the field of trans- medicine is constituted and how it has changed over
time (see Matte et al., 2009). Rather than asking after official definitions and
terminologies, or relying on expert claims, my approach to trans- genealogies is
one that centers surgical practices as themselves indicators of the bodily states
and body projects in which they are intended to intervene. What do patients

ask for in their process of surgical transition? How have those asks changed over time and what can those changes tell us about the kind of thing that *trans-* is and has been in the clinic?

In centring practices, I follow the work of medical anthropologist and science studies scholar Annemarie Mol (2002; Mol and Berg, 1994) to argue that the nature of a clinical object is best understood through attention to the clinical practices meant to respond to it. So, instead of assuming that *trans-* (or *transsexualism*, or *transgenderism*, or *gender identity disorder*, or *gender dysphoria*, or *gender incongruence*, or whatever label comes next) is a stable kind of diagnostic entity or body project to which particular hormonal and surgical interventions rationally respond, using Mol's approach I give the role of definition to clinical practices themselves. Attending to the numerous clinical practices aimed at 'changing' (or altering or confirming) sex or gender in the name of 'trans- medicine' brings two kinds of things into focus. First, the changing list of procedures that aim to change sex or gender is a great tool for understanding what sex and gender are as things that can be changed. Second, that as ideas about the nature of sex and gender change, so do the treatment rationales for how and why particular interventions can be regarded as good trans- medicine.

The emergence and growing popularity of facial feminisation surgery (FFS) demonstrates that profound changes in conceptualisations of *sex* and *gender* are being reflected in clinical responses to trans- women's desire to medically transition. No longer cleaving to the static divide between sex-as-physical and gender-as-social by which the concept of *transsexualism* first emerged in mid-century American sexology, trans- women's bodily practices reflect different stakes of what it means to transition and what role surgeons can play in that process. FFS is emblematic of a changing landscape of trans- medicine in America, one that is moving away from a myopic focus on genitalia as the location of bodily sex, and towards an understanding of sex as a product of social recognition. This latter mode, a surgical enactment of a performative model of sex/gender, not only rethinks the role of trans- medicine, but also makes it possible to see how conceptualisations of *trans-* are shifting away from the body-as-individual-given and towards the body-as-socially-lived-product. Rather than one model replacing another, these two modes of thinking sex/gender – and thus of understanding what interventions might constitute 'good trans- medicine' – are operating side by side, proliferating ideas about the role of trans- medicine and the kinds of things that sex/gender can and could be.

Before I go on, let me describe FFS and tell you, in the words of its patients and surgical practitioners, what FFS aims to do.

Facial feminisation surgery

Facial feminisation surgery (FFS) is a set of bone and soft-tissue reconstructive surgical procedures that aims to make trans- women's faces more feminine. Though each patient's treatment plan is different, bone procedures frequently employed include: reduction of the bony ridges above the eyes (bossing), setting back the frontal bone (forehead), rebuilding the nasal bones, reducing the width and squareness of the mandible (jaw) and reducing the height and shape of the chin. Soft-tissue procedures may include: advancing the scalp and reshaping the hairline, raising the position of the eyebrows on the forehead, rebuilding the tip of the nose, reducing the height of the upper lip, plumping the lips, reducing the thyroid cartilage (Adam's apple), hair transplant or removal, placing implants to augment the cheeks, reducing lines and wrinkles associated with aging and pinning the ears (see Plemons, 2017: 39–42). Some patients undergo most or all of these procedures, and some undergo only a few. Decisions about which of these are appropriate depend on the patient's goals, the surgeon's skills and recommendations, and the patient's physical and financial limitations. Given this wide array of procedures, FFS does not name a particular set of interventions, per se, but is instead defined by its animating goal: FFS aims to make trans- women who had, before surgery, been recognised by others as male, recognizable as female and, as such, recognizable as the women they know themselves to be.

Importantly, FFS is a procedure that is explicitly oriented to the perceptions of others. Calling on a long history of physiognomy and typological distinctions, the face is the site of our individual identities and a part of our bodies that signifies a great deal about us, from age to race and ethnicity to social class and more. When I conducted a year of ethnographical fieldwork in the offices and operating rooms of two American FFS specialists between 2010–11, both surgeons and patients consistently demonstrated the others-focused nature of FFS by narrating its efficacy through imagined or experienced scenes of social interaction.

I met Rachel, a trans- woman from New York in her mid-fifties, just five days after her surgery. Rachel had first decided that she wanted FFS 15 years earlier, as soon as she saw before-and-after photographs posted online. She said, 'From the moment I knew it existed, I thought, "Wow". I knew that I didn't have a pretty face. I'd get dressed up but I knew I didn't look like a woman. I could put all the makeup in the world on and nobody was going to mistake me for a girl. Maybe when I was like 16'.

When I asked her what it was about her face that she had wanted to change, she had trouble locating the problem that she hoped surgery could fix – though she could quickly recount the list of the procedures that had just been performed. She had had her forehead bone set back, her hairline reshaped and moved forward, her nose reduced at the bridge and raised at the tip, her jaw made more narrow at the back and shorter and more pointed at the chin, and her thyroid cartilage removed. In addition, her upper lip had been shortened and plumped.

'My goal, my ideal is that I could go out on the street dressed like I'm dressed right now – just a pair of pants and a t-shirt and some sneakers – and no gender markings other than I'd be wearing earrings, which I always wear, and that when I went into a grocery store the person would say, "Can I help you miss?" That's really what I want. I want to be read as, accepted as, and reacted to as a woman. So that is what I was hoping [the surgeon] would say he can do, and that's what he does say he can do. That *is* what he promises'.

In her grocery store fantasy, Rachel's face, unadorned by carefully styled hairdos, makeup or jewelry, would anchor a femininity so fundamental that an ordinary scene which might have previously instigated a tense exchange of suspicious glanced looks and bumbled pronouns, would became an opportunity for gendered deference: 'Can I help you miss?' In this moment, Rachel would get what she wanted, 'to be read as, accepted as, and reacted to as a woman'.

Helene, a Dutch attorney in her early fifties, also used scenes of shopping and examples of personal address to demonstrate first why she needed FFS, and then to prove that it had 'worked'. 'There is no question that I needed this operation', Helene explained of the FFS (brow, jaw, nose, chin, upper lip, hairline) she had had a year before. 'It was absolutely essential', she said, 'absolutely'. As we walked together through the narrow streets of a residential San Francisco neighborhood, Helene explained why she needed FFS by telling me a story.

> I was out shopping and two shop girls were talking. I heard them talking to each other and one of them said, 'I think she's a man'. And the other one said, 'No, no'. And the other one said, 'Look at her shoes'. And she said, 'No, they're quite normal'. But just the fact that they were discussing my gender just destroyed me completely. You just sink into the earth. It's the most terrible thing that can happen to you.

There was nothing that Helene could do about her shoe size, but she could make other changes. She had been on estrogen therapy for nearly two years and had undergone extensive facial and body electrolysis but she did not consider herself to really have transitioned. She had not discussed her intentions with her friends or business partners; only her wife knew of her plan to change her body. 'I had always thought that the face was the major barrier to a successful transition', she explained. 'Making other changes without changing my face just wouldn't work'. She found a surgeon online and began to research him. 'There was no hesitation' in choosing a surgeon, she explained. 'I was not picking who would do the job. I heard of [the doctor's] reputation and came here'. Helene opted to undergo a number of procedures. 'I had a typical male brow and the angular jaw and the nose was pretty masculine', she explained. 'It looked pretty badly from a female perspective. My wife would say, "But you are a beautiful man!" And I would say, "Yeah, but I'm not a man". So there you have it'.

Now post FFS, 'I'm always addressed as Mrs. So-and-so or madam', Helene told me. 'It's great. I'm so incredibly happy'. She described her FFS as 'miracle work'. 'It's from a fairy tale', she said. 'I'm stunned. You would not think that this could be done at all'. Helene's expressed need for FFS was a deeply personal one. Being recognised as female meant not being recognised as trans-, a change that kept her from 'sinking into the earth'. Now, a year later, she felt that her facial surgery had delivered on its transformational promise. It provided the crucial shift between perceptions of others that left her feeling humiliated and vulnerable and the self-assertion and ratification of her deeply felt identity.

Crystal explained that, for her, altering her face would make a much greater impact on her life than would GSRS. 'I received a gift that I was going to put some money towards doing the [G]SRS surgery', she said. 'But I realized that after having transitioned over ten years ago, [GSRS] is really not going to change my life a whole lot more at this point. What would change would be doing face work'. Denise was of the same opinion. She had not yet undergone genital reconstruction surgeries, though she did hope to do so at some point in the future. For Denise, too, FFS represented a life change that was more important than what genital surgery would provide. 'FFS will let me make the jump from man to woman, so I can live as a woman', she said. 'I'll deal with the lower parts later'.

Alison had not yet begun taking estrogens when she had her initial consultation for FFS. Her plan was to begin hormones, wait until her breasts had begun to develop and then undergo facial surgery. She planned to wait several years before undergoing any genital surgery; she hoped that the change she was seeking would mostly be accomplished through facial reconstruction:

> I think that [FFS] will be the key marker where I stop being Robert and start being Alison. When I walk into the surgery room and I walk in with a Robert face and whatever body I have at the moment, I walk in with that, even if I had Robert face and some small breasts, I'd still be Robert. And when I walk out I'll be Alison. The face will make that much difference to me.

For these patients, FFS was not complementary to (genital) sex reassignment; it constituted sex reassignment. Conceiving 'woman' as an accomplishment of social recognition, when FFS made them recognizable to others as women, they would be women, irrespective of their genital anatomies.

Surgeons who specialise in FFS also believe in its transformative promise, and also voice their beliefs through imagined scenes of social interaction in which it is some other viewer who recognises the post-op patient as a woman, thereby ratifying the effectiveness of the surgery. One prominent FFS surgeon explains the efficacy of FFS through the following scene: 'If, on a Saturday morning, someone knocks at the door and you wake up and get out of bed with messy hair, no makeup, no jewelry, and answer the door, the first words you'll hear from the person standing there are, "Excuse me, ma'am. . ."'. The story ends with the gendered term of address. 'Ma'am' is the crucial term that signifies not only the perceptions of the viewer on the doorstep, but also produces womanness through utterance. This is the quintessential performative scene: the making of woman in acts of social interaction and address.

The foregoing stories show a consistent understanding of social recognition as a 'woman' as the trans- woman's end goal and assert, therefore, that if facial surgery is the means to reach that goal, then it constitutes good trans- medicine. This is not a kind of trans- medicine that would have made sense in the genital-centric milieu in which *transsexualism* was defined and its attendant forms of therapy developed.

Trans- therapeutics

Like all forms of trans- medicine, FFS materialises 'masculine' and 'feminine', 'man' and 'woman' into action; it turns these contested terms into sets of bodily properties into which surgery can intervene (Plemons, 2014a, 2017). Surgical intervention requires an understanding of the ways in which the pre-operative body is unwell or undesirable (in this case, how and why a patient's face is 'masculine'), an end goal to which surgical intervention is oriented (the desirably 'feminine'), and a plan for how to get from the former to the latter. In and through each of these steps a therapeutic logic is enacted. That is to say, at each step – assessment, planning and intervention – links are made among the origins of the authorising diagnosis, treatment rationales and outcome measures. The implicit assumptions and explicit answers to each of these questions enact what I term *trans- therapeutics*. As patient-initiated surgical interventions in the name of trans- medicine change, they necessitate a reconsideration of aims, methods and logics of trans- therapeutics. What does the fact that more and more trans- women are seeking FFS instead of or before genital surgery tell us about the end to which their surgical engagements are oriented? What does it tell us about what they hope surgery can and will do? And if FFS counts as good trans- medicine, what kind of *trans-* does it assume and help to produce?

The growing popularity of FFS is not simply the newest way to create the same outcome that genital surgeries were once designed to create – namely, 'woman' defined as an individual, atomised bodily form. Instead, FFS aims to enact 'woman' as an effect of social recognition. In such a case, to say that FFS is effective is to indicate a different aim of trans- medicine from the one that genital surgeries have, for decades, been understood to confirm. To claim that FFS is 'therapeutic', that it is an efficacious and rational response to trans- women's request for medical transition, is to claim that the issue that those trans- women hope surgery can address is not only a facial one, but also one oriented by an aim of social recognition. It acknowledges 'woman' as a category constituted by social and subjective practices, rather than given bodily forms. Such a claim not only posits a different understanding of 'woman' as intersubjective and social rather than individual and anatomical, but by implication it also indicates the aim of trans- medicine as one that is not focused on individual bodies but conceptualises sex and gender as performative products. FFS engages performativity as a surgical philosophy and is, as a result, a significant departure from previous models of trans- therapeutics.

Original model: when changing sex meant changing genitals

Organised as they were by a genital-based understanding of sex, early clinical practices that aimed to 'change sex' focused on the reconstruction of genital and reproductive anatomies. Transsexualism, pioneering physician Harry Benjamin wrote in 1954, 'denotes the intense and often obsessive desire to change the entire sexual status including the anatomical structure. While the male transvestite *enacts* the role of woman, the transsexualist wants to *be* one and *function* as one, wishing to assume as many of her characteristics as possible, physical, mental and sexual' (Benjamin, 1954: 220). According to this foundational clinical model, the primary thing that a transsexual wanted and needed in order to be 'physically, mentally and sexually' a woman was reconstructive genital surgery.

It was based on this genital-centric understanding of sex, sex change and the therapeutic aims of intervention that university-based gender clinics began to offer psychological and medical services in the 1960s. Largely funded by a single trans- man who was the heir to an industrial fortune (Devor, 2002; Devor and Matte, 2007), American university clinics developed treatment protocols and began to conduct research on trans- medicine, ushering in a moment that Susan Stryker has called the 'the "Big Science" period of transgender history' (2008: 93).

The university-based gender clinics that had been the sole providers of psychological, endocrinological and surgical services to trans- patients beginning in the late 1960s, had, by the end of the 1970s, begun to close their doors. Their rapid closure was the result of diminished funding, clinical challenges to the benefits of surgical sex reassignment and refractions of their power because of the codification of *transsexualism* in the DSM-III and the establishment of professional best practices (APA, 1980; Irvine, 1990; Rudacille, 2005; Stryker, 1999; Devor, 2002). When the clinics dissolved, so did the restrictive power they held over who could access services for medical transition and how that transition would proceed. Now offered by surgeons working in private practice, patient narratives and goals that had been disallowed by strict diagnostic guidelines began to appear (Bolin, 1988). Historian Joanne Meyerowitz (2002) has argued that the shift of trans- medicine from university- based clinics to private practice in the late 1970s and 1980s is the event that has had the greatest impact on trans- health care in the United States. 'Suddenly the old morality tale of the truth of gender, told by a kindly white patriarch in New York in 1966 [Harry Benjamin], becomes pancultural in the 1980s', writes Sandy Stone of this dynamic moment in trans- medicine (2006: 229).

One effect of the shift to private practice is that patients were newly able to voice their own concerns and aims for transition-related surgical procedures. Though access to genital surgeries was still controlled by the processes outlined in the WPATH's Standards of Care, in the early 1980s, other kinds of body- and gender-altering procedures – such as facial surgery – were not. As I've described elsewhere in accounts of the development of FFS (Plemons, 2014b), in 1982, a trans- woman who had undergone genital surgery in a university clinic returned to her surgeon there with the request that her surgeon alter the sexed appearance of her face. This patient had found that the fact of her female genitalia did not change her life in all the ways she hoped 'transition' would. She was still recognised by others as male, despite her best efforts to cultivate a feminine appearance. She felt sure that altering the structure of her face would change all that. Adopting the then-current trans- therapeutics, the cranio-facial surgeon who took on this patient's case did not think of what he was doing as 'sex reassignment surgery'. To him, facial surgery was complementary to genital surgery – the 'real' sex-changing operation; it did not itself constitute sex reassignment. Over time, however, and in consultation with his patients, he has come to understand FFS as the most important surgery a trans- woman can undergo. If what a trans- woman wants from trans- medicine is to be a woman, he asserts, the most important change she can undergo is not one focused on hidden parts of her body, but on the part that others see the most: her face.

The claim articulated to me over and over by FFS patients and their surgeons – that FFS is a form of surgical sex reassignment because a trans- woman becomes a woman when others recognise her as such – is one that would not have made sense in the mid-century terms by which trans- medicine was first established. But in the contemporary FFS clinic, it was a claim that was presented as common sense. It was self-evidently clear to the trans- women who underwent it, and to the many, many people who view before-and-after FFS photos in awe of its transformational capacities. While there is no doubt that radical facial reconstruction enacts a dramatic change, to claim that enacts a change of sex is to posit a particular understanding of sex, a performative understanding. That performative logic – that woman is an effect of contextualised recognition rather than the ostensibly universalised fact of possessing female genitalia – is the logic that underwrites the power of FFS. Though neither patients nor surgeons ever used the language of 'performativity' in our conversations, it is the claim to performative efficacy that animates the project of FFS. It has become a surgical plan, a way of reframing trans- therapeutics tuned towards a different understanding of 'woman' and a different path to its enactment.

Trans- in the clinic

It is necessary to watch how trans- medicine gets done because the concepts at the heart of the definition of *trans-*, the concepts of disjuncture between physical sex and social gender, have been so fundamentally challenged that the foundational conceptualisation of two polar forces at odds is no longer tenable – from a psychological, biological or feminist point of view. What we can do is turn to ethnography to look at what people are doing in clinics. We can ask how the kinds of treatments people are seeking in the name of trans- medicine can help us understand the projects and ends for which they seek them. You have to go into the clinic and watch what people are doing. When trans- women seek FFS as a means of enacting 'woman', they're investing in a performative claim and taking up surgical interventions to realise it. FFS voices trans- therapeutics in terms of a performativity unmoored from its Butlerian concept work and used instead as a metonymic way to refer to conceptualisations of sex and gender that directly militate against the kinds of reductive essentialism that animated mid-century surgical projects.

The two modes of trans- therapeutics that I have contrasted here have not replaced each other in succession; they co-exist. There is no single thing that we can say all trans- people who seek it want from trans- medicine. That trans-medicine was ever one kind of practice or project was an artificial homogenisation of trans- ontologies that we know was never in fact that homogenous. As the university clinics closed and as American medicine became more available for (market-mediated) individual self-making, ideas about what people want from medical transition proliferated; they became more interesting, more unique, more self-directed. There are a lot of different things that trans- people want from medicine because *trans-* is a word that includes many different identities and body projects. GSRS is enlivened by a trans- therapeutics focused on the individual body, one that locates sex in anatomical properties. FFS, by contrasts, enacts trans- therapeutics as one oriented towards a transformation of the socially produced body, by an aim of intersubjective recognition.

Notes

1 I use the term *trans-*. Whereas Stryker, Currah and Moore (2008) use *trans-* with the open-ended hyphen in order to leave open the possibility of kinds of crossing that are not limited to gender, here I use it to draw attention to the multiple gendered endings to the word *trans* that have come to hold important personal and political stakes for those who use this word to identify themselves.
2 For an account of trans- men accessing medical intervention in the mid-twentieth century, see Rubin, 2003.
3 See Stryker and Sullivan (2012).

References

American Psychiatric Association (1980) *Diagnostic and statistical manual of mental disorders (DSM-III)*. Washington, DC: American psychiatric association.
Benjamin, H (1954) Transsexualism and transvestism as psycho-somatic and somato-psychic syndromes. *American Journal of Psychotherapy* 8: 219–230.
Berger, AE (2013) *The queer turn in feminism: Identities, sexualities and the theater of gender*. New York: Fordham Press.
Bolin, A (1988) *In search of eve: Transsexual rites of passage*. South Hadley, MA: Bergin & Garvey.
Butler, J (1990) *Gender trouble*. New York: Routledge.
Butler, J (1993) *Bodies that matter*. New York: Routledge.
Devor, A and Matte, N (2007) Building a better world for transpeople: Reed Erickson and the Erickson educational foundation. *International Journal of Transgenderism* 10(1): 47–68.
Devor, H (2002) Reed Erickson (1917–1992): How one transsexed man supported one. In *Before stonewall: Activists for gay and lesbian rights in historical context*. J Dececco and V Bullough, eds. pp. 383–392. Binghamton, NY: The Haworth Press.

Dolgin, JL (2015) Unhealthy determinations controlling medical necessity. *Virginia Journal of Social Policy & Law* 22: 435.

Irvine, J (1990) *Disorders of desire: Sex and gender in modern American sexology.* Philadelphia: Temple University Press.

Jones, DS, Podolsky, SH and Greene JA (2012) The burden of disease and the changing task of medicine. *New England Journal of Medicine* 366(25): 2333–2338.

Matte, N, Devor, AH and Vladicka, T (2009) Nomenclature in the world professional association for transgender health's standards of care: Background and recommendations. *International Journal of Transgenderism* 11: 42–52.

Meyerowitz, J (2002) *How sex changed: A history of transsexuality in the United States.* Cambridge, MA: Harvard University Press.

Mol, A (2002) *The body multiple: Ontology in medical practice.* Durham, NC: Duke University Press.

Mol, A and Berg, M (1994) Principles and practices of medicine. *Culture, Medicine and Psychiatry* 18(2): 247–265.

Plemons, ED (2014a) It is as it does: Genital form and function in sex reassignment surgery. *Journal of Medical Humanities* 35(1): 37–55.

Plemons, ED (2014b) Description of sex difference as prescription for sex change: On the origins of facial feminization surgery. *Social Studies of Science* 44(5): 657–679.

Plemons, ED (2017) *The look of a woman: Facial feminization surgery and the aims of trans- medicine.* Durham, NC: Duke University Press.

Rubin, H (2003) *Self-made men: Identity and embodiment among transsexual men.* Memphis, TN: Vanderbilt University Press.

Rudacille, D (2005) *The riddle of gender: Science, activism, and transgender rights.* New York: Pantheon Books.

Stone, S (2006 [1991]) The *empire* strikes back: A posttranssexual manifesto. In *The transgender studies reader.* Stryker and Whittle, eds. New York: Routledge. pp. 221–235.

Stryker, S (1999) Portrait of a transfag drag hag as a young man: The activist career of Louis G. Sullivan. In *Reclaiming genders: Transsexual grammars at the fin de siècle.* Kate More and Stephen Whittle, eds. New York: Cassell. pp. 62–82.

Stryker, S (2008) *Transgender history.* Berkeley, CA: Seal Press.

Stryker, S, Currah, P and Moore, LJ (2008) Introduction: Trans-, trans, or transgender? *Women's Studies Quarterly* 36(3/4): 11–22.

Stryker, S and Sullivan, N (2012) King's member, Queen's body: Transsexual surgery, self-demand amputation and the somatechnics of sovereign power. In *Somatechnics: Queering the technologisation of bodies.* Murray, S. and Sullivan, N., eds. New York, NY: Routledge. pp. 49–64.

World Professional Association for Transgender Health (2007) *Standards of care for the health of transsexual, transgender, and gender nonconforming people.* Seventh Version. www.wpath.org.

3   Becoming

Discourses of trans emergence, epiphanies and oppositions

Natacha Kennedy

This study constitutes a sociological analysis of how trans people experience epiphany stemming from cultural processes present in most European-based cultures, and contrasts with psychological gazes of the process of epiphany as an individualised phenomenon. Although it is likely that some trans people never experience an epiphany – for example, very young children, and those who die before they become fully aware they are trans – most will have experienced an epiphany of some kind; indeed, it may be one of the few experiences most trans people have in common. 'Epiphany' here is characterised as the process of coming to identify as transgender, and in this context does not necessarily refer to a sudden personal revelation. In some instances epiphanies may take some considerable time and their durations measured in months or years rather than minutes or hours.

This chapter examines data relating to the ways young trans people describe the experience of epiphany, suggesting that the processes by which trans people come to identify as transgender on a local or individual level are affected by obstacles to trans emergence on a general level, as well as resistance to these obstacles. Analysing data from a small-scale, in-depth qualitative study of 16 young trans people, relating to epiphany on an individual level provides evidence of the nature of the cultural processes constituting these impediments. The analysis draws on Social Activity Method (Dowling, 1998, 2009, 2013), a new sociological method which constitutes a deductive and inductive dialogic interaction between empirical and theoretical fields, regarding the social as constituting the formation, maintenance and destabilising of alliances and oppositions. A systematic mode of analysing qualitative data, Social Activity Method focuses on constructing an organisational language with the aim of presenting constructive descriptions as opposed to 'forensics' in social research.

Initially I present data to construct two axes of analysis to constitute a relational space with which to elucidate the processes involved and subsequently produce a constructive description of them. The relational space in Figure 3.1 consists of two axes and draws out the principal differences between the ways participants in this study experienced epiphany: modes of becoming and modes of identification. These are elaborated in the subsequent sections of this chapter.

	Mode of identification	
Mode of Becoming	*Opposition*	*Alliance*
Anaphoric	Affirming	Desubjugating
Cataphoric	Differentiating	Introducing

Figure 3.1 Modes of epiphany

Becoming: anaphoric and cataphoric

Deleuze (1991), referring to Bergson (1913), argues that, rather than regarding ourselves as 'being', it would be more appropriate to regard ourselves as perpetually 'becoming'. Understanding ourselves in this way has the advantage of de-essentialising trans people's experiences and representing a more neutral characterisation by acknowledging that *all* people – not just trans people – experience change, in different ways, during their lives.

The period of epiphany for trans people can be regarded as 'becoming' at possibly its most intense, however short or long this period is. According to the Deleuzian/Bergsonian view, epiphany will not occur in temporal isolation. It will either follow from less intense antecedent periods of prior becoming, constituted here as *anaphoric* becoming, or will constitute itself as a kind of 'new beginning' oriented primarily towards the future, characterised here as *cataphoric* becoming.

In the case of some participants, epiphany was experienced as a kind of revelation where something hitherto unsuspected was made clear to them; for example, in the case of participant SP:

> Well, I had no idea what it was until I was friends with this one trans woman and I was like 'OK. . .' and she would talk to me about her childhood and that kind of thing and I strongly identified but the opposite way.

His realisation that he identified as a trans man developed with no significant antecedent suspicions that he might be transgender. In this sense, it represented an orientation to the future as opposed to the past; consequently his experience is characterised as *cataphoric*.

In contrast, *anaphoric* becoming is exemplified by R's experience:

> I hate this as a cliché, but I always knew I was different from when I was young. From a very, very young age, my interests and that were different; I didn't like being with the boys I liked being with the girls.

She had some idea about her identification before an epiphany that included a re-examination of past experiences, but appeared not to have had access to the vocabulary with which to express these earlier (see Kennedy, 2014). The experience of another participant, F, who experienced a sudden epiphany upon being introduced to other trans women, contrasts with R's epiphany which took place over a much longer period of time:

> I kind of took one step and then I kind of took ten steps; yes, I sort of put one foot into the trans scene and very quickly I was ten steps into it. I didn't really have second thoughts about it.

These two oppositions form the vertical axis of the relational space in Figure 3.1: anaphoric and cataphoric becoming.

Modes of identification: alliance and opposition

The horizontal axis in Figure 3.1 is constituted by *alliance* and *opposition* modes of identification. It draws on Brubaker's and Cooper's (2000) attempt to arrive at a more rigorous characterisation of the term 'identity'. They characterise the two main types of identification process as 'self-identification and social location', which is predominantly dependent on establishing an identity in opposition to those who are different, and 'commonality, connectedness and groupedness' which emphasises alliances and likeness with similars. The first involves distinguishing oneself from other groups or situating oneself in relation to others in different groups; the second involves establishing a commonality between oneself and other groups. This establishes the horizontal axis of the relational space: 'Modes of Identification' constituted as 'opposition' for the former and 'alliance' for the latter.

Drawing on the data for illustration, participant H's experience of epiphany was predominantly characterised by an opposition to his birth-assigned gender:

> When I turned 14, over the summer in between year nine and year ten, I went on the internet and just typed in things like 'I don't like being a girl', 'I don't like. . .' things about not being a girl, and those searches led me to people's blogs who are transgender, you know I've never heard of that before.

His identification process was *oppositional* in the sense that he was, from the outset, rejecting association with his birth-assigned gender. This contrasts with participant I's identification process which was predominantly positively oriented towards female:

> I would associate with being female rather than . . . it probably would be a mixture of the two but leaning towards associating with being female.

Instead of primarily constituting an opposition between herself and others of her birth-assigned gender, as H does, participant I is principally concerned to construct an *alliance*, identifying positively with her real gender.

This completes the characterisation of the two axes of modes of becoming and of identification, and enables us to construct the relational space in Figure 3.1 with which to generate an analysis.

Modes of epiphany

The relational space in Figure 3.1 is constituted of a vertical and a horizontal axis based on the binary oppositions elaborated previously, and as a result constitutes the four different modes of epiphany: *affirming, desubjugating, introducing* and *differentiating*.

The top left corner of Figure 3.1 indicates the intersection of an oppositional identification process with an anaphoric becoming, which I have characterised as an 'affirming' epiphany. In this mode there is reference to antecedent experiences but there is uncertainty about identification and gender identity. Prior life experiences, which may previously have been disorienting, are reinterpreted. In this mode, the identification process is primarily oppositional, originating mostly from a rejection of one's birth-assigned gender. Participant P, for example, describes his prior experiences of being misinterpreted as a tomboy when he was younger, which later became relevant while experiencing epiphany:

> [My mother] told me that I started rejecting dresses at age 3, I don't remember it, I think what, the identity I remember having, the identity I was given by other people, was a tomboy.

These experiences helped provide him with a frame of reference when coming to understand himself as trans. However, they also represented an obstacle earlier on: being assigned the identity of 'tomboy' was considerably disorienting, as he found out after being introduced to another 'tomboy':

> I wasn't masculine at all; I'm still not very masculine at all, and she was just like, she was a girl who liked boy things.

Moving clockwise round the relational space, the top right corner is characterised as 'desubjugating': this represents an alliance mode of identification with an anaphoric becoming. M's experience exemplifies this:

> They could see it, everyone else could see it, but I was kind of really struggling with it, really fighting with it; it was, I mean, a massive internal fight, going, 'Oh fuck I've been a lesbian', you know. That's hard enough; do I have to . . . to . . . be weirder?

In this instance the obstacle M reports is the *notion itself* of accepting himself as transgender; he refers to his own resistance to identifying as a trans man, reflecting his earlier experience of coming out as a butch lesbian while he was at school. This mode of epiphany can be regarded as enabling him to overcome resistance to identifying as a trans man; a group of trans men helped him over-come the effects of prior negative experiences in a different context. Sub-sequently he reveals how this identification process primarily represented a positive orientation towards identifying as a man, as opposed to a rejection of femininity:

> I love the femininity that I have, but it's also coming from a masculine place, you know.

Moving clockwise round the relational space, the bottom right corner is char-acterised as 'introducing': a cataphoric becoming with an alliance identification process. Participant F describes her experience:

> I guess it just happened, I mean, I just went to one trans club one time and I met a friend there and he was really into trans girls and we dated for a while and he showed me all the other trans clubs. [. . .] I didn't know the scene at all; I didn't know any of the websites.

Here, she was quite literally introduced to trans people, with whom she very quickly came to identify, for the first time. In a not-dissimilar way to M's experience, F identified as a gay man before this; however, unlike M, she had no prior indication that she might come to identify as a trans woman. Her discourse is focused on the future; throughout her interview she often talked of medical transition and other aspects of her future life such as buying a place to live, enjoying herself while young and getting married. There was nothing trans-related from her pre-epiphany life referred to in her interview.

The final section, in the bottom left corner, is characterised as 'differentiat-ing'. Participant B, a non-binary person, describes how they related negatively to their birth-assigned gender:

> B: It's also been somewhat of a problem that he sees me as a woman because he can't really see me in another way because if he were to see me as a man he wouldn't want to . . . you know be doing stuff in the first place.
> INT: So it's important that he sees you not as a woman, for you to enjoy it?
> B: Yeah.

They describe how they found it became difficult to have sex with their hus-band because he needed to regard them as a woman in order to have sex with them, something which was problematic for them as a non-binary person who rejected their assigned gender. This is reflected in their attitude to wearing women's clothes for drag:

> INT: So you might consider doing drag at some point?

B:Yeah since I started identifying as trans I have a few times done … it's a bit difficult because when I put on women's clothes I look like a woman and not as a person in drag.

They also report having no antecedent conception that they might come to identify as trans, at least before they had been married for some time:

My husband didn't know from the start because I didn't know from the start.

This is characterised as *differentiating* mode since the principal issue here is to define themself apart from others, in this case from both cisgender people of the same birth-assigned gender and from binary-identifying trans people.

This relational space, constructed from the intersection of two binary oppositions derived directly from empirical data, enables us to produce a constructive description of trans people's epiphanies on a local level. The next section analyses how this might relate to trans emergence on a more general level.

Analysis: delegitimisation and erasure

This section argues that the modes of epiphany described here have all occurred as a consequence of cultural processes of obstruction. What follows is an analysis of the modes of epiphany characterised in the relational space in Figure 3.1, constituting a constructive description of the processes that result in these types of epiphany. By examining the ways participants have experienced epiphanies, we can describe the nature of this cultural obstruction.

Stryker (2008) noted how the decades between 1970 and 1990 were particularly difficult for trans people in European-based cultures, but that this started to change when a new wave of trans activism emerged during the 1990s. The process of epiphany manifests itself as an individual response to cultural processes, making it necessary for trans people to experience an understanding of their genders as a kind of revelation: established cultural mythologisations of gendering as an externally imposed, essentialised cultural process constitute an obstruction to identifying as transgender. If, in an ideal cultural environment, genders were not assigned at birth or perhaps only provisionally assigned, transgender people would not need to experience epiphany – at least not in the same ways they do in this analysis – because the assumptions of this process of 'cultural cisgenderism' (Kennedy, 2013) would no longer be made.

What is evident from the modes of epiphany outlined in Figure 3.1 is that they can be regarded as individual responses to the variety of sociocultural environments in which trans people grow up. Different trans people experience different kinds of epiphanies because we grow up in different cultural environments; these can erase and/or delegitimise trans people. Therefore, the

Introducing mode of epiphany can be regarded as occurring as a consequence of the cultural erasure of trans people; trans people are simply excluded from the general cultural milieu so the possibility of coming to identify as trans is much more restricted. This is evident in the case of F: the possibility that she might be a woman was not considered until she was introduced, in person, to other trans women.

Desubjugating and *affirming* modes can be regarded as most likely to be a response to delegitimisation through oppositional narratives that attempt to situate trans people as not legitimate, genuine, authentic, 'normal' or rational. The anaphoric nature of these epiphanies suggests that these participants' prior rebellions against their assigned genders are likely to have been delegitimised somehow; for example, through being regarded in ways that signified, for themselves and others around them, identities other than differently gendered ones:

> I do remember one day when I was walking to school in seventh grade, something not sure why I thought it was just a random thought, gender identity and sexual orientation I would probably think of myself as a butch lesbian or masculine lesbian but that's just wrong. . . . Does not compute.
>
> (participant D)

Differentiating mode is somewhat different and can be regarded as a response to a combination of both erasure and delegitimisation. Cataphoric becoming represents a consequence of erasure, while oppositional identification suggests that a reaction against birth-assigned gender is more significant than positively identifying with another gender. In this instance, erasure and delegitimisation combine against the possibility of identifying as genders other than those assigned at birth and, in this instance, non-binary genders also. In the case of participant B this is either because non-binary gender identification is both excluded and delegitimised at the most basic level of language, or because dysphoric feelings can be, and often are, misinterpreted as signifiers of other things such as homosexuality, as exemplified by participant D.

This analysis prompts the question: how has there been an apparent significant increase in numbers of trans people becoming more visible *as* trans people? While there appear to be no studies that can definitively tell us how many trans people there are (Nicolazzo, 2017), it is evident that increasing numbers of people are coming forward to ask for gender reassignment surgery (Lyons, 2016), and there is anecdotal evidence that many more than that are living their lives as a gender they were not assigned at birth, which includes a significant increase in the number of under-18s (Brinkhurst-Cuff, 2016).

Now that I have established a picture of trans epiphanies on a local or individual level, I use it to analyse the social and cultural milleux which have resulted in trans people needing to experience epiphanies in these ways, and how these relate to the recent emergence of trans people as a more widely recognised social group.

Emergence

Erasure, a mode of obstruction that was particularly prominent in, and before, the mid-twentieth century, remains as such today in some environments. In the past, trans people were advised to relocate to a different part of the country after transitioning, change their names and reconstruct a backstory for their earlier lives (e.g. Garfinkel, 1967). 'Stealth' remains an option today but probably by a declining proportion of trans people (Garfinkel, 1967; Shapiro, 2004; Lester, 2017).

While erasure may be less in evidence now (e.g. Steinmetz, 2014; Pesta, 2015; Mock, 2017; Bindel, 2016), delegitimisation is becoming more prominent (e.g. Greer, 1999; Jeffreys, 2014). Those opposed to the existence and well-being of trans people appear to have made the decision that delegitimisation represents the most productive strategy, from their perspective, particularly at the general level. Evidence from participant SH exemplifies how this subsequently affects the local:

> She moved house last September so I went round to help her move all her stuff and the old people came into the new property . . . just to pick up their post, and I'm standing there like this (points to bearded face) with a beard like this (points again) and she was just saying, 'Oh, this is my daughter'. I'd never met these people in my entire life.

Here, not only does SH's mother attempt to delegitimise her son by misrepresentation but also she attempts to invoke what she appears to perceive is a general non-acceptance of trans people from people who are, in this context, effectively random members of the public. Here, the move from a perceived general cultural mythologisation is mobilised into the local, in what SH constitutes as an opposition to him identifying as a trans man.

How this general-level opposition appears to affect the local is also exemplified by participant G's mother, who draws on the narrative of 'trans regret' by some journalists and media platforms as an opposition strategy:

> My mum, who is not equipped with any information, says, 'Oh, loads of people regret it' and I think the regret rate is probably the lowest of anything [. . .] I think she says it because it's . . . particularly when things are, you know, sensationalized by the media.

Material produced by journalists such as Jenni Murray, who in 2017 published a lengthy article in the UK newspaper *The Times* arguing that trans women are not 'real women', represents a topical example of a strategy of delegitimisation, based on misrepresentation of trans women (McCormick, 2017) in particular. Other journalists have attempted to misrepresent trans children and adults who campaign on their behalf (Butterworth, 2016) by employing narratives that are unsupported by data. The following example appeared in a UK tabloid newspaper and employs many traditional right-wing stereotypes regarding the supposedly nefarious influence of public-sector workers such as 'well-meaning liberal teachers' and 'social workers':

> If I were a teenager today, well-meaning liberal teachers and social workers would probably tell me that I was trapped in the wrong body. They might refer me to a psychiatrist who would prescribe fistfuls of hormones and other drugs. And terrifyingly, I might easily be recommended for gender re-assignment surgery . . . just because I didn't like the pink straitjacket imposed on girls.
>
> (Bindel, J. *Daily Mail* 24 October 2016)

Attempts to delegitimise trans people by such narratives appear to be one of the strategies of obstruction currently most in evidence (Brubaker, 2016), although these have a history dating back well into the 1970s and 1980s (e.g. Raymond, 1979; Blanchard, 1989; Greer, 1999). What is significant about these narratives is that whilst previously they tended to be less well known outside specific academic and 'feminist' groups, they have recently become more widely apparent in mainstream mass media (Guardian, 2016). This suggests that those who campaign against trans people's rights have perceived the need to import material previously only deployed in specialist domains into the general domain. In effect, they have drawn on existing arguments that were already available and popularised them. This move – distributing material which has been described by Lester (2017) as intentionally producing ignorance and by Lees (2015) as constituting hate-speech, to a much wider audience – can be regarded as a response to the emergence of trans people in the public consciousness.

We can see therefore how what previously constituted a more passive erasure appears to have been discarded in favour of a more active strategy of delegitimisation. Such delegitimising strategies have been heavily criticised for being divisive (Riddell, 1980), pathologising (Tosh, 2016), dishonest (Stone, 1996; Tosh, 2016), violent and abusive (Williams, 2016), bio-essentialist and harmful (MacKinnon, 2015).

Implications

To a significant extent the deployment of delegitimising narratives negates the possibility of maintaining the erasure of transgender identities as an effective anti-trans strategy.[1] There are fundamental differences between erasure and delegitimisation, in particular of motivation and activity. Stryker (2006) characterises a shift in wider cultural mythologisations that developed during the Renaissance. She argues that during this time Western culture moved away from a spiritual basis and became based much more on the material. This materiality had the side effect of introducing an element of cultural erasure in European-based cultures, in contrast to many other cultures (Williams, 1986; Wiesner-Hanks, 2011: 4), which resulted in the spiritual and psychological becoming subordinated to the physical.

As the general underlying basis for culture became more focused on the physical, claiming a gender identity at variance with that assigned according to an interpretation of one's physical body at birth would have become harder to conceptualise. It would have been in opposition to a more widespread assumption of gender as an essentialised quality based on one's physical body at birth produced by the wider material basis of culture in general. Not only would this have made it more difficult to regard oneself as trans but also the possibility of convincing others would also have seemed – and probably been – more difficult. As a consequence this produced an erasure, which did not necessarily affect other cultures until European colonial invasions and occupations took place. This essentialist materiality made it more difficult to identify in opposition to genders assigned at birth. To this extent erasure can be regarded as not intentionally targeted at trans people in particular, despite having negative consequences for trans people.

So whilst the erasure of trans people can be regarded as a largely passive and unintended cultural process, delegitimisation strategies should be regarded as purposely, actively and knowingly confected, distributed and maintained with the aim of specifically and deliberately affecting trans people's lives to their detriment (Dart, 2017). Erasure can be regarded as having arisen as the side effect of cultural processes not specifically directed at trans people, and against which trans activism has had to contend in the late twentieth and early twenty-first centuries, while delegitimisation can be regarded as the result of deliberately fashioned and targeted opposition (O'Shea, 2016).

Whether these delegitimisation strategies are pursued by those motivated by right-wing politics in the guise of religion, or whether the stated motivation is 'radical feminism', or, as appears to be more recently the case (Brydum, 2017), an alliance between these two apparently opposing ideologies manifest in the shape of a US-based group Hands Across the Aisle,[2] their effects are intentional. At the root of their deployment appear to be groups of people actively attempting to make the lives of trans people more dangerous, more stressful, more liminal, more isolated and less productive. If these very public attempts at delegitimisation are permitted to continue, the consequences are likely to be more trans people experiencing epiphanies, but subsequently finding an increasingly hostile environment created for them when they do.

The move from the predominance of the tacit/implicit erasure to the overt/explicit delegitimisation is significant, however. If erasure, the passive social/cultural resistance to trans people, is now less pervasive, the spread of delegitimising strategies can be regarded as a consequence of this. What may also be productive here is to consider the extent to which trans emergence on a general level can be characterised by this move. Could the decision by those opposed to trans people's existence to abandon the expression of explicit opposition in a relatively restricted domain in favour of its wider distribution in the public sphere be regarded as one of the defining features of trans emergence? What may also be important for further consideration is how significant this move from the tacit/implicit to the overt/explicit might be with respect to the future emergence of other groups, including intersex and asexual people.

The widespread availability of the internet has been credited with the emergence of trans people as a group (e.g. Whittle, 1998); however, it seems there is more complexity to this than mere technological determinism. Since the internet functions almost entirely through language, the development of a language which enabled trans discourses and the emergence of trans people was essential. Consequently the work of activists such as Feinberg (1992), Bornstein (1995) and Stone (1996) was probably more productive in this respect than previously considered. The development from largely localised and tacit expressions of trans identification to a more general and explicit discourse has facilitated wider coalescing of trans people into groups through online social media (Beemyn and Rankin, 2011: 160).

It is also possible that those apparently attempting to delegitimise trans people are, in no small measure, contributing to the process of emergence; their strategy is more likely to have the side effect of increasing trans visibility by facilitating explicit discussion and understanding by trans people and consequently enabling some modes of epiphany as well as supportive cohesive group formation. Those who oppose trans people's existence have, however, had to make a choice. On the one hand they could have attempted to maintain the existing passive erasure in the face of a larger and more visible trans population, or they could resort to delegitimisation. Ultimately it is likely that their hand has been forced: greater trans visibility has meant that erasure is no longer a viable option. The only choice available to them was whether to engage in delegitimising acts or not. However, let us be clear: this still represents a path these groups have actively chosen to take.

Those who have opposed trans people's existence and human rights and who have produced explicitly anti-trans material since the 1970s appear to be working harder to get these materials a much wider audience through mainstream media. It is also evident that their interests now coincide with those on the right of the political spectrum (Parke, 2016). While on the one hand is a group that claims to espouse a supposedly left-wing, 'radical', 'feminist' position, on the other is a more powerful and well-funded group of politically right-wing organisations which have recruited these narratives into their own propaganda efforts, including stochastic terrorism targeted at trans people (Tannehill, 2019). Not only do these narratives consist of largely unsupported, pathologising and disempowering narratives about trans people (Tosh, 2016), but also they appear to fit easily into the ideologies or methods of the political right (Eco, 1995, 2013: 2). Ultimately, prejudicial and discriminatory narratives misrepresenting minority groups are used to recruit support for oppressive ideologies, as has occurred in the past (e.g. Shirer, 1960). The way that this alliance appears to have been constructed with a group otherwise claiming to be opposed to their political aims is thus not insignificant, particularly when the right-wing organisations in question are opposed to many of the women's rights for which these 'feminists' claim to be campaigning (DiBranco, 2017).

Conclusion

Exploring what might appear to be individual instances of epiphany from a sociological perspective presents us with the opportunity to understand one element of the complex phenomenon that is trans emergence. This chapter suggests that these epiphanies may have become more common as a consequence of the move from the tacit to the explicit in terms of both discourses of emergence and narratives/propaganda of oppression. The discourses of emergence also need to be regarded as having themselves reflexively contributed towards that emergence. What may be more significant than previously assumed is trans people's own agency in achieving trans emergence at all levels through the facilitation of new discursive (and consequently cultural) possibilities, which function at many different levels, empowering trans people to become.

Notes

1 While the space to elaborate the nature of those delegitimising strategies is not available here, it would appear that misrepresenting trans people to a general population largely unfamiliar with trans people represents one of those most commonly used strategies, for example, as described by Julia Serano; https://medium.com/@juliaserano/transgender-people-and-biological-sex-myths-c2a9bcdb4f4a
2 https://handsacrosstheaislewomen.com

References

Beemyn, G & Rankin, S (2011) *The Lives of Transgender People*. Columbia University Press New York.

Bergson, H (1913) *Time and Free Will: An Essay on the Immediate Data of Consciousness*. George Allen New York.

Bindel, J (2016) I'm grateful I grew up before children who don't fit stereotypes were assumed to be transgender': Feminist activist Julie Bindel on the danger of playing gender politics with young lives. *Daily Mail* 24 October 2016. Available at: www.dailymail.co.uk/news/article-3865632/I-m-grateful-grew-children-don-t-fit-stereotypes-assumed-transgender-Feminist-activist-Julie-Bindel-danger-playing-gender-politics-young-lives.html (accessed 19 January 2019).

Blanchard, R (1989) The concept of autogynephilia and the typology of male gender dysphoria. *Journal of Nervous and Mental Disease* 177: 616–623.

Bornstein, K (1995) *Gender Outlaw: On Men, Women and the Rest of Us*. Vintage London.

Brinkhurst-Cuff, C (2016) Gender identity clinic for under-18s sees number of referrals double. *The Guardian* 11 April 2016. Available at: www.theguardian.com/society/2016/apr/11/gender-identity-clinic-under-18s-referrals-double (accessed 19 January 2019).

Brubaker, R (2016) *Trans: Gender and Race in an Age of Unsettled Identities*. Princeton University Press Princeton.

Brubaker, R & Cooper, F (2000) Beyond "identity". *Theory & Society* 29.

Brydum, S (2017) Right wing Christians and radical feminists form an odd (transphobic) couple. *Religion Dispatches* 19 January 2017. Available at: http://religiondispatches.org/right-wing-christians-and-radical-feminists-form-an-odd-transphobic-couple/ (accessed 19 January 2019).

Butterworth, B (2016) Daily Mail columnist says 'powerful transgender lobby' is threatening 'normal children'. *PinkNews* 14 December 2016. Available at: www.pinknews. co.uk/2016/12/14/daily-mail-columnist-says-powerful-transgender-lobby-is-threatening-normal-children/ (accessed 19 January 2016).

Dart, T (2017) Texas lawmakers clash over contentious transgender bathroom bill. *The Guardian* 17 July 2017. Available at: www.theguardian.com/us-news/2017/jul/17/texas-transgender-bathroom-bill-dan-patrick-joe-straus (accessed 19 January 2016).

Deleuze, G (1991) *Bergsonism.* Zone New York.

DiBranco, A (2017) Mobilizing misogyny. *Political Research Associates* 8 March 2017. Available at: www.politicalresearch.org/2017/03/08/mobilizing-misogyny/ (accessed 19 January 2017).

Dowling, P (1998) *The Sociology of Mathematics Education: Mathematical Myth/Pedagogic Texts.* RoutledgeFalmer Abingdon.

Dowling, P (2009) *Sociology As Method: Departures from the Forensics of Culture, Text and Knowledge.* Sense Rotterdam.

Dowling, P (2013) Social activity method: A fractal language for mathematics. *Mathematics Education Research Journal* 25.3.

Eco, U (1995) Ur-Fascism. *New York Review of Books* 22 June 1995. Available at: www. nybooks.com/articles/1995/06/22/ur-fascism/ (accessed 19 January 2019).

Eco, U (2013) *Inventing the Enemy and Other Occasional Writings.* Vintage London.

Feinberg, L (1992) *Transgender Liberation: A Movement Whose Time Has Come.* World View Forum Chicago.

Garfinkel, H (1967) Passing and the managed achievement of sex status of an 'intersexed' person. in Garfinkel, H (ed.) *Studies in Ethnomethodology.* Blackwell Oxford.

Greer, G (1999) *The Whole Woman.* Transworld London.

Jeffreys, S (2014) *Gender Hurts.* Routlege New York.

Kennedy, N (2013) Cultural cisgenderism: Consequences of the imperceptible. *British Psychological Society, Psychology of Women Section Review* 13(1): 10–16.

Kennedy, N (2014) Gefangene der Leksikon: Kulturelle Cis- Geschlechtligkeit und trans Kinder. in Schneider, E & Balthes-Löhr, C (eds.) *Normierte Kinder: Effekte der Geschlechternormativität auf Kindheit und Adoleszenz.* Transcript Verlag Bielefeld.

Lees, P (2015) On germaine greer and the hypocrisy of the 'left'. *Vice* 20 Novermber 2015. Available at: www.vice.com/en_uk/article/yvxxyy/germaine-greer-paris-lees-hypocrisy-left-free-speech.

Lester, C N (2017) *Trans Like Me: A Journey for All of Us.* Virago London.

Lyons, K (2016) Gender identity clinic services under strain as referral rates soar. *The Guardian* 20 July 2016. Available at: www.theguardian.com/society/2016/jul/10/transgender-clinic-waiting-times-patient-numbers-soar-gender-identity-services (accessed 19 January 2019).

MacKinnon, C (2015) Harm is harm, hello. *On Century Avenue* 9 March 2015. Available at: http://oncenturyavenue.org/2015/03/harm-is-harm-hello/.

McCormick, J (2017) BBC woman's hour host Dame Jenni Murray says trans women aren't 'real women'. *PinkNews* 5 March 2017. Available at: www.pinknews.co.uk/2017/03/05/bbc-womans-hour-host-dame-jenni-murray-says-trans-women-arent-real-women/ (accessed 19 January 2019).

Mock, J (2017) Janet Mock: Young people get trans rights. It's adults who don't. *New York Times* 23 February 2017. Available at: www.nytimes.com/2017/02/23/opinion/janet-mock-young-people-get-trans-rights-its-adults-who-dont.html (accessed 19 January 2019).

Nicolazzo, Z (2017) *Trans* in College: Transgender Students' Strategies for Navigating Campus Life and the Institutional Politics of Inclusion.* Stylus Sterling VA.

O'Shea, S (2016) I'm not that Caitlyn: A critique of both the transphobic media reaction to Caitlyn Jenner's Vanity Fair cover shoot and of passing. *Culture and Organization* 25(3): 202–216.

Parke, C (2016) The Christian right's love affair with anti-trans feminists. *Political Research Associates* 11 August 2016. Available at: www.politicalresearch.org/2016/08/11/the-chris tian-rights-love-affair-with-anti-trans-feminists/#sthash.odnFUK6W.dpbs (accessed 19 January 2019).

Pesta, A (2015) Chelsea manning shares her transition to living as a woman – Behind bars. *Cosmopolitan* 8 April 2015. Available at: www.cosmopolitan.com/politics/a38728/chelsea-manning-may-2015/ (accessed 19 January 2019).

Raymond, J (1979) *The Transsexual Empire: The Making of the She-Male*. Beacon Boston.

Riddell, C (1980) Divided sisterhood: A critical review of Janice Raymond's the transsexual empire. in Stryker, S & Whittle, S (eds.) *The Transgender Studies Reader*. Routledge New York.

Shapiro, E (2004) 'Trans' cending barriers: Transgender organizing on the internet. *Journal of Gay and Lesbian Social Services* 16:3–4.

Shirer, W (1960) *The Rise and Fall of the Third Reich*. Arrow London.

Steinmetz, K (2014) The transgender tipping point. *Time* 29 May 2014. Available at: http:// time.com/135480/transgender-tipping-point/ (accessed 19 January 2019).

Stone, S (1996) The empire strikes back: A posttranssexual manifesto. in Straub, K & Epstein, J (eds.) *Body Guards: The Cultural Politics of Sexual Ambiguity*. Routledge New York.

Stryker, S (2006) (De)subjugated knowledges: An introduction to transgender studies. in Stryker, S & Whittle, S (eds.) *The Transgender Studies Reader*. Routledge New York.

Stryker, S (2008) *Transgender History*. Seal Berkeley.

Tannehill, B (2019) Right-wing media are inciting violence against transgender people. *Media Matters* 10 January 2019. Available at: www.mediamatters.org/stories-and-interests/ transgender-rights (accessed 19 January 2019).

The Guardian (2016) Germaine Greer on difference between trans women and 'real women' – video. *The Guardian* 12 April 2016. Available at: www.theguardian.com/books/ video/2016/apr/12/germaine-greer-on-difference-between-trans-women-and-real-women-video (accessed 19 January 2019).

Tosh, J (2016) *Psychology and Gender Dysphoria: Feminist and Transgender Perspectives*. Routledge New York.

Whittle, S (1998) The trans-cyberian mail way. *Social and Legal Studies* 7.3:389–408.

Wiesner-Hanks, M (2011) *Gender in History: Global Perspectives*. Wiley-Blackwell Chichester.

Williams, C (2016) Radical inclusion: Recounting the trans inclusive history of radical feminism. *Transgender Studies Quarterly* 3.1–2:254–258.

Williams, W (1986) *The Spirit and the Flesh: Sexual Diversity in American Indian Culture*. Beacon Boston.

4   the seam of skin and scales

Elena Rose

I am not a woman trapped in a man's body. This body is no man's; it is mine, it is me, and there is no man in that equation. And I am not trapped in it. There are a million and one ways out of this body, and I have clung to it, tooth and claw, despite an endless line of people and institutions who would rather I vacate the premises, and have sometimes been willing to make me bleed to convince me they're right.

This body is mine, and I claim it and its bruises, and it is not a man's, and I am not trapped here. I have looked leaving my body in the eye and I have said, in the end, *hell no*. There is too much to do, too much to love, too many who need one more of us to say *hell no* and help them say the same.
You might not like it. It might be a wrongness to you.

I am done with traps. I am done with the philosophy of traps, and I am done with the feminism of who owns my body for what cause.
It is time for something that tells you that I am here for blood – my blood, the blood of my loved ones, the blood of the people who have battered themselves against my life and found me still here.

It is time for a feminism of the monstrous.

That is this body. That is this me. That is the voice that says get your names off of my parts and your hands off them too, that says stop colonising my reality and telling me what I mean without listening to a word I say.

What I say may be in a language incomprehensible, but there is a time for that, and it is right now, because this is a monster's creed. It is for the cobbled-together, the sewn-up, the grafted-on. It is for the golden, the under-the-earth, the foreign, the travels-by-night; the filthy ship-sinking blood-drinking cave-dwelling bone-cracking gorgeousness that says hell no, I am not tidy. I am not easy. I am not what you suppose me to be and until you listen to my voice and look me in my eyes, I will cling fast to this life no matter how far you drive me, how deep, with how many torches and pitchforks, biting back the whole way down. I will not give you my suicide. I will not give you my surrender.

This is for the Lilim, because you forget that the next part after your co-opted icon parts ways with Adam and goes her own way is *and she begat monsters*, and she becomes terrifying. This is for the Gorgons and the vampires and the chimaeras, for Cybele and Baba Yaga, Hel and Ashtoreth, for Lamia and Scylla, for Kali and Kapo 'ula-kina'u. This is for all of them with teeth.

It is time to look the monstrous in the eye. It is time. It is time to say that we are beautiful in our fierceness, and that we are our own. We are not the rejected of what we can never be. We are what we were meant to be. We are not pieces of wholes thrown together incorrectly. We are not inferior knockoffs of someone else. We are not mistakes.
If our monstrousness is frightening, then it is time we bare our teeth and draw that fear close to us and stop being so afraid of our fearsomeness that we fear everyone and everything else right back.

I am throwing my head back, here, and saying it: no more being afraid. Hell no. My monstrousness is not a place of shame. It is a strength. It is the power to say *I am mine*, and I will tell you what I mean. Not you. I am not any thing trapped in anyone's body. I am tougher than that, and I have plenty of blood to spare in this body of mine, and plenty more miles to go before any of you can bring me to my knees, and I dare you to try.

I am choosing to stay here, and it is mine to choose. And if that means changing shape, if that means putting together the unexpected, that is any monster's ancient right. It is damn well traditional.
The only ones setting traps are the ones in our way.
There. There's my teeth. There's my cause.

Boo.
Hiss.
Keep kicking: a thousand, thousand slimy things lived on. And so. Did. I.

Originally published online under the pseudonym 'little light' on 15 January 2007.

Part II

Trans as everyday culture

Foreword

The emergence of 'trans' identities, languages and discourses is entwined not just with the history of trans medicine, but also with the evolution of trans social networks, social movements and citizenship struggles. The chapters in this section reflect on the context and consequences of trans emergence for community groups as well as for individuals and their relationships with others. Key themes include communal, popular and 'everyday' repertoires of body, identity and feeling; transformations in everyday vernaculars of gender and sexuality; and 'on the ground' experiences within everyday lives and community events. A unifying element of these themes is the importance of *space*: space to be, space to explore, space to become; and what might happen when there is a *lack* of space for trans people and as their intimate others.

We begin this section with two chapters that explore trans cultural production. There have, of course, always been gender-diverse artists, musicians and performers; however, in recent years there has been an enormous growth in specifically *trans*-identified cultural production, a phenomenon that is impossible to disentangle from the rapidly increasing visibility of the trans population. In Chapter 5, Kat Gupta describes the creation of a trans space in the form of the 'Trans Tent' at Nottinghamshire Pride 2012. They reflect on how this was not just an important performance space, but also an important *conceptual* space, in which ideas about how a trans politics of diversity, inclusion and creation can be put into practice. This sets the stage for Chapter 6, in which Kirsty Lohman and Ruth Pearce provide a wider discussion of a DIY ('do it yourself') trans music scene in the UK during the early 2010s. The authors argue that modes of organisation and approaches to the creation of 'safe(r)' spaces within this scene ultimately reflected the approaches to gendered possibility inherent in the emergent gender-pluralist trans communities of the time, which emphasised genre evasion and 'cut-and-paste' approaches to identity formation.

In Chapter 7, the focus shifts to a less spectacular but no less important aspect of everyday trans cultures: that of intimate partnerships. Clare Beckett-Wrighton reports on the findings of a pioneering study examining the experiences of cis women in relationships with trans people in the UK. She explores the consequences of 'trans' emergence within a relationship, as partners work to come to terms with negotiating heterosexual fields of action while one individual is transitioning. Beckett-Wrighton observes that there is little conceptual space for trans people's cis partners within support groups, the medical arena, heterosexual traditions or homonormative lifestyles. Cis partners participating in the research describe feeling ungrounded by the absence of social recognition either for the kind of partnership they have transitioned into, or for the relational work undertaken in affirming their trans partners' lives and identities.

stef m. shuster and Ellen Lamont similarly explore how a lack of conceptual space for trans possibility can affect people's everyday lives in Chapter 8, through research examining non-binary people's experiences in the US. While possibilities for non-binary identification and understanding have expanded in recent decades with the emergence of trans language, cisnormative binary language continues to structure social interactions and shape the bounds of the possible. As with the cis partners in Beckett-Wrighton's study, shuster and Lamont's research participants find that breaking from the everyday rituals and assumptions of gendered belonging can result in the erasure of the lives and experiences, unless (and often even if) they are prepared to put much energy into asserting their right to recognition.

5   Creating a trans space

Kat Gupta

This piece was developed out of a blog piece originally published on 7 August 2012 on my academic blog, about the trans tent at Nottinghamshire Pride 2012. I present it to provide some context to the following chapter by Kirsty Lohman and Ruth Pearce, both of whom performed in the event I discuss and whose experiences at this event shaped their thinking about trans as a punk, DIY, fluid endeavour.

The trans tent came about through transphobia. The trans group I helped to run had a stall at the 2011 Pride event. However, the event itself was casually trans-unaware and we had to grapple with ignorance and obliviousness throughout the day. After the event we found out that a trans woman had presented as a woman for the first time at Pride, thinking that she would be in a welcoming and friendly environment. This was not to be: she was repeatedly misgendered by a performer as part of a set and she left Pride with her confidence shattered. As well as supporting her, we complained to the Pride committee and demanded better.

In 2012, the Pride organising committee offered the trans group our own tent and a small amount of money to start us off. This was tremendously exciting: the event had never had a dedicated trans area before. We were determined to showcase the talented, diverse and creative trans performers in our community; offer a space to our allies to perform in a friendly place where the complexities of their identities were welcomed; be a visible trans presence at Pride and, perhaps most importantly, reach out to people and make them feel a little less alone.

Performers were both trans and cis, and performed material ranging from punk to spoken word to opera. Many were part of the trans group itself or were local allies involved in queer and feminist activism, or were known to us through UK-wide networks of trans knowledge. Performers included:

Jennifer Moore (Single Bass)
El Dia (Sisters of Resistance)
Jase Redfield
Elaine O'Neill
Lashings of Ginger Beer Time

Dr Carmilla
Roz Kaveney
Sally Outen
George Hadden
Nat Titman
Trioxin Cherry
Jessie Holder (of Better Strangers Opera)
Not Right

Every single one of them was fantastic, bringing their words and music and loves and lives to the stage. Whether this was furious, fun punk, elegantly coiled poetry about the acronyms one must acquaint oneself with as a trans person, sweetly tender songs about growth and uncertainty, bawdily defiant poetry, eloquent fierceness about femme identity or subversively genderqueer readings of opera, our performers were both affirming and challenging.

There was something magical about being in a tent and being able to listen and watch people who articulated some of my fears and anxieties and desires. There were trans people speaking and singing and playing about trans experiences, and cis performers adapting, shaping and selecting their work to speak to us. Not us trying to eke out a trans interpretation of a song or a poem, but them finding the points where we could understand one another. It was people exploring gender and all that came with it: negotiating the National Health Service, the realities of genital surgery, the misery and joy we find in our bodies. When we started planning our tent, we were determined to bring a radical queer feminist perspective to Pride – something that we treasured in our communities but rarely found represented at Pride. In this tent we were able to do something special, and create a space that was visible and proud and joyful and intersectional and defiant.

Obviously things went wrong (technical hitches, delays, transport issues for some of our performers), and I can only thank our performers for being so patient with us. I learnt a lot about managing an event like this, even though the learning curve was so steep it felt more like a ski slope.

As an activist, I think about spaces. I think about the spaces that I challenge and create, and as I watched and applauded and ran around trying to locate performers, I thought about the space that I'd helped open up in Pride. The spaces I am talking about are both physical – like the tent – but also more abstract. Space is also about what is given voice, what is allowed to flourish, the possibilities that can be articulated. Much of my annoyance at the previous year's Pride was that it was a space for gay men, and possibly lesbians. This is important, and I'm not disputing the significance of a space where people can hold hands with their same-sex partners and not feel that tiny prickle of concern even at the best of times, that anyone, anywhere, could suddenly take it upon themselves to vocally – and perhaps physically – object to that simple, unobtrusive affection. However, other queer identities were less present or not acknowledged at all, and I found that really problematic. The LGBTQA community is a huge, diverse one, and it's really important to acknowledge and welcome that diversity. When that diversity is not embraced, it's not simply a matter of our experiences not being given a voice, as isolating and unwelcoming as that is. The lack of trans awareness at the previous year's Pride made the event a distressing, even dangerous, space.

This was an opportunity to put some of the things I had been thinking about into practice: not just in terms of thinking about what trans positive spaces might look like, but through actually trying to create one and working out what needs to be done to ensure a safe(r) and welcoming space. Theoretically, I wanted such a space to acknowledge the different and complex ways people identify, to encourage exploration of intersectional identities and to recognise that there is No One True Way of being trans. I wanted this space to provide information and offer solace, to be able to engage with people. What this meant in practice was looking carefully at who we'd invited to perform, having some basic guidelines for behaviour displayed in the tent, making information from a range of different organisations and about different issues available, and ensuring that the people covered in our trans history information were from a variety of backgrounds and reflected some of the ambiguities of posthumously assigning a trans identity to a historical figure.

It wasn't the most academic way to spend a weekend – I'm pretty sure most academics don't need to hastily hire drumkits the day before an event – but it had impact. Not just in a research sense, although I do work in areas of language and gender identity, but in the way we saw people come in to say hello or out of curiosity or seeking information, and leave feeling affirmed, moved, comforted.

A trans space was political for all the reasons I've discussed, but it wasn't until the day itself that I realised how very personal it would be too.

6 DIY identities in a DIY scene

Trans music events in the UK

Kirsty Lohman and Ruth Pearce

The past three decades have seen the emergence of an increasingly vigorous and outspoken trans movement in the United Kingdom. Resulting political and social changes have been accompanied by an increasing number of individuals willing to disclose their trans status and be publicly trans. With the development of 'new modes' and 'different codes' of trans identity and political activism (Whittle, 1998: 393), and an increasingly visible trans population, the stand-alone *trans* has also come to operate as an organising category for cultural forms. Whereas previous terminologies such as 'transsexual', 'transvestite' (and perhaps even 'transgender') provided more distinct categorical accounts of gender-variant possibility, 'trans' is intentionally open and – like 'queer' – refuses any clear or coherent definition (Pearce, Steinberg and Moon, 2019). In this chapter, we reflect on what it might mean to 'do' trans in a contemporary cultural context, in the tradition of recent accounts of trans music, theatre and performance (see e.g. Halberstam, 2005; Kumpf, 2016; Gossett, Stanley and Burton, 2017; Jaimie, 2017; Landry, 2018).

While there have always been trans performers, opportunities for their involvement in somewhat regular *trans events* have historically been limited. However, by the early 2010s there was a growing music scene in the United Kingdom. This was an exciting time to be involved in the creation of 'trans' arts and culture as new networks of trans activists, musicians and promoters emerged for the first time, linking semi-regular events across the country. Events such as Awkward Turtle, Bar Wotever, Transpose (London), Moulin Rage (Brighton, Cambridge and London), Cachín Cachán Cachunga (Edinburgh and Glasgow) and the Nottinghamshire Pride Trans Tent (Nottingham) effectively created temporary trans spaces within pubs, bars, small clubs and community centres, or as part of wider LGBT Pride programs.

Before this time, there was no pre-existing trans-oriented music scene for *new* performers to get involved with. High-profile figures were few and far between, either distanced by time (e.g. pioneering trans punk Jayne County predominantly released music in the 1970s and 1980s), or place (in the case of 2000s North American bands such as The Cliks and Coyote Grace, who never toured the UK). The so-called 'transgender tipping point' – the moment of heightened international media interest heralded by Laverne Cox's appearance on the cover of *Time* magazine in May 2014 – was yet to come.

This chapter offers insights into the emergence of a trans music scene at a key point in time (2010–2013) influenced by the emergence of 'trans' as a standalone identity. The events that this chapter discusses tended to draw small but enthusiastic crowds of 'underground' music fans, with typical audiences ranging between 20 and 100 people. They drew heavily upon a do-it-yourself (DIY) ethos most typically associated with underground scenes based around the genres of indie, punk or folk; however, the musical forms present at any given trans music event typically drew upon a far wider pool of genres. Efforts were often made by promoters (with mixed success) to ensure diversity in terms of age, class, dis/ability and race. Rather than being defined wholly by musical style or participants' cultural backgrounds, therefore, this scene coalesced largely through the notable presence of *trans* people as promoters, performers and audience members.

The starting point for the research project that forms the basis of this chapter was a process of critical reflection upon the authors' own involvement as performers and event promoters within a loose network of trans-oriented events. The scene we discovered through this network worked actively *not* to define itself, and was populated by individuals whose own identities were similarly complex. Our findings describe a scene in which flexible 'trans' approaches to gender are reflected in the *spaces* that participants created to share and experience music and performance. We argue that this is a de/constructive process by which participants draw upon practices of 'genre evasion' (Steinholt, 2012) and/or 'cut-and-paste' (Bornstein, 1994) in order to engage with complexity and possibility in a deeply personal – but nevertheless *social* – manner.

Entering the field

This paper is based on a small-scale ethnographical research project conducted in 2012–3. Our findings draw on materials associated with events, including gig posters, promotional websites, YouTube videos and blogs; four interviews with individuals deeply involved with the scene as musicians and/or promoters; and participant observation at a number of events that we attended as audience members, musicians and/or promoters. Both researchers are white, middle-class women who have long been involved in alternative music subcultures. Ruth is a trans woman; Kirsty considers herself to be a gender-nonconforming cis woman and was less involved with trans community events at the beginning of this research.

Ruth's trans identity has informed a long-running involvement with trans activism and associated cultural events, as an organiser and a DJ. The authors play together in a band (Not Right) which was part of the trans music scene at the time the research took place, and performed at a number of the events discussed in this chapter. This provided the inspiration for the research, offered access to the scene and provided a starting point for identifying the events that inform this paper.

Our entry to the field was through 'Wotever Rock', a gig hosted by Bar Wotever at London's Royal Vauxhall Tavern in May 2012. At this event we recognised for the first time that we were interacting with a wider community of trans artists, activists and promoters. The invitation to play at the Royal Vauxhall Tavern came after a member of the Bar Wotever team attended a fundraiser at the band's hometown of Leamington Spa for Godiva Young Gays & Lesbians (GYGL), a Midlands LGBTQ youth group; this was another event which, we noted on reflection was organised by a trans promoter and featured a substantial number of trans performers from a range of artistic and demographic backgrounds.

In the months that followed, we found ourselves increasingly invited to play at similar events across the UK, where a high proportion of performers, organisers and attendees were trans. The questions we began to ask ourselves provided the original basis for this research project. Is there a trans music scene? If so, how might it be characterised; are there common elements beyond the prevalence of trans performers and organisers?

The design of our project was informed by grounded theory (Corbin and Strauss, 1990): the findings presented in this paper were generated and refined in an ongoing, back-and-forth process of data collection, analysis and theory generation. Our aim was to inductively and reflexively produce theory that prioritised participant voices. This was important for two interrelated reasons. Firstly, we wanted to look empirically at how the events we were interested in were understood by those who participated in them, and construct the conceptual categories at the centre of our analysis accordingly. Secondly, trans people's cultural histories are all too often subject to erasure or appropriation (through theoretical abstraction) by cis academics who have had no direct involvement in them (Namaste, 2000; Serano, 2007). By focusing our research on trans people's activities and understandings, we work to actively resist these tendencies through constructing new narratives and offering alternative cultural accounts. We further wish to move beyond tropes of trans victimhood in order to refocus on the rich cultural realities and possibilities of trans lives.

Through an initial process of analysis we quickly answered our original research question: the proliferation of events and the network of performers and promoters who linked these events indicated that there *was* a 'trans' music scene. We therefore shifted our focus towards understanding how the scene operated, and how it was understood by participants.

During the research process we drew upon a range of qualitative data, including cultural artefacts[1] produced by individuals who participated in and/or organised events, as well as a small number of semi-structured interviews. We later coded our data using a thematic analytical approach (Braun and Clarke, 2006).

We recognised our *own* participation in this scene as relevant for our analysis, and therefore draw on participant observation as well as analytical autoethnographical reflection (Anderson, 2006). Both researchers kept notes on our (trans-oriented) cultural participation, detailing (for instance) the atmosphere at events we attended, the nature of the performances and the purpose of the events. These were informed by participant observation at ten events, plus a critical reappraisal of four events we had attended in the past. The autoethnographical element of this project was therefore retrospective as well as continuous: this enabled us to draw critically on our past experiences in the same way that we would ask our interviewees to do.

Our contacts from the events we attended formed a basis from which to recruit interviewees. We interviewed four individuals who had, like us, been involved in performing at and/or organising trans-oriented events across the country. These individuals came from a range of different social backgrounds, but were all in their 20s or 30s and shared a thoughtful and reflective approach to gender that is common within the activist networks from which the trans music scene emerged. To ensure the anonymity of interview participants we have used pseudonyms, and do not share explicit demographic information on these individuals.[2]

Coming to terms with 'trans'

Whilst 'trans' is sometimes used as a shorthand for individuals who undergo a medically supervised transition from male to female or vice versa, in this paper we use the term in a broader sense. Whittle (2006) argues that: '[a] trans identity is now accessible [. . .] to anyone who does not feel comfortable in the gender role they were attributed with at birth, or has a gender identity at odds with the labels "man" or "woman" credited to them by formal authorities' (xi). In this sense 'trans' is oppositional: individuals move through the world as trans do so because their behavior and/or bodies do not conform to normative ideas of binary sex and/or gender. Thus, while 'trans' does operate as a 'politicised identity category', it can also be understood more widely as something that people *do* (Enke, 2012: 236; West and Zimmerman, 1987).

We argue that this *doing* of trans moves beyond the way in which people express gender, to incorporate the way in which people engage more widely with the politics and possibilities of gender. Within the spaces of the trans music scene we observed many examples of this. Acts such as the queer cabaret collective Lashings of Ginger Beer Time and our own band Not Right exhibited a trans feminism through critiques of sexist objectification and transmisogyny (Serano, 2007). Performers such as Lashings comedian/singer Sally Outen very explicitly discussed being trans within their acts, thereby countering tropes of transfeminine passivity and the notion of authenticity through 'passing'. Conversely, musicians such as CN Lester and Seth Corbin expanded gendered norms through performances in which they brought genderqueer bodies into the public sphere *without* their trans experience being a specific focal point for their performances. In claiming space *as trans* on their own terms within a public sphere, all of these performers worked towards an oppositional de-subjugation of trans identity.

An alternative engagement with trans politics and possibility could be seen in acts such as The Mechanisms and Dr Carmilla. These performers drew upon iconography of science fiction and fantasy to deconstruct gender norms. For instance, the character of Dr Carmilla (played by singer-songwriter Maki Yamazaki) is a lesbian vampire from outer space; in songs such as 'Exhumed', she describes being awoken from the dead and experimented on in a laboratory, before escaping and joyously embracing her monstrosity. In this way, Yamazaki's storytelling reflects a celebration of disruptive 'cyborg' possibilities within the literatures of feminist and trans theory, with technologically enhanced bodies posing a threat to the patriarchal divide between 'man' and 'woman' (Haraway, 1991; Stryker, 1994).

A range of oppositional engagements with gender could similarly be seen in our interviews. In addition to providing an in-depth, complicated account of gendered identity and selfhood, each participant described being 'trans' in terms of their relationship to others. For instance, Pat stated, 'I definitely see myself as being "trans" insofar as it means being in constant opposition to current/historical norms of gender/sexed bodies/behaviours'. Similarly, Robin explained, '"[t]rans" is a useful shorthand I can give if I don't feel like telling people the long and involved story of my gender dysphoria, gendered expression, etc. etc[.]''. Both Pat and Robin understood their identities in terms of a non-binary paradigm, entailing a rejection of 'female' and 'feminine', 'male' and 'masculine' as the only possibilities for gendered understanding and expression. By contrast, Ruth's identity as a trans *woman* entails – for her – a different kind of non-conformity: a rejection of the normative cisgenderist link between apparent physical sex, assigned gender, gender identity and gender presentation (Kennedy, 2013). Within the trans music scene, there was conceptual space for these different approaches to 'trans' to exist alongside one another, in what Monro (2007) describes as a 'gender pluralist' approach: 'conceptualizing gender as "fields" or "groupings" of – in some cases overlapping – masculinities, femininities, and gender diverse identities' (6.10).

Pat, Robin and Ruth's various understandings of themselves as 'trans' demonstrate the innate ambivalence of an oppositional trans identity. Within a different social world, they (like Dr Carmilla, and some of The Mechanism's non-gendered characters) might not be trans: they therefore recognise the conditional nature of this identity. However, this also imbues the term with a queer fluidity: Pat, Robin and Ruth use the term 'trans' to describe the way in which their gender/sex does not mesh with (cis)normative understandings of body/behaviour.

Like Pat, and also Enke (2012), we regard trans identities as socially and historically contingent. That is to say: we believe that categorical distinctions between 'trans' and 'cis' are inherently problematic because they result in an artificial binary that is insensitive to the complexities of gendered diversity. A trans identity does not, therefore, *necessarily* follow from a flouting of (cis) normative sex/gender standards. Other terminologies of gendered dissent that exist alongside and can intersect or diverge complexly from 'trans' include (but are not limited to) butch, femme, dyke, fairy, drag kings and queens (Halberstam, 1998; Nestle, Howell and Wilchins, 2002; McKay, 2019). What trans offers is a specific organising principle for people whose gendered identity and/or experience differs from what they were assigned at birth, grounded in the social circumstances of the here and now.

The emergence of 'trans', then, offers a means by which individuals might label their own complexly embodied relationship to both social norms and external social actors, *and* means by which people with differing experiences of gender but a shared experience of exclusion and oppositionality might come together to organise, socialise and indeed perform. This use of 'trans' for both individual identity and as an umbrella term for multiple experiences was certainly the case amongst our research participants and within the trans music scene, reflecting the multifaceted use of the term by activist-academics such as Whittle (2006).

'Trans' as de/construction

'Trans' does not, therefore, have a single, fixed meaning; it instead incorporates a multiplicity of meanings that vary according to both individual and social context, and might shift over time. Drawing upon the interviews undertaken for this project as well as wider observations within the trans music scene, we argue that these meanings are negotiated through a process of simultaneous deconstruction (through 'genre evasion'), and construction (through 'cut-and-paste'), with trans identity existing in the space between the two. Like our wider observations of the music scene itself these are snapshots from a particular point in time and space, capturing individuals and communities amidst ongoing processes of identity formation.

In describing their gendered identities, we saw performers and interview participants employing similar discursive practices of 'genre evasion' to those noted by Steinholt (2012) in his research with Russian punks. Steinholt's participants tended to either avoid genre labels or choose their own ways to define themselves. In this way they sought to avoid being pigeonholed or judged alongside others: '[g]enre evasion becomes necessary in order to protect the notion of an authentic voice that is not ensured by reference to generic convention' (Steinholt, 2012: 282). In a similar manner, participants in the trans music scene frequently sought to evade generic conventions of gendered possibility:

> I'm not sure that there's any one thing we can agree on in terms of meaning when we speak of 'gender' – and maybe that's the best way of saying how I understand my own gender? [. . .] On a personal, philosophical level I'd say that I think the concept of 'gender' is so multitudinous and resistant to fixed definition that it ceases to have any 'true' meaning whatsoever.
> (Pat)

Pat questions the very *idea* of gender: or, at least, the idea that 'gender' can have any 'true' meaning. In this way, they seek to evade defining their own gender identity in any way that is fixed or absolute. We argue that this is a broadly *deconstructive* strategy, used to question and break down the rigidity of (cis)gendered language.

A second example of genre evasion from our findings entailed the use of a wealth of seemingly contradictory terms to distance oneself from the fixedness of these labels. An example of this can found in Robin's description of their trans gender identity. Robin ascribes the following terms to themself: nonbinary, genderqueer, gender-fluid, androgynous, 'an effeminate queer man, a butch woman, a totally genderless thing, a person with [an] excess of masculine AND feminine traits'. In this way, Robin refuses to be bound by the limitations typically associated with these terms, and also seeks not to be 'pinned down' by a single gender(ed) identity. As Steinholt (2012) noted in reference to his interviews with Russian punks: '[e]vasion, it appears, is the point in itself. In this particular case the refusal to be pinned down reaches an extreme' (278).

In the process we describe as 'construction', our participants drew on a range of pre-existing ideas regarding gendered possibility in order to build understandings of their (trans)gendered selves. This typically took place even as participants *also* engaged in genre evasion. Robin describes their aforementioned list of descriptive terms as: 'picking up loads of different words and smushing them together until they reach an approximation of what I'm looking for'. Similarly, Maki Yamazaki's Facebook artist page describes her as 'queer, trans, grey asexual, genderqueer and thoroughly nerdy'. In this regard, we see parallels with Bornstein's (1994) conceptualisation of transgender identity 'based on collage. You know [. . . sort] of a cut-and-paste thing' (3). A complex identity that reflects the specific experiences and feelings of the individual can therefore be discursively *constructed* in a DIY fashion from whatever language is available. 'Trans' can be understood in this context not as a fixed identity, but as an oppositional movement away from rigidity and towards the creation of new possibilities through the acknowledgement of gendered (and sexual, and social) complexity and fluidity. This offers an alternative to the limited possibility of normative (cis)gendered language, whilst utilising discursive tools that are already available. Our participants sought to redefine language, rather than be defined by it.

For some participants this de/constructive approach appeared to be the outcome of years of reflection. However, in one case we witnessed de/construction *during* the interview itself. Whilst Riley initially asserted that his gender identity was 'male', he almost immediately called this definition into question as he realised that 'male', as a lone descriptor, was too prescriptive to fully describe his gender identity:

Interviewers: What pronouns would you prefer us to use?
Riley: Male if you please.

Interviewers:	[. . .] would you describe your gender identity as male?
Riley:	Yes.
	Actually wait, no
	[. . .]
Riley:	I feel like I have multiple gender identities running parallel to each other and how I feel on a day-to-day basis contradicts identifying purely as 'male'.
Interviewers:	Is 'male' a large part of your gender then, rather than the whole of your gender?
Riley:	It's part of it, maybe not a large part but it's definitely in the mix.
Interviewers:	What genders do you see as being in the mix?
Riley:	Transgender, transmasculine, male, female.

Whilst Riley started out describing himself as male, he continued to add description to add further meaning to his male identity, whilst simultaneously destabilising the boundaries of 'male' possibility. We also see again the de/constructive use of seemingly contradictory identities ('male'/'female') in a manner similar to the approaches taken by Robin and Maki Yamazaki. In this way, the binary logic of 'male' and 'female' as necessarily distinct is discarded as participants seek recognition as (in some sense) both. This also opens up the possibility for (some) individuals to be *neither* 'male' nor 'female'; as with Yamazaki's character of Dr Carmilla (who notably uses a non-gendered title), there are more meaningful ways by which people can be defined.

Indeed, some participants sought to deliberately move the conversation away from gender as we discussed identity. For instance, Alex explained: 'I might sooner be labelled by what I do, how I think, my loves and passions which is too complex to actually be readily appraised by visual scrutiny alone', describing themself as a '[m]usic lover, punk, techie, scientist, writer, reader, sibling'. Just as Robin and Riley utilise long lists to a build a description of themselves, Alex here produces a list of identities tied to their greatest interests. This, too, is arguably a de/constructive approach to personal identity, with Alex seeking to define themself through a complex interaction of activities rather than be 'pinned down' and defined in terms of their being visibly (gender)queer, in a similar manner to performers such as CN Lester.

For our research participants, being 'trans' can be understood as an outcome of *simultaneously* evading gendered definition, and constructing new gendered possibilities in a 'cut-and-paste' manner. Trans identities come to be in the space between these processes. Gender pluralism is hence not simply an interpersonal phenomenon, but also a means by which *individual* engagements with gender might draw upon a great range of possibilities for being. These strategies work to create space in which trans people might express and understand themselves and communicate with others in a more authentic way.

'cut-and-paste'
definition
labelling

CONSTRUCTION

'TRANS'
IDENTITY

DECONSTRUCTION

'genre evasion'
fluidity
ambivalence
redefinition

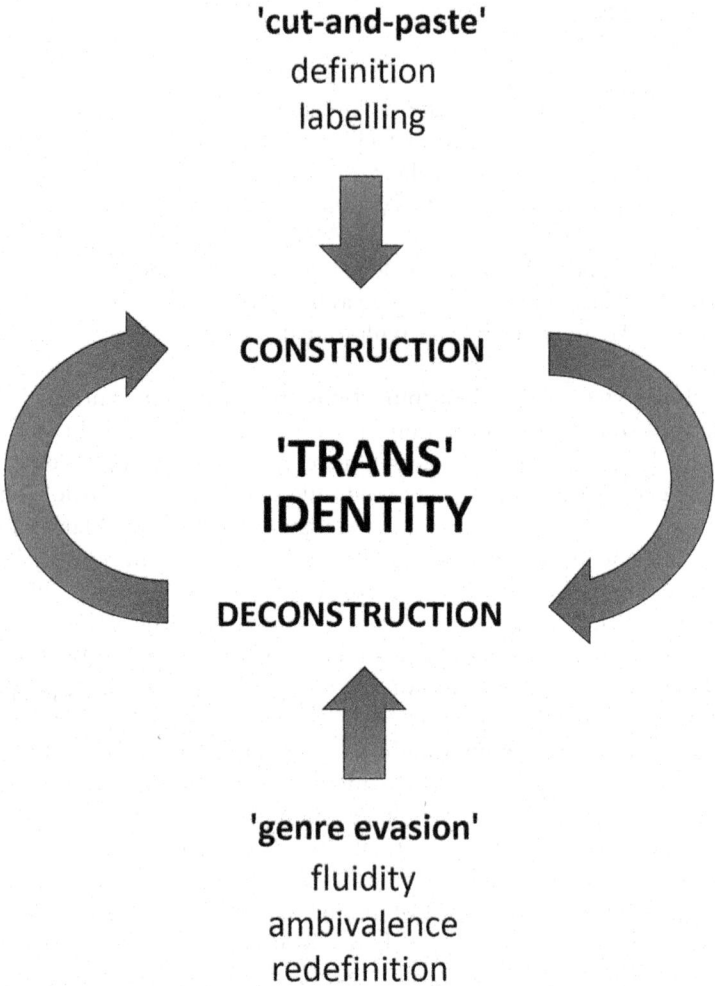

Figure 6.1 De/construction theory of trans

A trans music scene

In his seminal account of the emergence of new forms of trans identity
in the context of internet communities, Whittle (1998) describes how a
'reconstructive project of "new modes" and "different codes"' came to
shape innovative and 'exceptionally influential' forms of activism (393). In a
similar manner, our findings show that the de/constructive, gender–pluralist

approaches to 'trans' employed by trans music scene participants came to shape their *cultural* engagement. As we examined scene participants' de/constructive approaches to (trans)gendered identity, we began to observe parallels with the manner in which they approached their involvement in cultural events.

Individual events constituted a scene that was linked by more than just a network of (trans) promoters, performers and audiences; they also shared an approach that complicated notions of trans space. Just as participants' trans identities existed in a space created through both deconstructive genre evasion and cut-and-paste construction, the very way in which the events (and wider scene) in which they were involved might be understood as *trans* similarly relies upon de/constructive logics.

We observed that trans music scene events shared the following elements:

- The events foregrounded trans performers.
- The events were not restricted by genre.
- The events were open to all even as they aimed to be a 'safe space' specifically for trans people.
- There was an overarching theme at most events that was often *not* related directly to a specifically trans identity or politic.
- The events were run along DIY principles.

For example, the July 2011 Cutlery Drawer event *Moulin Rage* was organised by a trans promoter, and featured a lineup consisting primarily of trans solo performers (CN Lester and Ruth Pearce) or groups prominently featuring trans members and themes (Lashings of Ginger Beer Time and The Mechanisms). These acts represented a range of genres: Lashings of Ginger Beer Time put on a musical burlesque show, CN Lester performed a number of piano ballads rooted in alternative rock and The Mechanisms were a space opera/fairytale-themed folk band. A great many trans people were present at the event, at which the promoter had (intentionally) created a 'safe space' in which attendees felt comfortable expressing gender diversity. However, this was not a trans-only event: indeed, it was not even advertised as a trans-oriented event, with promotional materials instead focusing on the night's role as fundraiser for Rape Crisis South London (the 'overarching theme' of the night). Instead, the presence of so many trans performers communicated the nature of the night to those 'in the know', even as a cis audience was explicitly invited and welcomed into the space. Finally, this was not a 'professional', for-profit event, with the promoter and all of the acts contributing in a DIY, non-profit capacity for the sake of both the music and the cause.

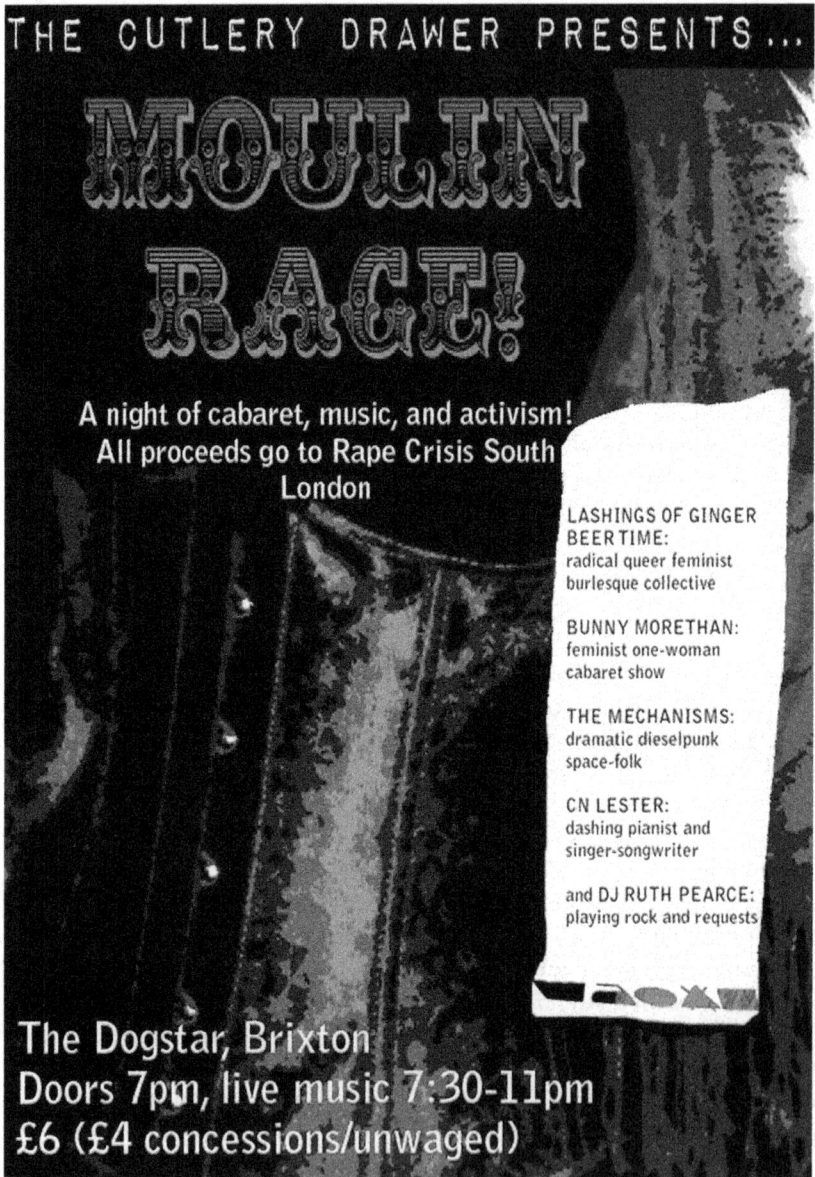

Figure 6.2 'Moulin Rage!' poster by The Cutlery Drawer, London July 2011

De/construction in and through the scene

To unpack how these elements can be viewed through a similar lens to the de/constructive approaches to gender identity, we turn now to an analytical discussion of further events. We focus in particular on the Trans Tent at Nottinghamshire Pride 2012 as a running example. Organised along DIY grounds by local trans group Recreation Nottingham, the Trans Tent provided a trans-oriented space within the wider annual LGBT Pride event in the city of Nottingham. As with Moulin Rage, it shared the defining elements of the trans music scene, as well as considerable crossover in terms of the performers who were present.

The majority of individuals who performed in the Trans Tent were trans. In this way, Recreation Nottingham ensured that trans people and their creative projects were prioritised and given a specific platform within a wider LGBT event. The Trans Tent was therefore a space constructed *by* and *for* trans people. Importantly, this afforded the organisers an opportunity to define the parameters of 'trans' for the event. The trans people who were invited to perform in the Trans Tent represented a great range of (female, male, genderqueer and non-binary) gendered identity and expression, in addition to a considerable variety of intersecting identities in terms of age, class, dis/ability, race and sexuality. The organisers therefore took an intersectional (Crenshaw, 1991), gender-pluralist approach, rejecting more prescriptive approaches to 'trans'.[3] Moreover, the lineup was not exclusively trans. A number of cis people performed alongside trans bandmates, or were booked as solo acts. This was a trans event where you didn't have to be trans: the boundaries of identity were not strictly policed. The 'trans' label for the event was thereby simultaneously constructed (in an intersectional, gender-pluralist manner) *and* deliberately destabilised by the organisers, through practices akin to genre evasion. This was a strategy we'd similarly seen employed at Bar Wotever, where the emphasis at Wotever Rock was on trans-fronted bands The Makeshifts and Not Right, in a lineup organised by a trans promoter. However, there were also acts on stage who played with the possibilities of gender from a 'cis' perspective, including anti-macho male singer-songwriter Killer's Riches, as well as Battle Of You, fronted by two queer women and also known as 'B.O.Y.'. Echoing the way in which individuals might de/construct their 'trans' identities, events such as the Trans Tent and Wotever Rock de/constructed the very notion of what a 'trans' space might look like.

The Trans Tent also featured examples of (quite literal) genre evasion. In contrast to most of the other tents and stages at Nottinghamshire Pride, which were usually organised around a specific genre – for example, the acoustic stage, the dance tent and the burlesque tent – the Trans Tent took a cut-and-paste approach to its artistic offerings: 'a little bit from here, a little bit from there' (Bornstein, 1994: 3). Our punk band Not Right followed an opera singer from the Better Strangers collective, there was acoustic rock from Dr Carmilla, comedy from Sally Outen, hip hop from El Dia, burlesque from Lashings of Ginger Beer Time, poetry and spoken word from performers such as Roz Kaveney and Elaine O'Neill. This genre-evading element of the trans scene varied depending in part on the size of the event: an event with a larger lineup was more likely to have a greater diversity of cultural forms than a shorter night with a more cohesive focus such as Wotever Rock. Some promoters address this by holding a series of events to ensure variety over time. For example, CN Lester's event Transpose has been run on an occasional basis in London since 2011. While particular iterations of Transpose might focus more upon one musical genre or another (or upon non-musical forms such as spoken word), the series has featured a similar range of acts to Nottinghamshire Pride's Trans Tent over time, for example, taking in folk from Wild, genrefucking rock from Squid and the Krakens and Lester's own classically informed alternative music. Such events therefore transcend genre; the unifying feature is 'trans', *even as* promoters seek to avoid any kind of prescriptive approach to the term (and sometimes, as with Moulin Rage, avoid the term altogether in promotional material).

Both the organising committee for the wider Nottinghamshire Pride event and the organisers of the Trans Tent claimed a commitment to community 'safety'. For Pride, this involved hiring private security services. Recreation Nottingham, however, took a different approach to providing a 'safe space' in their tent. The tent *itself* was seen as an investment in 'safety', a response to transphobic incidents at previous Pride events in the city. It was, nevertheless, open to all attendees of Nottinghamshire Pride, with a whole 'wall' of the tent removed to make the space literally open. Instead of closing down the space, a number of strategies were employed by the organisers to create and maintain 'safety' for the exploration of trans issues. Firstly, there was the aforementioned commitment to inclusivity and intersectional diversity. Kat Gupta was a member of the organising team; they explain in Chapter 5 that, 'I wanted such a space to acknowledge the different and complex ways people identify, to encourage exploration of intersectional identities and recognise that there is No One True Way of being trans'. Moreover, the safety afforded by this approach extended beyond trans identity: as Gupta describes, 'we were determined to [. . .] offer a space to our *allies* to perform in a friendly place where the complexities of *their* identities were welcome' (emphases added). Secondly, a range of informative materials were made available, with resources and contacts for trans people and their families and friends, as well as facts about a diverse range of historical figures who might be understood as trans. Finally, a code of conduct for the space was prominently displayed, with basic guidelines for behaviour. The Trans Tent at Nottinghamshire Pride therefore operated to construct a trans-specific safe space, even as it deconstructed the very notion of 'trans space' by being open to the general public and not being exclusively 'trans'. In this way, the de/construction of 'trans' spaces within the scene was very much about *extending* the liberatory potential of gender pluralist trans discourse beyond the boundaries of personal identity and particular trans communities, and into the wider material world.

Approaches to the space in which events were run varied according to the availability of suitable venues across the country. Some events were held in 'trans-friendly' venues: for instance, Queer We Go was located in Leeds' Wharf Chambers, which has a trans-inclusive 'safer space' policy on its website, and non-gendered toilets within the building itself. However, we consistently saw that in spaces which were not *already* set up in a specifically trans-safe way, promotors would often seek to *trans* the spaces they occupied. For example, Transpose was often (and increasingly) held within 'mainstream' venues such as Hackney Attic. At these events temporary toilet signs were created to 'neutralise' the toilets. A similar measure was undertaken at the authors' feminist punk event Revolt in Coventry, with both trans-inclusive women's toilets and gender-neutral toilets created, and signs prominently displayed to explain to cis attendees why this was happening. In this way, the politics of trans diversity, inclusion and visibility can be brought into wider public spaces as part of a commitment to trans attendees' safety.

A 'trans' approach was therefore very explicitly drawn upon as an organising principle of trans scene events, with the promotion of a diverse range of trans performers and the creation of a safe trans space being the *purpose* of the scene. However, just as we saw in our interview participants' reflections upon their gendered identities, there was a simultaneous process of deconstructing what it means to 'be' trans, and – by extension – what it means to create and participate in a 'trans space' or 'trans event'. This was done by ensuring that 'trans' was communicated in the broadest possible way, and in making the space not solely 'about' or 'for' trans. This both provided space to individuals who might have a 'trans' experience without identifying explicitly as such, and – as Gupta notes in Chapter 5 – meant that a trans recognition of *complexity* could be extended to cis allies. To promoters within the scene, trans discourse was seen to be of benefit to the wider world, not just to trans audiences; and in turn, it was beneficial for trans people to engage with wider communities and socio-political issues. For this reason, it made sense to organise the Trans Tent under the wider umbrella of LGBT Pride: 'trans' alone was *not* the overarching theme of the event. Instead, the Trans Tent was just one part of a large celebration of diversity, inclusivity and openness within a community-oriented, 'family-friendly' setting. Similarly, events such as the GYGL fundraiser, Queer We Go, Revolt and Cutlery Drawer gigs were organised in a manner that emphasised 'LGBT', 'queer' and/or 'feminism' as wider themes, even as these events are created by trans people and brought together a wide range of trans performers.

Conclusion

The very concept of 'trans' is fluid and contested. Its meaning(s) have shifted and evolved considerably during the past couple of decades, just as the meaning and possibility of preceding/coinciding concepts (such as 'transsexual', 'drag' and 'butch/femme') have also undergone significant changes. However, the emergence of 'trans' as both umbrella term and unitary identity offers individuals the means to conceptualise a particularly wide range of understandings and engagements with gender, both *as* individuals and in solidarity with other gender-diverse people. Whilst some community groups use 'trans' effectively as a shorthand for transsexual, transvestite and/or transgender, and some focus upon non-binary, genderqueer and genderfluid identities, others take a gender-pluralist approach that provides a more open space for engagement with gendered possibility. Within the latter camp we found the communities that constituted and contributed to the trans music scene discussed within this paper. Both the interviewees in this study and the wider body of promoters and performers encountered by the authors were keen to avoid prescriptive notions of 'trans' possibility and identity. This, of course, raises the question: how can we even understand something as 'trans' if the very object of discussion refuses definition?

In this chapter we have provided a response through examining connections between the (trans)gendered identity of individuals involved in the trans music scene, and the manner in which the scene itself is organised. We argue that within this scene, 'trans' exists in the space between deconstructive strategies (grounded in genre evasion) and constructive strategies (grounded in a cut-and-paste approach): this is the case for events as well as personal identity. In this way, 'trans' performance comes to reflect personal approaches to identity formation. Just as our interview participants and many of the performers described 'trans' in terms of opening up space for diversity and gender pluralism through genre evasion and cut-and-paste, the raison d'être of the events in which they are involved is to open up space for gendered possibilities.

The trans performance community was only a few years old at the time of research, with new events and spaces emerging all the time. Since our research project was conducted, the scene has grown and diversified, intersecting in particular with pre-existing queer and feminist punk scenes. From 2014, numerous all-day and weekend queer punk events took place across the UK, under the banner of 'Queer Fest' (there have also been 'Bent Fest' events in London, and a 'Glitterfest' in Leicester). These frequently drew upon processes of DIY de/construction in a similar manner to the events examined in our research, and offered a platform to a growing number of punk bands with trans members and lyrical/musical themes, including groups such as Slum of Legs, Jesus and His Judgemental Father, Daskinsey4, Faggot, Twinken Park, T-Bitch, Screaming Toenail, Dispute Settlement Mechanism, Tuck and the Binders, Anatomy and Kermes. In 2013, the UK's first Trans Pride was held in Brighton; this has become an annual event, with other Trans Prides later organised in cities such as Belfast, Bristol, Glasgow and Leeds. At these events, the cabaret format of Transpose and 'trans tent' approach of Nottinghamshire Pride are increasingly replicated for performance spaces in parks, bars and arts centres.

As we write in 2018, there are now more openly trans people in the UK than ever before, coupled with an increased awareness of trans arts and music among the cis population. There is, therefore, a far larger audience for trans cultural participation, with more scope for cis audience support. Openly trans celebrity musicians have seen a growing visibility and success, with Laura Jane Grace of US punk band Against Me! receiving critical acclaim for her band's albums *Transgender Dysphoria Blues* (2014) and *Shape Shift With Me* (2016), and UK singer-songwriter Anohni earning an Oscar nomination in 2016 for her song 'Manta Ray' (although she would later boycott the awards ceremony after not being invited to perform). Some events that were 'underground' when our research took place have now gained a far larger audience, with Transpose taking place in more high-profile venues such as London's Tate Modern museum of modern art and Barbican cultural centre in recent years. Queer Fest alumni The Spook School, who explicitly addressed trans themes on their albums *Try*

To Be Hopeful (2015) and *Could It Be Different?* (2018), have increasingly had their music played on national radio and featured on popular TV shows such as *The Only Way is Essex*.

Our research provided a snapshot of an emergent scene at a particular moment in time; however, this moment was an important one. The events and processes we describe in this chapter could not have happened much sooner: the scene required recent conceptual shifts and developments within trans theory and social movements and the emergence of the stand-alone 'trans' itself to create the kind of space we saw in the Trans Tent at Nottinghamshire Pride, for instance. It is exactly this productive commitment to inclusive, community-oriented diversity and de/construction that reinforces the importance of a non-prescriptive approach to trans possibility.

Notes

1 Including event pages on social media, posters, blog posts, lyrics, band and promoter websites.
2 Venue locations and the names of club nights, bands and solo performers have, however, been preserved in this chapter; we consider them vital for contextualisation and capturing the character of the scene.
3 Whilst Recreation Nottingham's intersectional approach was fairly typical in the trans scene, the Trans Tent was arguably more successful in implementing this than some other events. Our interviewees and a handful of bloggers noted that many events featured predominantly youthful, white performers and audiences and/or oppressive behaviours such as 'skeezy class drag'. We observed that the diversity of performers and audiences was often linked to the diversity of music genres at any given event: for instance, predominantly 'indie' lineups at events such as Coventry's Ditch Your Boyfriend club night tended to attract predominantly white audiences, reflecting a broader lack of diversity within the wider indie rock scene.

An earlier version of this article was published in the journal Sexualities, entitled 'De/constructing DIY identities in a trans music scene'.

References

Anderson, L. (2006) 'Analytic Autoethnography', *Journal of Contemporary Ethnography*, 35(4): 373–395.

Bornstein, K. (1994) *Gender Outlaw: On Men, Women and the Rest of Us*. London: Routledge.

Braun, V. and Clarke, V. (2006) 'Using Thematic Analysis in Psychology', *Qualitative Research in Psychology*, 3(2): 77–101.

Corbin, J. M. and Strauss, A. (1990) 'Grounded Theory Research: Procedures, Canons, and Evaluative Criteria', *Qualitative Sociology*, 13(1): 3–21.

Crenshaw, K. (1991) 'Mapping the Margins: Intersectionality, Identity Politics, and Violence against Women of Color', *Stanford Law Review*, 43(6): 1241–1299.

Enke, A. F. (2012) 'The Education of Little Cis: Cisgender and the Discipline of Opposing Bodies', in S. Stryker and A. Z. Aizura (eds.), *The Transgender Studies Reader 2*. New York: Routledge, pp. 234–247.

Gossett, R., Stanley, A. E. and Burton, J. (2017) *Trap Door: Trans Cultural Production and the Politics of Visibility*. Cambridge: MIT Press.

Halberstam, J. (1998) 'Transgender Butch: Butch/FTM Border Wars and the Masculine Continuum', *GLQ: A Journal of Lesbian and Gay Studies*, 4(2): 287–310.

Halberstam, J. (2005) *In a Queer Time and Place: Transgender Bodies, Subcultural Lives*. London: NYU Press.

Haraway, D. (1991) *Simians, Cyborgs and Women: The Reinvention of Nature*. New York: Routledge.

Jaimie, K. (2017) '"Chasing Rainbows": Black Cracker and Queer, Trans Afrofuturity', *TSQ: Transgender Studies Quarterly*, 4(2): 208–218.

Kennedy, N. (2013) 'Cultural Cisgenderism: Consequences of the Imperceptible', *Psychology of Women Section Review*, 15(2): 3–11.

Kumpf, T. (2016) 'From Queering to Trans*Imagining: Sookee's Trans*/Feminist Hip-Hop', *TSQ: Transgender Studies Quarterly*, 3(1–3): 175–184.

Landry, O. (2018) 'On the Politics of Love and Trans-Migrant Theatre in Germany', *TSQ: Transgender Studies Quarterly*, 5(1): 30–48.

McKay, F. (2019) 'No Woman's Land? Revisiting Border Zone Denizens', *Journal of Lesbian Studies*. Pre-published online 31 January 2019. Available at: https://doi.org/10.1080/108 94160.2019.1565521.

Monro, S. (2007) 'Transmuting Gender Binaries: The Theoretical Challenge', *Sociological Research Online*, 12(1). Available at: www.socresonline.org.uk/12/1/monro.html. [10/11/2015].

Namaste, V. K. (2000) *Invisible Lives: The Erasure of Transsexual and Transgendered People*. Chicago: University of Chicago Press.

Nestle, J., Howell, C. and Wilchins, R. (2002) *GenderQueer: Voices from Beyond the Sexual Binary*. New York: Alyson Books.

Pearce, R., Steinberg, D. L. and Moon, I. (2019) 'Introduction: The Emergence of "Trans"', *Sexualities*, 22(1–2): 3–12.

Serano, J. (2007) *Whipping Girl: A Transsexual Woman on Sexism and the Scapegoating of Femininity*. Emeryville: Seal Press.

Steinholt, Y. B. (2012) 'Punk is Punk but By No Means Punk: Definition, Genre Evasion and the Quest for an Authentic Voice in Contemporary Russia', *Punk & Post-Punk*, 1(3): 267–284.

Stryker, S. (1994) 'My Words to Victor Frankenstein Above the Village of Chamounix: Performing Transgender Rage', *GLQ: A Journal of Lesbian and Gay Studies*, 1(3): 237–254.

West, C. and Zimmerman, D. H. (1987) 'Doing Gender', *Gender & Society*, 1(2): 125–151.

Whittle, S. (1998) 'The Trans-Cyberian Mail Way', *Social & Legal Studies*, 7(3): 389–408.

Whittle, S. (2006) 'Foreword', in S. Stryker and S. Whittle (eds.), *The Transgender Studies Reader*. New York: Routledge, pp. xi–xvi.

7 On being a 'wife'

Cis women negotiating relationships with a trans partner

Clare Beckett-Wrighton

Introduction

Israel (2005: 1) argues that 'even one supportive family member' can ensure successful gender transition. In adult couples, this role usually falls to a cis partner. Califia (1997) names partners as providing direct communication between cis and trans worlds. Despite identification of this role, little is known about partners' negotiation of transition.

The genesis of this chapter was a group meeting open only to people who were considering, in the process of or had undertaken a gender transition and identified themselves as 'trans'. The group met in a UK community centre for lesbian, gay, bisexual and trans (LGBT) people. This centre provided a support and outreach programme for the trans community as well as space to meet. Group members were discussing actions that could be taken by lesbian and gay members of the centre to support their experiences of transition.

The trans group's discussion centred on support for their own partners before, during and after transition. Group members felt that their partners were invisible in the LGBT centre and in other environments offering support to trans people. This included hospital and clinic appointments, family and social relationships. Transition impacted on these partners by changing external perceptions of their gender identity. Heterosexual partnerships became less welcome in heterosexual space when both partners were identified with the same gender. Partners who had been gay were no longer straightforwardly members of a gay community after transition. These changes were not always congruent with the choices of partners. Partnerships were recognised as a foundation to the everyday experience and support networks of group members, and lack of recognition for partners was identified as a major weakness in support given generally and by the community centre in particular. Among other things, members reported that their needs during transition could be incompatible with the lives their partners lived and the relationships that supported the couple.

This conversation began a journey of discovery in which I explored the lived experience of transition from the perspective of intimate partners, developing the research project 'In step with my trans partner', or 'In step'. In this chapter I raise particular themes from that research to consider how intimate relationships and partners are supported, or not, as transitions are facilitated. The word 'partner' is used here specifically to describe male or female cisgender partners whether heterosexual or lesbian or gay, with or without legal marriage (although this chapter reports specifically on the experiences of female partners). Cis is used to indicate a person for whom assigned sex and lived gender match. It is not always a popular description among a group who have never questioned their own identity position. My own research journey included learning to accept 'cis' as a way of describing myself despite my own uncertainty about embracing an identifier that could be felt to diminish membership of the universally understood category of 'woman'. In this research, many women, both trans and partners, objected strongly to being described in this way because, among other things, the definition can be seen to create different categories of 'women'. For partners, this was an unacceptable position. While I am aware of difficulty in using this description, it does allow me to write clearly in an arena where pronouns and descriptions may otherwise be confusing. The signifier helps to describe the paradox of cis partners who enter a relationship with recognisable features reflecting their own identity as women and as lesbian, gay or heterosexual (again, terms used reflect the language given by research participants) and find external recognition of that relationship changed. Transition requires adaptation of at least the outward expression of partnership in an arena where gender is not only the subject of theoretical analysis but also the focus of public policy. Living through transition as a partnered couple challenges conceptual norms of gendered behaviour across different cultural sites in theoretical, professional and everyday practice.

Of course, it can be argued that the experience of cis partners who identify as gay or lesbian would be fundamentally different from that of partners who identify as heterosexual. Eliding the two, as I have done here, risks incorporation of gay experience into heterosexual assumptions and thereby, as Plumwood (1992) would argue, backgrounding sexuality. However, exploration of *gender* is the foreground of this study. Foregrounding gender allows me to take a biographical approach to the experience of negotiating private and public relationships in this arena. Such intimate relationships are founded in sexual behaviours that are private but which cross into the public gaze *because* assumptions of gender, sexuality and identification are public and cultural and endorsed by social expectations.

The proposal for the 'In-step' research project was developed with and by a small group of trans people and their cis partners. Members of this small group reported that they felt silenced and made invisible by lack of support and lack of recognition of cis partners' unique position. Invisibility was reflected in negotiating personal life, personal relationships, family, friends and others. This included interaction with formal institutions such as health centres and less formal structures such as community centres or support organisations. In particular, little attention was paid to existing partnerships during any medical process, and lack of formal support from health authorities or community groups led to invisibility. This in itself is no surprise: trans experiences of health care are frequently negative (Bachman and Gooch, 2018). This lack of support is distressing in itself, but it can be argued that it is so dissonant with common practices towards intimate opposite-gender partners in heterosexual settings that it also reflects a process of exclusion for the idea of close relations among trans people. Ignoring the support that partners provide threatens to undermine specific 'intimate labours' (Ward, 2010) that include recognition and support of gendered identity. Here, 'the power of silence as discursive practices (that) eliminate certain issues from arenas of speech and sound' (Simpson and Lewis, 2005: 1253) works to deny recognition of trans partnerships. This is despite, or possibly because of, the primary focus on gender in any transition process. This is not a simple equation, however. Partners who identified as lesbian before their partner's transition and could be perceived as heterosexual after transition identified similar exclusions to partners who identified as heterosexual before their partner's transition. This similarity in experience between heterosexual and gay couples may indicate an area where mechanisms of heterosexuality as *social organisation* can be separated from ideas of heterosexuality as *sexual practice*.

The process of transition (as experienced through access to health and community provision) runs in parallel to changes in visible constituents of partnership. During this period heterosexual couples become recognised as single-gender couples and single-gender couples begin to appear as heterosexual ones. Cis partners often approve changes but only on rare occasions would actively choose them. Often a change that may seem minor and is accepted, like changing hairstyle, has unexpected impact on the visual identity of a couple. Gender as an action, or 'doing gender' (West and Zimmerman, 1987: 1) is a complex process, but being recognised as having gendered identity was unquestioned among the cis partners. Gender is also performative (Butler, 2006) and relational (Alegria and Ballard-Reisch, 2013) such that cis partners adapt and react to changing performances of gendered identification. Recognising the complexity of this adds to understandings of how the emergence of 'trans' challenges, develops and extends understandings of gender and sexuality, and begins to offer insight into the reconfiguring of everyday lives and new normativities. Ways of talking about transition indicate ways in which trans appears in everyday lives and repertoires, both in the experience and language of partners and in the reflection of that experience from social networks and health practitioners. Hence, this chapter also looks at ways in which partners articulate transitions.

In this chapter I concentrate on mechanisms of regulation for female partners' position, identity and work in supporting and caring for their significant others before, during and after transition, because this is an issue around which the trans group at the LGBT centre originally expressed disquiet. Women entering into active transition with their partners may also enter into medical arrangements for transition. Medical transition runs in parallel with appearances in public as a changing couple: because of this Brown (2009) titles her work about sexual-minority women in relationships with transsexual men 'I'm in Transition Too'. It might be more accurate for the 'In-step' participants to say 'my relationship is in transition too'. Understanding this relational impact helps to inform understandings of gender in a heterosexual field of action. The experience of these cis women illuminates accounts of partnership and marriage as transitions are completed.

The 'In-step' research took place in the United Kingdom, where rights and processes supporting gender transition are relatively new, and this project may reflect that. Theorisations and understandings of 'trans' have changed and are changing over time. Dominant paradigms based in biological difference are less present in analytical frameworks but are still utilised in everyday understandings. This has fundamentally influenced lived experience of intimate partnering. Partners' understanding and description of their own identity may help to shed light on the utility of different approaches understanding and describing trans identity.

Perspectives on trans people's partners

It is hard to identify a theoretical approach to partners of trans people, even though their position is potentially central to understanding transition processes. Partners are not only the knowing bystanders of transition, but also they are projected into change. West and Zimmerman's (1987) active analysis of 'doing gender' in an interactive tradition is helpful here, as is their identification of the difference between the *role* of gender in an institutionalised social world and the *display* of gender in enacting that status in a dual-gender heterosexual theatre. In understanding partners, the role of gender can be seen as explicit in negotiations around care, while displays of gender are implicit in the negotiation of a social role before, during and after transition. Whitley (2013) also uses a relational approach, drawing on West and Zimmerman (1987) in identifying the position held by a group identified as 'SOFFAs' (Significant Others, Family Members, Friends and Allies). He discusses the potential for SOFFAs to experience misreadings of their sexual orientation based on the perceived gender of their partner in much the same way as experienced by cis partners in the 'In-step' project. For instance, a 'heterosexual' woman can be read as a lesbian and vice versa dependent on the gender of her partner.

Understanding gender and sexuality as relational rather than individual is not a new method of analysis. Since early recognitions of a separation between sex and gender (Oakley, 1972), many analyses have focused on how gender positions locate men or women. Useful examples include Dworkin's (1987) work placing sex acts into a framework of power, and Rich's (1980) argument placing heterosexuality into a relational and capitalist context. Both frameworks help to understand the position of cis women partnering trans people, in that being a female partner is theorised within an analysis of power. Going further, Jackson (2006: 106) sees gender as both social, in the sense that it affects relationships, and cultural, in the sense that it is embedded in structural responses 'given meaning and substance in the everyday actions, interactions and subjective interpretations through which it is lived'. There is little doubt that gender as a fundamental social division creates, reflects and supports heterosexual norms and, as Jackson (2006) also argues, can promote theoretical acceptance of heterosexuality. It is gender, not sexuality, that is described here although, possibly, these experiences could only take place in the field of heterosexuality. Accepting a heterosexual background to experiences that reflect negotiations of binary gendered roles risks a tacit assumption that heterosexuality is not problematic while gender is, or as Ingraham (2006) put it, 'thinking straight'. The hegemony of heterosexuality acts as the field of action or the backdrop to discussion of gender, or as Weigman (2006: 100) says in debating concepts of heteronormativity, 'there seems to be only one thing of which we can be certain: that the desire for gender will leave none of us alone'.

To Halberstam (2005: 49) transgender describes 'not simply an identity, but a relation between people, within a community, or within intimate bonds'. Halberstam recognises the journey of gender change as both individual and relational with respect to private partnerships, public community and social organisation. Cis partners' recognition and support for transition is an *active* contribution. Drawing on this understanding, Ward (2010: 240) uses the term 'gender labour' to describe 'the act of giving gender to others' or the active recognition and support of another's gendered actions and behaviours. She sees part of the role for cis women in trans relationships as providing support for re-gendered behaviour in their partners. She identifies 'the duties that comprise gender labor – witnessing, nurturing, validating, fulfilling, authenticating, special knowing, and secret-keeping' as specifically feminised forms of work, which support the transitioning partner in their new role but are bound up with feminised performances of love, intimacy and caring (Ward, 2010: 240). Seeing gender in this way, as an active part of partnership, is a helpful tool in understanding the actions of cis female partners. Going further, Butler's (2006) work unpins gender role and activity from gendered identity and introduces an element of performativity to the picture. If gender is made up from a repetition of gendered acts that both create and reinforce a gendered position, then the recognition and understanding of those acts must also reinforce recognition of gender. The role of the viewer was understood also by cis research participants. For them, the struggle was both about being seen themselves and supporting their partner's gendered position.

There is also a literature specific to understanding transgender families. Notable among these are Hines (2007, 2010) in the UK and Pfeffer (2008, 2010) in the United States. Hines' work offers insight into ways that transgender individuals negotiate their status and relationships. She offers valuable discussion of negotiation of gender in family and community settings and, unusually, locates elements of her discussion in the policy field (Hines, 2010). Her work, which argues that negotiations of gender can be subversive but are specifically located by culture or place, is dominated by concepts of community care. Pfeffer (2010) interviewed 50 female partners of transgender and transsexual men. Her contribution to debates on gender work included discussion of emotional work, including responsibility to sympathise or empathise. Both researchers are explicit in recognising that the experiences they relate take place in the context of heterosexuality. Their studies demonstrate ways in which active parties to transition negotiate between each other as partners, and explore how these relationships are located within a network of established structures with recognised expectations. Their reading clearly accepts gender as performative and relational and is concerned with specific and culturally located experiences of cis partners. This offers valuable insights with which to continue the 'In-step' research.

In this research, gender is explored in the context of heterosexuality: not just in terms of sexual relationships but also as an 'ordering not only sexual life but also domestic and extra-domestic divisions of labour and resources' (Jackson, 2006: 107). Explorations of heterosexuality as the context of gendered actions follows Diane Richardson's (1996) analysis of heterosexuality as encoding and structuring everyday life. Jackson (2006) offers analyses of debates regarding the borders or boundaries of heterosexuality and heteronormativity, which also help to identify heterosexuality as a field in which gendered behaviours are located. That none of the research participants explicitly discussed heterosexuality is, I think, a result of the universality of heterosexuality as a normative context. In this chapter I therefore examine how heterosexuality provides the *field* in which gendered behaviours are seen, understood and accepted.

There is also a growing literature on the specific experiences of cis partners. Notable among this is interest in potential for transgression of gender and sexuality boundaries among partners (Pfeffer, 2008; Brown, 2009; Joslin-Roher and Wheeler, 2009). There is also work that focuses on one aspect of intimate relationships: Meier et al. (2013) focus specifically on romanticism, Chase (2011) takes a psychoanalytical approach which prioritises mental health implications of transition, Alegria and Ballard-Reisch (2014) foreground identity formation and reformation in both partners during transition. However, in the body of literature there is very little that addresses the constant work of negotiation and renegotiation of gendered roles, a daily lived reality in a predominantly heterosexual capitalist economy. This work involves not only the reproduction of tasks but also the recreation of social values and norms. In this way cultural expectations of gender roles are cultivated and passed on.

The research

Initially, data were collected in 2014 through an online survey distributed through forums that represented, advised or supported trans people. Survey participants were asked if they would be willing to be interviewed in order to gather deeper data. Little is known about numbers of trans people and small groups – for example, the research steering group which was based in one geographical location – may not reflect a range of experiences. Using online data collection allowed a wide spread of responses. Surveys may encourage responses from stigmatised and isolated groups like this because the researcher is absent (Beckett and Clegg, 2007). Online distribution encourages a wide geographical spread. Implications of this method include the possibility that trans people act as unofficial gatekeepers for their partners. It may be that some or many did not pass on the link to the research, but anecdotal evidence suggests that trans people are deeply concerned about the practical position of their partners and happy to facilitate access to the questionnaires. Chase (2011) also recruited partners through existing LGBT organisations and identified several factors that might prevent partners coming forward to discuss transition, including inaccessibility and the potential for discussion to affect their partners' transition process. She does not mention the potential for gatekeeping as an issue but, in common with my findings, found difficulty reaching male partners of trans people, whether in gay or heterosexual relationships.

In my experience, respondents were anxious to contribute. For many, this appeared to be the first opportunity to discuss their position. I asked that trans partners be out of earshot during the interview, which took place mainly face to face but sometimes through Skype. I conducted one interview with each partner who declared themselves willing to talk. An unexpected feature of the negotiation process for interviews was that I was frequently asked about my own attitudes, as respondents expressed concern that I would use the research material to damage trans people. This was a question about broad issues rather than about specific partnerships and may have been raised more often because I am an older lesbian woman who identifies as feminist. As such, I developed my feminist understandings in a historical period that foregrounded and prized the identity of 'woman' as a social group and a political power base. This understanding includes the prioritising of gendered social positions and the learning and understanding that go with growing to womanhood in a particular culture, physical form and power structure. Understanding the development of womanhood in this way challenges an acceptance of gender as potentially transitional. Often, the political position is more developed in that it rejects men as always subject to male social positioning and therefore antagonistic to women. In this way, transition is not recognised as bringing entry to the position of 'woman'. I do not share this position, but I do understand the arguments that lead to it and recognise that the possibility of my researching from that position could be damaging to trans people. I did not make my personal information explicit, but it is easy to find. This may have contributed to wariness in discussing any difficulties with me.

This chapter draws on all survey responses. These provide structured demographic information and long answers to four questions about events or landmarks during the journey of transition, feelings about social presentation and interaction, what was important to include in the research and what sources of help there had been. The responses to this last question were unanimous: From the unequivocal 'There aren't any' to the more textured 'None available; tried one and they said leave my partner as it wouldn't work' to the considered 'I did a lot a research on the internet, even joined transgender sites, just looking for answers and to understand it', none of the responses recorded finding help or support. However, this in itself may have changed the situation: there were five new groups for partners identified in the survey and supported by partners known to the respondents.

In drawing on interviews for this chapter I have selected cis women who share 'common ground' in that their partners have been or are undergoing medical treatment, and that they have been in a married or settled partnership before, during and after the process and were not aware that their partners wished to transition until the relationship was well established. Some of the women identified as heterosexual and others as lesbian; their partners variously identified as trans women or men. This group of women is also identified by Alegria and Ballard Reisch (2013), who look specifically at changes in sexual identity among cis women. Their observation, that cis women questioned their sexual orientation after their partner's transition, was not apparent in my research.

At the time of writing I have conducted ten interviews in different parts of the UK. All interview respondents provided a name they wished to be known by in any work drawn from the research and used here. The interview schedule was as broad as possible, with an opening invitation to 'tell me everything I should know about your journey'. Subsequent questions mirrored areas highlighted in interview responses. All of the interviews have included expressions of surprise and pleasure that someone was asking about their experience. One participant ended the interview with an emotional expression of how good it had been to talk about it, that no one had ever asked how she was before.

The research was conducted during a period when many media accounts of partners' experiences were negative. A condition of undertaking the research set both by myself and the steering group was to obtain and offer an image of trans partnerships that was realistic and unsensational. In the end, it was easy to do this: participants documented long and difficult journeys but were not critical or dismissive of the transition process undergone by their partners even where their own experience had not been positive. Of the partners quoted here, all are expecting to continue in close and intimate relationship after transition. This, in itself, offers a real lived critique to models of gender, heterosexuality and partnership that require a binary gender split.

Entering the medical arena

In both surveys and interviews, women identified partnership, whether married or not, as including responsibilities. One area of responsibility foregrounded by all participants was a need to provide physical and emotional support during medical experiences. Providing physical and emotional care to partners can be seen as part of a gendered field of action, where love and intimacy are accompanied by practical and supportive tasks of caring and organisation. There is little work looking specifically at the experience of supporting transition processes that are medical but not usually connected to illness. Pfeffer's (2010) discussion is an attempt to bridge this gap by asking what the narrative of work and care given by cis partners has to contribute to knowledge of gendered care and women's work. Cis partners in the 'In-step' project entered into long-term relationships with implicit expectations that physical intimacy would include caring tasks. Their difficulty appears to have been in negotiating their expectations of providing care for their transitioning partners in relation to the expectations of medical providers.

Partners interviewed identified areas in which care was needed, in both public and private arenas. Often, the first contact with explicitly transition-related medical arrangements was through a gender clinic. Contact would be made with a clinic after a long process of 'getting used to' the idea of physical transition, and after the trans partner had made a visible change in their identification in the couple's social location. One survey respondent commented, 'If I wasn't willing to be part of the process, I wouldn't have been there' (meaning the clinic). Clinical policies explicitly state that the relationships trans people form are important. However, partners reported at best a lack of clarity about their position, and at worst direct exclusion from interviews and decisions. One area of consternation for several cis women was when or how hormone treatment would begin. This had often been discussed by the partners in advance of clinical appointments but was not a shared decision in the medical environment. Women reported occasions where both partners were expecting to be included in the consultation but the partner was left outside, or where requests for help or information made in the presence of the trans partner and with their support were ignored. For example, one woman reported being in the waiting room with her trans partner, who expected her to be present at the consultation. The trans partner was called through but the cis partner was explicitly asked to wait.

Some medical processes, conducted on a body familiar and intimately known to the cis partner, and carrying gendered implications, brought unexpected complications. One survey response reported:

> Then the chest surgery was another difficult time. I always knew that he would have this surgery but when it came time to have the consultation with the surgeon I found myself quite distressed at what was discussed. I was also concerned that this surgery would take place in [redacted for anonymity] where we didn't know anyone and I would be alone while he was in hospital.

Another survey response raised similar issues: 'Partner being put on Decapetile was scary – decisions being made that will affect me – but I have no control over'. The respondents are clearly supportive of medical intervention, but resentful of what they perceive as side-lining. Some responses couched this in terms of the information and knowledge they had about their trans partner which might have facilitated the process. Jenny, in her interview, reported feeling that the medical profession was uninterested in her, that she was 'nothing to do with it'. On one occasion, counselling was offered to both the trans person and their cis partner, but the couple turned this down because they felt that any response they made could affect the availability of the transition process.

Despite difficulty in contributing to formal medical decision-making, cis partners reported engaging in considerable emotional caretaking and actual physical care during this period:

> Testosterone injections. I was expected to administer these. I had never had any medical training, and a few demos at the local GP's surgery didn't make me feel confident. I really didn't like doing it as I was terrified every time that I would cause him some harm.

One interviewee reported the level of physical care she provided after her partner underwent 'bottom surgery' (surgery to alter genital sexual characteristics). She identified this as one of the most positive periods of the whole experience of transition, because she could go in to the room and lie on the bed with her partner, look after her if she was in pain or depressed, make sure that she ate and took her medication. Rebecca reported paying for her partner's chest surgery because they wanted to ensure it was at a time she would be available to provide care.

This level of care for a partner in hospital is not unusual among relationships. It is a part of the normative intimate labour of a socially accepted partnership. Dunscombe and Marsden (1993) identify differences between the amount and types of emotional labour completed by men and women in supporting their partners, but in doing so they also identify a place for and recognition of this emotional work. Arguably, Khor (2007) recognises this divide in lesbian arrangements as well. Pfeffer (2010: 174) describes the kind of labour involved in supporting a transitioning partner and locates that labour in gender roles. The feminist women she interviewed:

> Detailed elaborate routines of attending to (and being accountable for) both the mundane and extraordinary organisation of the details of their partner's personal lives in ways that revealed traditionally gendered roles.

This kind of involvement in the process of transition is not questioned by partners. They often describe themselves as 'glad to do it', having 'one way of supporting him', and a way of 'keeping in touch with' partners. Providing physical and sometimes financial care, and contributing to the emotional well-being of the couple, is part of their understanding of the relationship they entered in to as partners. As one member of the initiating group explained, 'If I had had cancer, or needed any other kind of service from the doctor, my wife would be included'.

Cis women in this research felt that their treatment by external agents such as medical practitioners stood in marked contrast to the experiences of female partners in non-trans relationships, where a 'wife' has a recognised role and place at the partners' side. This invisibility can be felt very deeply: one woman talked about feeling that everyone was rooting for the beautiful woman her partner had become, while 'I went through the hell with no one rooting for me or telling me how brave I was'. This has personal repercussions. The lack of attention paid to women fulfilling a traditional gender role is so marked that it is indicative of external agencies' inability to see how it is possible to present gendered boundaries as permeable while also accepting a partner with an emotional and intimate life. In this sense the discipline of heterosexuality establishes who can be a 'partner'. Butler (2001: 621) writes, 'What, given the contemporary order of being, can I be?' It seems that trans people cannot claim the ordinary social relationships of partners, and their cis female partners in turn cannot rely on the solidity of completing expected labour. In this sense what appears to be happening is that the agencies located at the crux of transition are effectively reinforcing a heterosexual matrix of binary gender, in which a trans patient's perceived gender instability means there is no intelligible role for a partner.

Gender as a relational concept

Cis partners in this research did not question their own gender identity as women. Identifying commonalities in partners' understanding of 'being a woman' may have been complicated by the respective heterosexual or lesbian status of different participants, but regardless they shared identifiable locations of care. Since West and Zimmerman's (1987) work, it has been possible to think of gender as actively constructed through interaction, rather than as a single entity with constant expression. Lloyd (2007: 54), following Judith Butler, argues that 'it is precisely the repetition of acts, gestures and discourses that produces the effect of identity at the moment of action'. Franklin (2014) draws on Ward (2010) to relate relational practices to gender labour. Ward (2010: 238) herself connects gender labour to the support of gender in intimate partners, identifying 'tedious acts of emotional, physical and sexual "support" that are undertaken to co-produce the gender coherence and/or transgression of others'.

However, Franklin and Ward are interrogating positions taken by sexual-minority women supporting trans partners, and so are concerned with the development of the concept in relation to transgressive (LGB) performance. This is not the focus of concern reported in this research: here, cis women are describing their (gendered) experience as women, rather than recognising themselves as located in sexuality.

For partners involved in this research, providing support to gendered practices is possibly the location of greatest change. The shift from supporting one gender performance to recognising and supporting another, often with little time to make the change and in a period where hormonal and other treatments create different currents, was always recognised as problematic even when the process of medical transition took a long time or was incomplete. This moves beyond the caring tasks recognised in Pfeffer's (2010) account and speaks to ways in which gender change impacted on interpersonal incidents in public and private.

One interview summed up accounts of concern about gendered identity. It discussed a trip away, taken to celebrate a specific event. It was long planned, and both partners had looked forward to it. In the event, it coincided with a period where the trans partner still had some facial hair growth and was wearing thick foundation to conceal it. Her own view of her female gender was firm and she was confident. The cis woman in the relationship was deeply upset by the reactions of other women in public situations, who clearly identified her partner as 'trans' rather than 'female' and whose body language and unspoken reactions were not accepting:

> I was so uncomfortable. I just wanted to shrink into myself. I couldn't bear it. I couldn't bear it for her, and I couldn't bear it that I was so embarrassed.

This incident was not discussed by the couple until a long time after the event, and this discussion did not reach any clear conclusions. It seems to lie comfortably alongside accounts given in the research that cis female partners may no longer 'make the best of themselves' when going out with a trans partner, or are concerned about trans partners who use too much jewellery, or wear tight or revealing clothes. For one participant, supporting her partner meant that her own style of presentation had become less 'feminine – you know, all styled up to look good' while her trans partner was portrayed as 'ultra-feminine – a real head turner'. In these examples the relational labour of supporting transition into a female social role seems to create questions in cis partners about their own ability to fulfil that role. However, for some women, transition opened up welcome opportunities. In particular, one participant described how she loved going to a health spa with her partner as two women, or getting dressed up with her and going out. Here, the labour of supporting female change was welcome.

There were two accounts of cis women supporting male partners. Neither of these accounts focused on relational gendered practices in the same way. These two women talked much more about the intimate bodily changes their partners undergo. For instance, one participant focused on whether her partner would undergo bottom surgery to create male-gendered genitalia. There is insufficient evidence to locate this difference in approach in a gendered or sexualised context, but the contrast with accounts from cis women in relationships with trans women was marked.

At the end of the transition process, identified by research participants as the point where their partner looked, behaved and was accepted as holding a binary gendered identity different from that held at the start of the partnership, there were also distinct difficulties. Partners who had whole-heartedly supported change, often for many years, found themselves struggling to find a role at the end of the process. One interviewee summed this up in an emotional interview: 'Now she's off and going out and having fun, and I'm just here on my own and fat'. Another described her experience very fully. At the start of the process she had looked forward to transition as a way of changing her relationship with her partner. She saw it as completely beneficial to the relationship. Through the year of transition (an unusually short period) she became exhausted by her partner's need for support and her own unexpected emotional reactions to physical change. At the end of the process she saw herself as still in a committed relationship, in which her religious marriage was important and lifelong commitment was expected. She talked about being disappointed in the changes, which had not lived up to her expectations of change for herself, although her partner was completely satisfied.

The end of transition was sometimes marked in UK law through the trans partner applying for or gaining a Gender Recognition Certificate. At the time of writing, a married couple in the UK must apply for a Gender Recognition Certificate together and must show that they are likely to stay together. In England and Wales the marriage must then be dissolved and reconstituted, as 'gender-neutral' marriages are not recognised in these jurisdictions, but instead must be explicitly *either* heterosexual or homosexual. This provision may change as gender recognition laws are under review, but currently it has a marked impact on couples. Two members of the trans support group involved in this research described their marriages ending at the point where they collected their certificate. One interviewee described the day the couple received the gender recognition certificate as:

> The worst day of my whole life [. . .] it was all over then, you see.

Her relationship continued but she found it hard to develop a role and way of communicating once the focus on transition was gone.

This research relies on too small a sample from which to draw an inference on the impact of gender recognition (and the associated dissolution of marriage) as a final marker of transition and in any case since this chapter was written before the law has been reviewed. Nevertheless, participants' responses are concerning. One participant contacted me after the research was completed to report that she had left her partner once the certificate was provided, even though she had not had any intention of leaving the relationship until that point.

In these examples there is evidence of support for a trans partner's new identity in ways that help to re-affirm their gender identity. Reciprocity is not as clear. It is possible that these comments show evidence of the enforcement of heterosexual binary norms in a context where relationships cannot live up to these norms, where it is important that partners should evidence different gender positions but these positions rebound on cis partners. It may be that the ending of the external identification process leads partners to enter a fundamentally different relationship with each other, as well as to the mechanisms of gendered location. However, for many individuals their participation in this research was possibly undertaken before their partnerships had continued long enough to develop new ways of relating.

Promises and partnership

If a transition is to move forward, result in new family forms and encourage transgression across the binary of heterosexual partnerships, then how trans partners understand the process and name themselves within it may be the trigger for change. Already, the cis partners interviewed were intending to continue their partnership in a changed gender and sexual context, and may be developing ways to relate to their trans partners that inform expectations of gendered behaviour. Here, the contexts of marriage, partnership and of being a wife are related but not the same. A married identity was a statement of religious and/or social intent and had implications for some partnerships, but other cis women rejected formal marriage. These women, however, reported their care and support role in the same way as married women. Being a wife and able to call oneself 'Mrs' may be a potent identity in formal settings but, in this research, did not mean that women's expectations of themselves to provide care and support were different from unmarried partners.

An unexpected but welcome finding from the research was that different and specific understandings of 'marriage' relate to negotiations of gendered behaviour. One woman wrote in her survey response that 'getting married was a promise I meant to keep for the rest of my life'. Many women commented on marriage 'meaning something', but what was meant and how that impacted on their own identity differed. Sometimes, marriage was a specific relationship placed in social expectations. One older woman married young, divorced, then lived with and ultimately re-married the same partner. She had children and grandchildren with her partner and had close ties with extended family and the local community. Shortly after the second wedding her partner entered a transition process. This had huge impact on the participant. While she continued to negotiate contact between her partner and the extended family, she became isolated from the community because she insisted on retaining her identity as married by using the title 'Mrs' and attending events usually limited to married couples. There was no doubt in her account that her second marriage had been a final act and that she was totally committed to her partner. For her, this position was contradictory. She had great difficulty accepting her partner's transition, although she had given her enormous support. She found using her partner's female name difficult and often used male pronouns. To her, her husband was still her husband. She identified this opposition herself and presented her difficulty with considerable humour. She identified a particular picture of her partner as a (male) child and said:

> Oh Clare, if you could have seen it! It was picture of a girl with that beautiful red hair.

This respondent found considerable comfort in a discourse of her partner having been 'made' one gender or another 'all along'.

Other participants found a married identity less contradictory. A much younger participant described being married as being, for her, a religious experience that could not be dissolved by social processes in which she included gender. Her wedding day had been sanctioned by her church and was, in her view, irrevocable. It committed her to providing support for her partner through intimate physical care and public loyalty. For her, her partner remained the person to whom she was wedded regardless of gender. Her account indicates that gendered behaviour was, in her view, backgrounded compared with the reality of her partner as a specific person. Another story also illustrates this way of seeing marriage as to a person, with gender as a permeable category. Here, the cis partner entered into an intimate relationship with a college friend. She saw this relationship as private and not open to public sanction. She and her friend were moving to a different continent partly for work and partly so that the trans partner could begin medical processes. Nothing would begin until after the move but the potential move away from both a geographical place and a gendered identity prompted her community to demand a wedding ceremony and legal recognition of marriage between the couple. This was described as being a way in which the community could ensure that the cis partner would have the care and support of her trans partner regardless of gender transition.

Marriage was regarded as a private rather than publicly sanctioned statement for other participants. There is no evidence in this research that formal marriage processes were the only, or even the main reason for partnerships to continue after transition. With or without the recognisable identity of being 'married', cis women saw themselves as in a partnership, with that partnership having private and public connotations. This may be most apparent in an account from a cis woman who identified herself as a politically active lesbian. She had entered partnership with a person she identified as being a 'butch' (potentially male-appearing) woman, who later came out as a man. Because her partner was identified as butch and both were active in LGBT politics, she expected that her partner's transition would be accepted by others. Instead, she found that some areas of her previous political activity were closed to her, either because they no longer resonated or because she was now publicly identified as heterosexual rather than lesbian. She indicated frustration and uncertainty in how to proceed. Her trans partner was reported as moving away from lesbian society and political activity because these no longer had personal relevance. The cis partner was not happy about this, reporting that it impacted on her friendships and her activities, but was not able to see an immediate answer. For her, 'I thought being together meant sharing things. When we got together for me it was forever'. While this account is presented and understood in a political context, it chimes with other accounts of lost friendships or changed activities. Another woman spoke about becoming isolated from the local games club she and her partner had contributed to for several years because members, old friends of the couple, had trouble relating to her partner's transitioned status.

Even where cis partners understood gender boundaries as permeable, external social responses could be problematic. One participant started the interview by explaining that gender identity was not a fixed concept. Her approach to her relationship and to gender transition had always been that you could 'do what you like with your own body', and so her trans partner's chest surgery had not, in her view, changed the relationship in any way. For her, the fundamental issue in the relationship was how she was now perceived as a cis woman in partnership with a male-identified person. She had lost friends in the gay community where she had previously felt well positioned. She identified herself as a 'lesbian who lives with a man' but had problems being seen by others as holding that identity.

In a world of changing conceptualisations of gender, recognising that these relationships call into question expectations of married couples and of partners would be useful in that it allows for a more nuanced understanding of those relationships and of gendered behaviour. No account placed responsibility with trans partners for supporting cis partners or recognising any difficulties a new sexual identity might cause. One cis woman described the journey of transition as being so fraught with misunderstanding and constant battles that it 'had' to be a selfish journey, and used that reasoning to explain her partner's lack of support. However, perhaps a conceptual issue in understanding this process can be seen in the difficulty of unpicking separate implications of gendered or sexual identity. Transition takes place within heterosexual gendered assumptions. This chapter has focused on the implications of and for gender, but that has necessarily meant leaving some interactions with heterosexuality unfocused.

It is worth noting that the foregoing comments do not coincide with Franklin's (2014) or Alegria and Ballard-Reisch's (2013) findings that partners' transitions encouraged minority-sexuality partners to question their own sexual identity. The sample generated in that research focused on US-based cis women whose partners transitioned from female to male. That research cohort could be expected to have identified as lesbian before their partner's transition and as heterosexual afterwards. The differences in findings could be related to the geographical location of the participants, as well as to the predominance of cis women in relationships with trans women in the 'In-step' sample. This British sample were not considering changing their own gendered identity in response to transition and were struggling with, rather than questioning, changes in sexual identification caused by their partners' transition. Visible gender change in the partnership strengthened partners' original identification as a 'wife', as a heterosexual or as a lesbian. Women in partnership were unshaken in their continued identification as such, despite the perceived gender of their partners and how they might articulate their understanding of transition or of gender as potentially at odds with this.

Conclusion

The findings in this project may be influenced by the location and timing of the research. All respondents quoted here live either in the industrial north of England or in Scotland. None live in capital cities, and some reside in isolated rural areas. The data were gathered in 2014, when protections from discrimination for trans people in the Equality Act (2010) were relatively new, and gender recognition certification based on the Gender Recognition Act (2004) was becoming widely known. Any or all of these factors may have influenced the cis women contributors to come forward. However, this focused research does raise some specific issues and themes for further discussion and exploration.

Perhaps the most important finding is the lack of engagement with partners of people entering a transition process from social networks and institutional agencies. This may be simply due to a lack of attention to the matter in institutional policies, but the outcome is a silencing of both trans and cis people's real lived experience. If there is no place for partners, is it because there is no name for this kind of relationship, and no acceptance of trans people as individuals whose gender and social identity encompass both continuity and change? A focus on gender change rather than the emotional processes of living reflects (and so supports and reinforces) a heterosexual matrix of understanding, where relationships can only exist in a gendered binary.

Lack of understanding of the relational work done by intimate couples in supporting and affirming gender identity leads to a diminished and partial view of trans relationships. Acceptance of the real-life experience of couples should lead to development of health-care policy that includes cis partners of trans people in the same way that partners are accepted and encouraged in other areas. The lack of support services and community groups is also a factor in the experience of isolation and invisibility for this group. Moreover, a lack of recognition for the changes in social position resulting from transition leads to further side-lining the real lives of trans people and their partners. Exploration of this dynamic could lead to fundamental changes in ways that gender identity is theorised and understood.

Lastly, partners here theorise trans in a heterosexual binary divide without question. Tacit acceptance of this divide also works to reinforce it and reduce the potential for other, more transgressive understandings of relationship dynamics. If trans partnerships are to fulfil their potential for destabilising heterosexual norms and introducing new forms of intimate being, then a wider understanding of these processes needs to be developed.

References

Alegria, C.A. and Ballard-Reisch, D. (2013) Gender Expression as a Reflection of Identity Reformation in Couple Partners Following Disclosure of Male-to-Female Transsexualism, *International Journal of Transgenderism*, 14: 49–65.

Bachman, C. and Gooch, B. (2018) *Trans Report*. London: Stonewall.

Beckett, C. and Clegg, S. (2007) Qualitative Data from a Postal Questionnaire: Questioning the Presumption of the Value of Presence, *International Journal of Social Research Methodology*, 10(4).

Brown, N.R. (2009) "I'm in Transition Too": Sexual Identity Renegotiation in Sexual-Minority Women's Relationships with Transsexual Men, *International Journal of Sexual Health*, 21(1): 61–77.

Butler, J. (2001) Doing Justice to Someone: Sex Reassignment and Allegories of Transsexuality, *GLQ: A Journal of Lesbian and Gay Studies*, 7(4): 621–636.

Butler, J. (2006) *Gender Trouble: Feminism and the Subversion of Identity*. London: Routledge.

Califia, P. (1997) *Sex Changes: The Politics of Transgenderism*. Minneapolis: Cleis Press.

Chase, L. (2011) Wives' Tales: The Experience of Trans Partners, *Journal of Gay and Lesbian Social Services*, 23: 429–451.

Dunscombe, J. and Marsden, D. (1993) Love and Intimacy: The Gender Division of Emotion and 'Emotion Work': A Neglected Aspect of Sociological Discussion of Heterosexual Relationships, *Sociology*, 27(2): 221–241.

Dworkin, A. (1987) *Intercourse*. New York: Free Press.

Franklin, K. (2014) Gender Labor, Assimilationism, and Transformative Practices: The Relational Negotiations of Cisgender Women and their Transgender Men Partners, *Sociology Compass*, 8(6): 648–659.

Halberstam, J. (2005) *In a Queer Time and Place: Transgender Bodies, Subcultural Lives*. New York: NYU Press.

Hines, S. (2007) *TransForming Gender: Transgender Practices of Identity, Intimacy and Care*. Bristol: Policy Press.

Hines, S. (2010) Recognising Diversity? The Gender Recognition Act and Transgender Citizenship, in: Hines, S. and Sanger, T. (eds.) *Transgender Identities: Towards a Social Analysis of Gender Diversity*. New York: Routledge.

Ingraham, C. (2006) Thinking Straight, Acting Bent: Heteronormativity and Homosexuality, in: Davis, K. and Lorber, J. (eds.) *Handbook of Gender and Women's Studies*. London: Sage, pp. 307–321.

Israel, G.E. (2005) Translove, *Journal of GLBT Family Studies*, 1(1): 53–67.

Jackson, S. (2006) Gender, Sexuality and Heterosexuality: The Complexity (and Limits) of Heteronormativity, *Feminist Theory*, 7(1): 105–121.

Joslin-Roher, E. and Wheeler, D. (2009) Partners in Transition: The Transition Experience of Lesbian, Bisexual, and Queer Identified Partners of Transgender Men, *Journal of Gay and Lesbian Social Services*, 21(1): 30–48.

Khor, D. (2007) 'Doing Gender': A critical Review and Exploration of Lesbigay Domestic Arrangements, *Journal of GLBT Family Studies*, 3(1): 35–72.

Lloyd, M. (2007) *Judith Butler: From Norms to Politics*. Cambridge: Polity Press.

Meier, S.C., Sharp, C., Michonski, J., Babcock, C. and Fitzgerald, K. (2013) Romantic Relationships of Female-to-Male Trans Men: A Descriptive Study, *International Journal of Transgenderism*, 14(2): 75–85.

Oakley, A. (1972) *Sex, Gender and Society*. Aldershot: Ashgate.

Pfeffer, C. (2008) Bodies in Relation – Bodies in Transition: Lesbian Partners of Trans Men and Body Image, *Journal of Lesbian Studies*, 12(4): 325–345.

Pfeffer, C. (2010) Women's Work? Women Partners of Transgender Men Doing Housework and Emotion Work, *Journal of Marriage and Family*, 72: 165–183.

Plumwood, V. (1992) Feminism and Ecofeminism: Beyond the Dualistic Assumptions of Women, Men and Nature, *Ecologist*, 22(1): 8–13.

Rich, A. (1980) Compulsory Heterosexuality and Lesbian Existence, *Signs*, 5(4): 631–660.

Richardson, D. (1996) *Theorising Heterosexuality: Telling It Straight*. Buckingham: Open University Press.

Simpson, R. and Lewis, P. (2005) An Investigation of Silence and a Scrutiny of Transparency: Re-examining Gender in Organization Literature through the Concepts of Voice and Visibility, *Human Relations*, 58(10): 1253–1275.

Ward, J (2010) Gender Labor: Transmen, Femmes, and Collective Work of Transgression, *Sexualities*, 13(2): 236–254.

Weigman, R. (2006) Heteronormativity and the Desire for Gender, *Feminist Theory*, 7(1): 89–103.

West, C. and Zimmerman, D.H. (1987) Doing Gender, *Gender and Society*, 1(2): 125–151.

Whitley, C.T. (2013) Trans-kin Undoing and Re-doing Gender: Negotiating Relational Identity Among Friends and Family of Transgender Persons, *Sociological Perspectives*, 56(4): 597–621.

8 Sticks and stones break our bones, and words are damaging

How language erases non-binary people

stef m. shuster and Ellen Lamont

'Do you know what I'm fucking sick of?' Jax asks as ze gulps more coffee, getting amped up to respond to zir own question:

> I am motherfucking sick and tired of having to tell strangers that I am not a woman. And I am not a man. I am a genderfucked person, and 'lady' is not a respectful way of acknowledging my queered out gender and 'sir' is not a respectful way of rendering my genderfucked self as simply a kooky man who wears dresses.

As a 22-year-old American Indian genderfucked-identified person, Jax embraces a non-binary gender identity and is often misread in social life. Indeed, Jax, and many of the trans★ people interviewed for this study, told countless stories of negotiating social life, their on-the-ground experiences that are met with humor, anger and sadness because of the persistent assumption that all people are either cisgender women or men. This assumption translates to non-binary people feeling erased from much of social life, and with few options to respond to misgendering in these interactional moments.

Here, we use 'trans★' as an inclusive word for individuals who identify with a gender that does not correspond with the gender assigned at birth (i.e. not cisgender) and 'non-binary' to denote gender identities not located within a normative binary gender system (e.g. beyond or outside of women and men, and correspondingly hegemonic femininity and masculinity). There are countless possibilities for those who claim non-binary identities, such as genderfucked, genderfluid or genderqueer. And yet, despite the proliferation of gender identities in contemporary U.S. culture, they are rarely acknowledged in everyday interactions.

This chapter, then, is guided by a simple question: what are the challenges that non-binary people experience in everyday life in the United States? Yet while the question holds the illusion of provoking a 'common-sense' explanation, we show that how non-binary people negotiate gender in social interaction is a complex process that involves the intertwining relationship between cultural norms and an Anglophone linguistic system built upon the assumption of a two-and-only-two gender system (Lucal, 1999). Within deeply entrenched culturally normative gender systems in the US, no other possibilities beyond the gender binary are commonly recognised in social life. How people use language reifies binary gender categories in interaction, further perpetuating the assumption that all people identify as (cisgender or transgender) women or men.

A growing body of scholarship on trans★ people's experiences with inequality has documented several key areas in everyday life imbued with inequity and normative pressures to maintain gender binaries. From institutional domains such as the workplace (Schilt, 2010), legal classification (Spade, 2015) and health care (shuster, 2016), to public sites such as bathrooms (Westbrook and Schilt, 2014) as well as in the intimate spaces of relationships (Pfeffer, 2014) and parenting (Hines, 2006), trans★ people routinely confront cultural norms that restrict the range of gender identities commonly recognised in interaction. These persistent cultural norms come to shape normative gender-based expectations (e.g. sex assignment at birth and gender assignment at birth are seamless and correspond). In social interaction, in particular, these norms perpetuate trans★ oppression, but also reflect how all individuals – regardless of gender identity – experience the constraints of gender in everyday life.

Despite this growing body of scholarship on trans★ people, there remains a dearth of empirical data explicitly focusing on non-binary people's experiences in social life. To begin filling this gap in knowledge, we focus on language systems. Language and talk are inescapable features of social life. Because the English language is predicated upon binary gender categories, it is used to communicate and enforce norms while creating a liminal space for non-binary people in social life. Using in-depth interviews, we find that social interaction is fraught with tension for non-binary people in negotiating their self-identification and how others identify them. Within these gender determination processes (Westbrook and Schilt, 2014), or the interactional relationship between one's gender identity and how people determine others' gender, non-binary people are typically not recognised in their self-identified gender.

In this chapter, we present vignettes from in-depth interviews with non-binary people, to bring to light how gender determination processes break down for non-binary people in interaction. We demonstrate how non-binary people confront the constraints of English language by consistently having to self-disclose one's gender identity to strangers, remind familiars of their genders and engage with and resist the attempts of others to fold them into binary genders. As a consequence, people who identify with a gender outside of the binary are rendered invisible in social life, as there are no commonly recognised ways to interact and no existing cultural schemas with which to make sense of non-binary people.

Background

In the United States, widely shared cultural beliefs about gender are core components of maintaining social order. Dominant gender norms are built on the presupposition that the assigned sex at birth, assigned gender at birth, gender identity and gender expression correspond in straightforward ways (West and Zimmerman, 1987). These expectations of congruence among gender, identity and expression are governed by cultural norms that imply everyone *should* be able to meet them. Those who do not (or cannot) meet these norms are regulated in an effort to restore gender-based expectations in interaction (see Speer, 2005; West and Zimmerman, 1987).

At the interactional level, gender norms are (re)produced and shape how people negotiate cultural rules regulating gender identities, behaviors and expressions (Davis, 2009; Namaste, 2000). Social-relational contexts are the arenas in which these rules are brought to bear on the behaviour and evaluation of individuals (Ridgeway and Correll, 2004: 514). In interactions with strangers, gender is a classification mechanism that facilitates social order, as it operates as a taken-for-granted assumption that helps simplify interactions (Ridgeway and Correll, 2004). In using culturally bound schemas to create order in social life, individuals avoid cognitive overload in attempting to classify each person they pass in everyday life, as gendered. Within social-relational contexts, gender determination processes (Westbrook and Schilt, 2014) translate to people moving through social interactions unaware that some may identify outside of gender binaries. Kennedy's (2013) work on a culture of cisgenderism similarly demonstrates that it matters not how an individual identifies, but rather how an individual is *identified*. A culture of cisgenderism contributes to trans★ people's identities being dismissed, in favor of maintaining the status quo that is built upon binary and cisnormative assumptions, and thus, leaving non-binary people with few ways of being recognised as their self-identified gender in interaction.

Like gender, language systems form a foundation for social order and shape expectations for interactions (Speer, 2005). As people construct their social worlds through interactions with others (Eder, Evans and Parker, 1995), it is often through language that expectations about gender are communicated and reinforced. Language signals assumptions about social life and maintains social order by contributing to a sense of shared understanding of social life (Eder, Evans and Parker, 1995: 8; Speer, 2005). For example, gendered language systems are shaped by two interlocking cultural norms which uphold the assumption that identifying an individual's gender is a relatively easy process (Friedman, 2013; Lucal, 1999), and all people are cisgender (Kennedy, 2013). As documented by previous scholars (Pascoe, 2007; Speer, 2005), systems of language also symbolise and transmit cultural values surrounding the place of social groups For example, the words 'congressman' or 'fireman' convey assumptions about these occupations wherein men are assumed to be the proper people to hold these jobs, as men have historically been recognised as more qualified for state governance and risky occupations. In contrast (and in a traditional gender ideology), women are assumed to be more qualified for matters of the home and service-based occupations (Correll, 2001). Consequently, qualifiers are frequently used to delineate and emphasise nonnormative behavior, as with *male* nanny or *female* doctor (Hamilton, 2010).

Within cisnormative and binary spaces, language demarcates the 'normal' from the 'abnormal' through small cues such as the assumption that all people in an audience, for example, are 'women and men' or 'ladies and gentlemen'. As language structures interactions, and continues to reflect the assumption of a binary gender, how language and binary assumptions intertwine produces for non-binary people a double standard in everyday life. Non-binary people are either rendered invisible by interactants or must call attention to the fact that interactants have glossed over their non-binary gender identities. This double bind of invisibility or hyper-visibility reinforces 'difference' in the self-concepts of non-binary people in social interaction.

Methods

Data

This research project was motivated by a scholarly concern regarding trans★ people's experiences in everyday life, and a recognition of the importance of interviewing a wider range of trans-identified individuals who are otherwise absent from social scientific research on trans★ people. The first author conducted in-depth interviews with 18 non-binary people in a Midwestern US metropolitan area (named here 'Metromidwest'). Of these individuals, 60% were between the ages of 18 and 25, with the remaining 40% between ages 26 and 34. Of the younger non-binary people, many were actively enrolled students in area colleges and universities. Yet, college attendance was not a proxy for class, as 70% of non-binary participants came from working-class and/or poor backgrounds, with 30% identifying their families of origin as being middle to upper-middle class. In addition, 65% of non-binary people were white, approximately 20% identified as black or African American, 10% as Latinx and the remaining 5% as mixed race.

To find interviewees, the first author began with personal networks in trans★ communities in the Midwest, and then used a snowball sampling method to find additional interviewees. Interviews ranged in length from one to three hours. The average interview time was 115 minutes. The interviews were semi-structured and organised by broader categories of questions related to trans★ people's communities, relationships to others, and experiences in gender-segregated spaces. The first author met with people across Metromidwest, in a location selected by respondents.

Analytical Strategy

We used a recursive process to analyze data from the interviews. This entailed moving back and forth among the data, coding schema and existing literature, with the goal of further refining codes into sub-categories and looking for patterns in the data. Beginning with the interview transcripts, we noted that many trans★ people narrated challenges with language systems in everyday life. We examined the literature on language and culture, and returned to the transcripts for a second pass of coding. We identified three domains of social life where language erases the existence of non-binary people: having to self-disclose to strangers one's gender identity, reminding familiars of their genders and being folded into binary gender categories.

We crafted three vignettes as exemplars of these three prevalent themes, defined by at least 85% of respondents giving voice to the experiences coded in a theme, to demonstrate how language transmits cultural norms about gender as a two-and-only-two system (Lucal, 1999) while simultaneously erasing the existence of non-binary people. As other feminist scholars have suggested (e.g. Sprague, 2016), presenting data with vignettes enables a participant-focused narration of one's experiences in everyday life and exemplifies the meaning-making processes. This approach prioritises the voice of the participants, an important intervention in the existing scholarship on trans★ people in the social sciences, given that most of this research is conducted, analyzed and composed by cisgender people.

Results

A central theme that shaped non-binary people's experiences in everyday life was how language itself could not accommodate the existence of people who identify outside of gender binaries. The experiences that non-binary people shared exemplify how language systems are structured to perpetuate assumptions regarding dichotomous gender identities, and the expectation that all people should be able to meet these normative standards. We demonstrate that the common experiences iterated in the interviews are consequences of the language system and translate to non-binary people having to manage their gender identities in social life in order to create a space for them to exist as non-binary people.

Self-disclosing gender identity to strangers

Jax and I (the first author) have been engrossed in a discussion for the past 45 minutes on zir experiences in social life.[1] Like many of the non-binary people interviewed, Jax shared stories of putting in significant emotional labour to take care of other people in everyday interactions. As ze suggested, it is like 'a collision of emotions all wrapped up into me sometimes feeling like I am losing my fucking mind'. Jax continues to reflect on the emotional labor ze has to do that usually translates to zir taking care of others – strangers in fact – over zir own mental health in 'just getting through the day with my heart intact'. I ask if Jax would mind sharing a little more about those moments where ze is toggling between taking care of others, and one's self, and ze shares the following story:

> The other day on my way to school I stopped by a local coffee shop before heading to class. We went through the usual routine that you go through

in ordering a coffee. And at the end of our transaction, he says, 'Is there anything else that you would like, sir? No? OK, thanks man. Have a great day'. And I sort of lost it. It's a hard time right now, you know? I don't usually do this but there was just something about the smugness of this person referring to me as a guy twice in just a few sentences. So yeah. I lost it and yelled at him that I'm not a man. I'm a fucking gender-fucked identified person. As it was happening I felt bad, but also good that I was reclaiming space for myself with this stranger.

This interaction in the coffee shop is an interpretative process for both Jax and the barista. From Jax's perspective, the barista is understood as smug because he has rendered Jax's identity as a binary 'man' while Jax moves through social life as a genderfucked person. A history of interactions like these has resulted in Jax employing a lens of intentional culpability when strangers make incorrect gender determinations and brings to the interaction the full wrath of zir anger with the accumulation of similar experiences. To close the interaction, ze asserts a genderfucked identity. Disclosing zir gender is, for Jax, a way to reclaim space and re-balance the power dynamic that ensues when an individual unreflectively determines another's gender. Yet while Jax successfully calls attention to the barista's assumption, and we might imagine that the barista might be inspired to be more mindful of non-binary people in future interactions, the larger linguistic structure that shapes everyday interactions is left intact.

I asked Jax to reflect upon these kinds of interactions with strangers, and to share how ze imagined a different scenario playing out, if these gendered terms of sir and ma'am were not so pervasive. Taking a long moment to reflect on the question, ze stated matter-of-factly:

I honestly don't even know what that would look like. I mean, on one hand I am a genderfucked person and I don't expect people to know that about me in their first encounters. But also, why do we have to use these terms anyways? Like – what would actually be lost if we stopped making assumptions about people's genders? In that same interaction, what if the coffee shop person had just said, 'Would you like anything else, and have a great day?' It gets tiring to have to correct strangers, and disclose my gender identity just to have people properly interact with me. I know that to some I look like a freak with my bright blue flip-over hair with shaved sides, eye makeup and glitter nail polish, with skirts and hoodies and combat boots. But to me, fucking with gender is what my identity means . . . What information are they gleaning from me that points to either 'man' or 'woman' rather than just avoid gender all together?

As Jax suggests in this poignant commentary, the assumptions regarding gender, transmitted through a binary language system, translate to Jax and other non-binary people feeling compelled to disclose their gender identities to be recognised and acknowledged correctly by strangers. As a result, Jax must either confront potentially hostile strangers to claim social space, possibly compromising zir safety, or struggle with zir social invisibility (Lucal, 1999). Either approach requires significant emotional output on Jax's part in order to assert zir identity and manage the reactions of those ze confronts.

Reminding familiars of gender identities

When Remy and I met, they had been out as a genderqueer person to their family of origin for a few years, and as a queer person for even longer. Remy shared that this was a difficult process for them. At the time they came out in the early 2000s, the term 'genderqueer' was not as widely used as it is now in contemporary US society, and Remy's parents were 'fairly checked out' of Remy's life anyways, which they shared was partly a result of the parents ignoring or 'forgetting' those coming-out conversations. Indeed, Remy's father made explicitly homophobic comments to them about 'those gays', signaling to Remy that their father was dismissive of their queer identity. In response, Remy began disconnecting from their family of origin, and stopped visiting and calling to check in.

Two years had passed after coming out to their parents as genderqueer. Emboldened by their new job working at an LGBTQ center, with homeless LGBTQ youth whose stories resonated for Remy on the challenges that LGBTQ youth face with their families of origin, Remy decided to go home for the holidays to see if they could begin repairing the fractured relationship. As Remy was chatting with their mom, the following conversation took place:

> I was hanging out with my mom in the kitchen talking about [Metro-midwest] and she was like, 'I would respond positively if I had a child that was trans'. And I was like, 'Mom. Hold on. I am a trans person. You know this. I told you this several years ago, and have told you several times since then'. And she was just like, 'Are you trying to tell me that you are trans?' I was so angry and I was just like, 'Mom, this is not OK. You have to stop pretending that I'm a girl'. I think part of the confusion for [my parents] is that I don't have a typical trans* narrative of medically transitioning from one binary to the other.

In a follow-up conversation with the first author six months after the initial interview, Remy shared that they were in the process of changing their name and had told their parents, but that their parents didn't understand why they would want a name change, 'I had to remind them again that I'm a non-binary person and my assigned-at-birth name didn't make sense anymore. They once again pretended to not know that I was trans'.

Although popular media discourse has drawn attention to the existence of trans* people, trans* representation is typically defined around binary, normatively gendered trans people's experiences (see Gray, 2009) and an overtly fetishising fascination surrounding medical interventions. This lack of diverse representation was reflected upon across the interviews as non-binary people sought to claim a space in community, friendship, romantic and family contexts. As many participants noted, 'everyday' people often understand what it means to be trans through a transnormative narrative. This narrative transmits an oft-cited discourse in mainstream media of 'being born in the wrong body' and where it is assumed, and reified, that trans is equated with medically assisted transitions from one gender to the other (i.e. transitioning from woman to man, or man to woman), a focus that reinforces the binary (shuster, 2016). An unintended consequence of this transnormative narrative is that many non-binary people have to engage in significant identity work to remind familiars of their gender identities, which are often met with skepticism that identifying as non-binary is a real' thing. Remy's story shows how the identity work engaged in by Jax to claim some space in social life for non-binary people is not relegated to interactions with strangers. Indeed, some familiars will interpret 'non-binary' as an illegitimate gender identity and view their responsibility to recognise and affirm someone's non-binary identity as a personal preference.

Remy's story is a striking example of how non-binary people confront language barriers with familiars who have a surface understanding of what it means to be trans. In having to remind their family of origin of their gender-queer identity, Remy was, like Jax, involved in a process of identity work that required an ongoing negotiation to legitimate the existence of a non-binary identity. While Remy helped their family of origin save face by making sense of the constant reminders as the result of them 'pretending' not to remember, this story points to the ways in which existing gender-based cultural schemas are mapped onto people's identities, regardless of how people identify. Language systems shape cultural categories regarding gender, and subsequently limit understandings for who might fit within the category of 'trans'. Further still, the consequences of transnormativity are far reaching in that these familiars are not only determining the gender of people in their life (Westbrook and Schilt, 2014), but encouraging conformity to a binary system. Cisgender people, perhaps even unintentionally, mandate compliance to proper (trans)gender expression and anyone outside of this normative narrative is met with suspicion, and rendered invisible.

Being folded into binary genders

One late fall evening, I met up with Casey at a local coffee shop. As one of the last interviews conducted for this research, I was feeling disheartened by the gender policing rampant in Metromidwest, even within trans-specific spaces. I had heard countless examples of trans★ people feeling like there was no place to call 'home' even within a city that had gained a reputation as a place where trans★ people could go to find community. Casey said that they had only recently moved to Metromidwest and were having a hard time finding other genderfluid people to hang out with. The difficulties that Casey had in locating queer and trans★ community in Metromidwest struck me as exemplifying the collective stories of non-binary people negotiating social life. How is it that in a place known for an extensive and (from first glance) affirming queer trans★ community, a new transplant like Casey can feel isolated and alienated? I followed up on this thought, which tracked through the interview, by asking Casey to reflect upon the circumstances under which they had tried to tap into a trans★ community, and where they felt alienated in social life as a non-binary person. Casey shared:

> It tends to happen in two areas that I keep noticing over and over, whether in River City (where they had just recently moved from) and here in Metromidwest. In my romantic relationships and within community spaces defined as trans★ I feel incredibly frustrated, put out and alienated. It seems that the world cannot comprehend non-binary genders, and I'm fucking sick and tired of it. My introvert self just wants to hunker down into a cave and stop interacting with people. Maybe it's because it comes from within supposedly queered and trans-affirming spaces. These are the places where we shouldn't be policing each other and our genders.

Non-binary people's negotiation of community spaces is fraught with assumptions regarding who has access to those spaces, and the specific norms that govern them. Within trans★ community space specifically for non-binary people, Casey further reflected:

> It just seems like there is a lot of pressure on people to transition here. There was this one trans guy at the genderfluid meeting who was telling me that I was actually a man, I'm going to eventually transition, and I need to stop kidding myself. I was shocked that this person felt like it was OK to tell me that I'm 'really just a guy'. Especially because this is supposed to be a queer and trans space. I felt betrayed, I guess. Like how can you say that to me? I am a part of your community.

Despite the potential that genderfluid and genderqueer-marked spaces hold to affirm people's gender identities, even within trans★ communities, non-binary people are told by others what their gender 'really' is. Some binary trans★ people, active in the broader trans★ community in Metromidwest, engage in gender policing of other trans★ people's experiences. This policing was accomplished by wielding a transnormative narrative about the proper way to express and understand one's self as trans★, while simultaneously pressuring non-binary people to 'fall in line' with the status quo. As a result, Casey and others with similar experiences feel betrayed when they are folded back into a binary gender, based on the assumption that they are 'eventually' going to transition.

Casey, like others, also shared how romantic relationships can become fraught with tension as lovers and partners, in scrambling to make sense of their own identities, may erase the complexity of non-binary people's gender. Casey explained:

> My last relationship was with a queer-identified cisgender woman. She had had a previous relationship with a trans* person, who ended up beginning a social transition as a non-binary person and eventually came to understand himself as a trans man, and chose medical interventions. My ex-partner carried a lot of baggage from that relationship into ours. When I told her that I was beginning to identify as genderfluid, she became really concerned that I was going to eventually identify and transition to a male identity. This became a central point of tension in our relationship. Like, she didn't believe that genderfluid was an actual identity, and that instead it was something I was using as a short-term solution to eventually identifying as a guy.

While their partner had some knowledge of trans* experience, even she leaned on existing binary structures as a lens through which to understand Casey's identity. As a result, Casey was compelled to do a lot of work persuading their partner that they were 'really' a genderfluid person, perpetuating a pattern of inequality in which a marginalised person has to do emotion work for the dominant group. Furthermore, non-binary people are forced to make space for themselves in public and private life, requiring significant emotional output on their part. As a result, like Jax and Casey, many of those interviewed reported emotional exhaustion and a desire to temporarily retreat from social life as a consequence of this effort. And, as demonstrated in all three vignettes, many discussed how their emotional output extended beyond self-care, and emphasised the well-being of those who cast judgements (e.g. parents, partners or strangers) on the identities of non-binary people.

Casey's experiences, like those of other non-binary people interviewed, reflect how trans* communities might not be as inclusive as they seem, and involve a reciprocal process as trans* communities teach cis people the normative narratives within trans* spaces. Indeed, cis people may feel that they are being inclusive in mirroring the narratives of (binary) trans* people, and placing these binarist expectations onto *all* trans* people. In this manner, trans* normativity spills over into cisgender people's understandings of trans* experience and embodiment, further perpetuating the regulation of 'proper' trans* expression and dismissal of non-binary people's identification in both cis- and trans-specific spaces. As Remy shared, 'Even though I had identified *with* the trans community for a long time, I didn't think I *could* identify as trans because I wasn't transitioning per se. Like I wasn't trans enough in my mind, you know?' For Casey, and other non-binary people, language renders non-binary identities as a stepping stone or gateway identity to identifying as a binary trans* person and subsequently folds them back into a binary gender system.

Conclusions

Our work was provoked by broader theoretical questions about how non-binary trans★ people negotiate social life in the US, given the persistence of binarist language systems that shape social interaction. We show that within a hierarchical power structure of gender, where those 'determining' the gender of others are people in higher positions of power (Westbrook and Schilt, 2014), their determinations will trump a non-binary person's claim to a gender identity outside of the widely recognised binary trans★ narrative. This finding is in line with Kennedy's (2013) observation that within a culture of cisgenderism, 'the responsibility for determining gender is placed on the observer rather than the individual' (p. 5). With strangers, familiars, lovers and even trans★ community members, despite their best efforts to resist, negotiate and work around the English language, non-binary people have little recourse to change a linguistic structure that is fundamentally built upon the assumption of a two-gender system. Without an existing language to make sense of non-binary people's identities, many people cannot cognitively hold the possibility of those who might exist beyond dichotomous categories. Indeed, language is a foundational part of a US cultural assemblage that offers not only the tools for individuals to communicate, but pre-packaged cultural schemas to make meaning of their social world. In the process, language delineates acceptable gender identities, and subsequently erases non-binary people from social life.

Individuals who identify within the binary gender system take for granted their right to a visible and socially recognised identity, while those who break with the rituals and norms governing social space make 'difference' apparent and call attention to the assumptions embedded in social life. In these everyday encounters with a binary language system, non-binary people are then subject to gender sanctioning and consistently reminded that they are 'different'. Without social recognition, non-binary people are left with few options to assert their own right to recognition. Efforts to challenge the gender binary are interpreted by dominant social groups as 'flaunting' one's difference (Sherry, 2004), provoking hostility rather than deeper reflection, and insinuating that any negative reactions to non-binary people are a consequence of their own actions (Schilt and Westbrook, 2009). Thus, both the onus for change and any outcomes, including those that are negative, are placed on the subordinated person rather than the dominant group. This sends the message to those lacking social recognition not to expect the support, understanding and even legal rights that are taken for granted by those in the dominant group.

While here we examined the constrictions of binarist language in the everyday lives of non-binary people, similar processes unfold in social institutions where language and cultural norms intertwine to produce the double bind of hyper-visibility or erasure for non-binary people. In the current political landscape of the United States, for example, states have begun to reify the culturally constructed gender binary into law and consequently, trans★ people are coerced into living out their lives according to cisnormative standards. As demonstrated by recent legislation in the US, such as House Bill 2 in North Carolina, legislators have begun a dangerous process of mandating compliance with a law where the message is that one may change a gender presentation, and possibly even a sex marker on a birth certificate, but 'sex' categories are innate, stable and biologically determined. North Carolina House Bill 2 mandates trans★ people use the bathroom that corresponds with the sex assignment that appears on their birth certificate regardless of their gender identity or presentation. This simplistic understanding of sex and gender perpetuates the assumption that these two categories are one and the same. These assumptions are built from culturally specific contexts and ways of understanding gender, upheld by systems of language and reified in legislation. While this bill specifically targets binary trans★ people whose legal documents do not coincide with their birth-assigned sex, and much US public discourse emphasises the consequences of those who inhabit hyper-visible trans★ identities, what has been left out of these conversations is how the bill codifies the gender binary into law, while simultaneously erasing the existence of non-binary people from legal discourse and definitions of sex and gender.

Language is the delivery system for communicating cultural expectations regarding the immutability of biological processes and the stability of sex categorisation based on genitals. Trans★ people disrupt these cultural norms and expectations which serve as a catalyst for more formalised discrimination. These processes are not relegated to legal institutions. Future research should thus clarify how and to what extent non-binary people are erased from other social and institutional domains through the intertwining of language and cultural norms, and in linguistic systems that are not bound by the same gendered assumptions as English. In this lose-lose situation in the current political and popular cultural landscape, trans★ people's needs, safety and bodily integrity will continue to be undermined, and non-binary people remain linguistically erased from social life, community spaces and institutions.

Acknowledgements

We are grateful for the editors and reviewers for engaging this work with such deliberate critiques. We also warmly thank Laurel Westbrook, Teresa Roach, Laura Hamilton, Erin C. Davis and Mara Buchbinder for offering constructive comments on working drafts of this chapter.

Note

1 In the presentation of vignettes, the 'I' referent denotes the first author who conducted the interviews.

References

Correll, S.J. (2001) Gender and the career choice process: The role of biased self-assessments. *American Journal of Sociology* 106: 1691–1730.

Davis, E.C. (2009) Situating "fluidity": (Trans)gender identification and the regulation of gender diversity. *GLQ: A Journal of Lesbian and Gay Studies* 15: 97–130.

Eder, D., Evans, C.C. and Parker, S. (1995) *School talk: Gender and adolescent culture*. New Brunswick, NJ: Rutgers University Press.

Friedman, A. (2013) *Blind to sameness: Sexpectations and the social construction of male and female bodies*. Chicago, IL: University of Chicago Press.

Gray, M.L. (2009) *Out in the country: Youth, media, and queer visibility in rural America*. New York, NY: New York University Press.

Hamilton, L. (2010) Family names count. In: Powell, B., Bolzendahl, C., Geist, C. and Steelman, L.C. (eds.) *Counted out: Same-sex relations and Americans' definitions of family*. New York, NY: Russell Sage Foundation.

Hines, S. (2006) Intimate transitions: Transgender practices of partnering and parenting. *Sociology* 40: 353–371.

Kennedy, N. (2013) Cultural cisgenderism: Consequences of the imperceptible. *Psychology of Women Section Review* 15: 3–11.

Lucal, B. (1999) What it means to be gendered me: Life on the boundaries of a dichotomous gender system. *Gender & Society* 13: 781–797.

Namaste, V.K. (2000) *Invisible lives: The erasure of transsexual and transgender people*. Chicago, IL: University of Chicago Press.

Pascoe, C.J. (2007). *Dude, you're a fag: Masculinity and sexuality in high school*. Berkeley, CA: University of California Press.

Pfeffer, C. (2014) 'I don't like passing as a straight woman': Queer negotiations of identity and social group membership. *American Journal of Sociology* 120: 1–44.

Ridgeway, C. and Correll, S. (2004) Unpacking the gender system: A theoretical perspective on gender beliefs and social relations. *Gender & Society* 18: 510–531.

Schilt, K. (2010) *Just one of the guys? Transgender men and the persistence of gender inequality*. Chicago, IL: University of Chicago Press.

Schilt, K. and Westbrook, L. (2009) Doing gender, doing heteronormativity: "Gender normals," transgender people, and the social maintenance of heterosexuality. *Gender & Society* 23(4): 440–464.

Sherry, M. (2004) Overlaps and contradictions between queer theory and disability studies. *Disability & Society* 19: 769–783.

shuster, s.m. (2016) Uncertain expertise and the limitations of clinical guidelines in transgender healthcare. *Journal of Health and Social Behavior* 57: 319–332.

Spade, D. ([2011] 2015) *Normal life: Administrative violence, critical trans politics and the limits of law*. Durham, NC: Duke University Press.

Speer, S. (2005) The interactional organization of the gender attribution process. *Sociology* 39: 67–87.

Sprague, J. (2016) *Feminist methodologies for critical researchers: Bridging differences*, 2nd edition. Lanham, MD: Rowman & Littlefield.

West, C. and Zimmerman, D. (1987) Doing gender. *Gender & Society* 1: 125–151.

Westbrook, L. and Schilt, K. (2014) Doing gender, determining gender: Transgender people, gender panics, and the maintenance of the sex/gender/sexuality system. *Gender & Society* 28: 32–57.

Part III

Trans in popular representation

Foreword

The emergence of 'trans' is a cross-media phenomenon. In the introduction to this book, we explored the complexities of trans visibility within and beyond the popular medium, which have only become more pronounced in an era of trans tipping points and bathroom bills.

As we put the finishing touches to this book, the continuing contradictions of trans emergence within the context of popular representation could not possibly be more evident here in the UK. The past two years have seen an enormous upsurge in anti-trans reporting in mainstream media platforms such as *The Times*, *The Guardian*, *The Telegraph* and *The Sun*, accompanied by an increase in hostility towards trans people on social media platforms such as Twitter and Facebook. This has included extensive harassment of high-profile trans people and allies, plus concerted campaigns against trans people's access to health-care services and gendered spaces.

In December 2018, a £500,000 grant was awarded by the Big Lottery Fund to Mermaids, a charity that works to support young trans people and their families. Within days, the grant was withdrawn pending review, following a letter-writing offensive by members of the parenting discussion site Mumsnet. Just one month later, Mermaids found an unexpected benefactor in YouTube personality Hbomberguy. Over a weekend in January 2019, Hbomberguy undertook a sponsored gaming session, playing *Donkey Kong 64* to completion to raise money for Mermaids while sharing his exploits on the live video-streaming platform Twitch. With the support of trans organisers such as Irish campaigner Casey Explosion and American activist Chelsea Manning, Hbomberguy hosted conversations with numerous trans activists, plus a range of increasingly high-profile celebrity guests, including video game designer John Romero and US Congresswoman Alexandria Ocasio-Cortez. This event received an unexpected amount of attention and eventually raised approximately $340,000 (£264,000) for Mermaids. The relentless positivity of the stream was warmly welcomed by an enormous number of trans people across a range of social media platforms. However, some commentators argued that a possible emphasis on cis celebrities, donations to a cis-led organisation and the logics of charity itself might come at the expense of building a trans-led liberation movement that is attentive to existing power dynamics and economic inequalities (Chican3ry, 2019).

Such events would have seemed inconceivable when we were preparing the early drafts of this book. They serve to illustrate the increasingly unexpected and unpredictable consequences of trans emergence within ever-more entangled media terrains, celebrity cultures and rapidly shifting discursive landscapes. Trans is not simply a point of contestation in and of itself: it is a nexus through which wider cultural anxieties, political possibilities and forms of media convergence to play out. At the centre of these extraordinary events, however, are ordinary people: the anti-trans activist furiously accusing Mermaids of child abuse on Twitter, the desperate parents hoping to find advice and support in raising a child distressed by cis gender norms, the lone man in a darkened room attempting to herd digital beavers in front of 25,000 remote spectators while guests on a chat client discuss trans political economy.

The first of the two chapters in this section examines one iteration of this lopsided intersection of the individual and the collective, whereby the weight of an entire media culture may come to bear on an individual. In Chapter 9, Kat Gupta discusses the tragic case of Lucy Meadows, a primary school teacher who died by suicide after her transition was subject to substantial media attention, including an exceptionally hostile column written by *Daily Mail* journalist Richard Littlejohn. Gupta digs deep into the complexities underlying the extensive misgendering of Meadows both before and (to a lesser extent) after her death, demonstrating how selective quoting and the repetition of transphobic narratives was perpetuated across a range of publications.

The question of how trans children in particular might be best supported through popular representation is effectively explored in Chapter 10. Clare Bartholomaeus and Damien W. Riggs undertake a nuanced examination of trans characters in children's books published between 2004 and 2015 in Australia, Canada and the US, analysing how these characters are represented in terms of their gendered appearance and interests, and the role of medical discourse in their lives. The authors note the potential importance of these works for exploring trans issues with children and creating inclusive school cultures, but also critique them for reproducing certain forms of normativity. The trans characters in question mostly adhere to female/male binary gender norms, rely on medical professionals for diagnosis and affirmation and are typically also white and abled. Here, again, we see interrelated questions raised about who, ultimately, is telling the stories of trans emergence – and in turn, whose stories are told.

Reference

Chican3ry (2019) 'Trans Allies and the Society of the Spectacle', *Medium*. Published online 20 January 2019. Available at: https://medium.com/@Chican3ry/trans-allies-and-the-society-of-the-spectacle-760e39b54972.

9 Response and responsibility

Mainstream media and Lucy Meadows in a post-Leveson context

Kat Gupta

Introduction

In March 2013, a woman named Lucy Meadows was found dead at her home. Meadows, a teacher, was transitioning from male to female. In December 2012, the school announced her decision to return to work after the Christmas break as Miss Meadows. This was reported in the local press and quickly picked up by the national press. Three months later, Meadows was found dead. Her death came at a time when the press was under intense scrutiny because of the Leveson Inquiry, and prompted discussions of responsible media reporting, press freedom and the contributions of transgender people to society. I focus on Lucy Meadows, and her pronouns in particular, for three reasons. Firstly, as just outlined and in Part I, her life and death was reported at a sociopolitically significant time. Secondly, I offer a case study of British reporting rather than US reporting (c.f. Capuzza, 2015; Schlit and Westbrook, 2009). Thirdly, by focusing on pronouns, I offer a detailed, systematic examination of easily identified and socially significant lexical items. Pronouns are words that can replace proper nouns; for example, *she, him, they* and *it*. In English, third-person singular pronouns are usually gendered as *she, her, he, his* and *him*. There is also increasing use of non-gendered singular pronouns such as *zie, hir* or singular *they*. Pronouns are especially significant for trans people: many trans people change their pronouns during their transition to better reflect their identity. Pronouns also reflect other people's perceptions of our gender, something particularly salient in this study. Wayne (2005: 87) locates pronouns as a particular site for erasure, non-signification and violence, observing that '[i]f transgendered people cannot speak they are nonetheless spoken to and about, and here pronouns not only fail to signify but can lead to violence against the subject who is estranged within the binary sex/gender system'.

Within a journalistic context, pronouns are one of several strategies that are used to question, undermine or validate a transgender person's gender identity – and, indeed, impose limits on what gender identities it is possible to express (Barker-Plummer, 2013; Squires and Brouwer, 2002). Barker-Plummer (2013: 717) argues that pronouns in news media serve to establish a 'dynamic of (unintentional?) gender containment by journalists and sources' in which pronouns reflect political, as well as linguistic, choices about which genders are recognised, validated and made visible in culture. Billard (2016) also addresses issues of validation in discourse in mainstream US media; in the article, pronouns are one of 15 key 'legitimacy indicators' examined. Billard (2016: 4198) identifies use of a transgender person's preferred pronouns as a legitimising strategy and use of those reflecting the gender they were assigned at birth a delegitimising strategy.

An examination of pronouns, therefore, not only reveals how Meadows was perceived before and after her death but offers an insight into the violence, erasure and invalidation enabled by such perception.

The Leveson Inquiry

Prompted by the revelation that phones belonging to family members of people dead as a result of murder, terrorism and war had been hacked by journalists, the Leveson Inquiry, chaired by Lord Justice Leveson, was set up to investigate 'the culture, practices, and ethics of the press' (Leveson, 2012: 5). Part I of the Leveson Inquiry was opened on 14 November 2011; Lord Justice Leveson published the report resulting from the first part of the Inquiry on 29 November 2012. Trans Media Watch submitted evidence as a specialist organisation monitoring newspaper reporting of transgender people and offering advice to journalists. Three pieces of evidence were submitted: 'The British Press and the Transgender Community' in December 2011, an additional submission in February 2012 (Trans Media Watch, 2012) and oral evidence by Helen Belcher of Trans Media Watch on 8 February 2012. The Leveson Inquiry report (2012: 448) highlighted their evidence, noting that:

> Transgender people are subject to disproportionate and damaging press attention simply by dint of being members of that group, rather than in consequence of anything they might have said or done, and because of what they describe as an obsession in parts of the British press with 'outing' members of the transgender community.

In the 'The British Press and the Transgender Community', Trans Media Watch outlined four key strategies used by the British press: the routine use of previous names; the routine use of 'before' photos; demeaning and intimidating language for comic effect; and misgendering. Trans Media Watch (2011: 11) identified misgendering as follows:

> Using inappropriate pronouns or placing the person's identity in quotation marks to dismiss the veracity of the subject's identity. This approach [. . .] serves to invalidate the individual's experience, expressly to give the writer an implicit licence to demean. It makes of the transgender person a liar – and liars are ripe for parody and ridicule.

As I argue, misgendering through pronoun use is not necessarily straightforward. Instead of being solely enacted through the journalists' use of misgendering pronouns in their own writing, I argue that selective, repeated quoting of key interviewees contributes to tabloid misrepresentation of trans people's authentic, lived genders.

Negative media representation's effect on mental health

It is important to note that negative media representations have a devastating effect on an already vulnerable population. The Trans Mental Health Study (McNeil et al., 2012) is a detailed insight into the mental health of British transgender, non-binary and agender respondents. It found that ideas concerning the abnormality of trans people were pervasive, with 92% of respondents having heard such (McNeil et al., 2012: 41). Trans Media Watch's Leveson submissions (2011: 8) highlighted the emotional effect of negative media representation on respondents:

- 67% of respondents said that seeing negative items in the media about transgender people made them feel 'angry'.
- 51% said that these items made them feel 'unhappy'.
- 35% said that they felt 'excluded'.
- 20% said that they felt 'frightened'.

Trans Media Watch's survey also found that trans people linked representations of trans people in the media to negative reactions from family and friends (34%) and at work (19%), and to verbal (21%) and physical abuse (8%). As these figures indicate, negative media portrayals of trans people have consequences. Family, friends, colleagues and wider communities are often informed by media representation of trans people – and this has tangible, devastating consequences for trans people when these portrayals are poor.

Using corpus linguistics to examine social discourses

In this chapter I use corpus linguistics, an approach that, very broadly, utilises computer programs to search for patterns in large collections of machine-readable text. These patterns may focus on the lexis used, grammatical functions or semantic associations of the words. Hunston (2002: 109) explains that '[p]atterns of association – how lexical items tend to co-occur – are built up over large amounts of text and are often unavailable to intuition or conscious awareness' and as a result, 'can therefore convey messages implicitly and even be at odds with an overt statement'. In contrast to traditional ways of reading a text horizontally, as a whole, coherent and unique piece, and for its content (Tognini-Bonelli, 2004: 18), corpus linguists read texts as mediated through computer programs such as WordSmith (Scott, 2012) or AntConc (Antony, 2014) to identify these recurring patterns.

Corpus linguistics is often combined with other approaches to analysis. A particularly useful approach has been to combine corpus linguistic and (critical) discourse analysis: an online bibliography lists some 600 items (Gabrielatos, 2016). As Mautner (2009: 32) argues, these two methodologies for analysing texts have 'a shared interest in how language "works" in social rather than merely structural terms'. This focus on naturally occurring language and reading for language as a social, discursive phenomenon is at the heart of both approaches.

One way in which these two approaches can be used together is by acknowledging ways in which their strengths can be used to complement each other. Corpus linguistics, in its focus on large collections of texts, avoids some of the issues of researcher bias and cherry-picking data associated with discourse analysis. Because so many texts make up a corpus, it is necessary to form interpretations which account for frequent patterns in the data. Corpora are also invaluable for searching for very subtle patterns in language use. For example, Baker (2006) offers the example of a sailor who uses a wheelchair praised in a newspaper article for their courage; it is only when looking at a large collection of texts that the assumption that wheelchair users are not expected to be physically active and independent becomes clear. Baker (2006) argues that the use of corpora enables the researcher to examine the incremental effect of discourse and explore resistant and changing discourses – both areas that critical discourse analysis has investigated extensively.

In turn, critical discourse analysis (e.g. Fairclough, 1992, 2000, 2001; Reisigl and Wodak, 2009) often supplies the concepts and intellectual framework used in this 'methodological synergy' (Baker et al., 2008). A considerable body of work utilising critical discourse analysis and corpus linguistics demonstrates that combining these approaches can reveal different features and thus complement each other in linguistic analysis. Approaches combining corpus linguistics and (critical) discourse analysis[1] have been used to explore the discursive construction of concepts or groups of people. Recent work focusing on the media representation of (often minority) groups includes work on refugees, asylum seekers, immigrants and migrants (Baker et al., 2008; Gabrielatos and Baker, 2008), feminism (Jaworska and Krishnamurthy, 2012), Muslims (Baker et al., 2013a, 2013b), migrants (Taylor, 2014) and the suffrage movement (Gupta, 2015). While corpus linguistics have been used to explore gender (c.f. Baker, 2005, 2008, 2014), these have tended to focus on the construction of cisgender gay identities,[2] with little attention given to transgender identities.

Using corpus linguistics, I am able to explore the cumulative effect of misgendering. As I demonstrate later, there are consistent patterns in what pronouns are used to describe Meadows at different points in the news narrative. However, it is only when looking at a lot of news texts reporting Meadows' transition, death and its aftermath that striking changes can be revealed.

Lucy Meadows

Lucy Meadows was a primary school teacher working in Accrington, Lancashire. In winter 2012 she stopped working in a male role; in December 2012, the school newspaper announced her decision to return to work after the Christmas break as Miss Meadows. Three months later, on 19 March 2013, she was found dead at her home. The coroner leading the inquest into her death recorded a verdict of suicide, but condemned the media response as intrusive, sensational and a factor in the distress she had experienced in the months leading up to her death. The coroner was rebuked for his comments in August 2013.

Lucy Meadows' death and the inquest into it came at a time when the press was under intense scrutiny in the Leveson Inquiry. Meadows' transition had been reported in the local press in December 2012 and the story was picked up by the national press. The initial reporting was swiftly followed by commentary, most significantly by Richard Littlejohn, about the suitability of transgender people for teaching in schools. Littlejohn's comments, published in the *Daily Mail* and titled, 'He's not only in the wrong body . . . he's in the wrong job', argued that pupils would be 'forced to deal with' Meadows' transition which would have a 'devastating effect' on them. Littlejohn concluded that rather than transition at work, Meadows should have resigned from her job, 'disappear[ed]' and reappeared as Meadows in a different school. He concluded that Meadows' failure to do so indicated a lack of concern for 'the sensibilities of the children he is paid to teach'. Littlejohn's comments attracted vigorous rebuttal online but, at the time, attracted little press attention.

Meadows' death three months later was also reported in the local and national press. Many news sources discussed the announcement of her transition in December 2012 and revisited older articles written about her. Littlejohn's comments were also revisited, this time in the context that they were not only transphobic, but were implicated in Meadows' suicide. After her death was reported, an online petition for the withdrawal of Littlejohn's article and protest outside the *Daily Mail* offices was organised; both the *Independent* and the *Guardian* reported on this response.

As discussed above, considerable numbers of transgender people reported anger, unhappiness, exclusion and fear as a result of poor media reporting on transgender issues. This link was made by Michael Singleton, the coroner in the inquest into Meadows' suicide. *The Times* quoted him extensively, describing his comments as 'a tirade against journalists':

> It seems to me that nothing has been learnt from the Leveson Inquiry,
> [. . .] I'll be writing to the Government to consider now implementing in full the recommendations of the Leveson report in order to seek to ensure that other people in the same position as Lucy Meadows are not faced with the same ill-informed bigotry as seems to be displayed in the case of Lucy.

Following these comments, the *Daily Mail* and *Daily Telegraph* reported that Singleton had been rebuked. However, *Media Lawyer* reported that he had received informal advice from the Chief Coroner, explicitly identifying this as not a disciplinary sanction.

As this brief description of events shows, Meadows' transition, death and the aftermath of her death were widely reported in the UK press. By focusing on an individual trans person rather than commenting more widely on transgender issues, the press has the ability to discuss Meadows' experiences – and Meadows herself – in individual, personal terms. As I show, this makes pronouns an illuminating part of speech to examine in greater detail.

Data

I use two corpora: a small, focused corpus (166 texts, 108,643 words) of news texts reporting on Lucy Meadows between October 2012 and October 2013, and a reference corpus (7000 texts, 3,954,808 words) of general news texts. The Lucy Meadows corpus was collected from Nexis, an online database of news stories, using the search term 'Lucy Meadows', and were collected from the UK newspaper section. They include broadsheet, tabloid, local and online news reporting, and include articles published both in print and on UK newspapers' websites. The reference corpus is composed of news texts sampled within the same time frame, also from Nexis, also from the UK newspaper section and also including broadsheet, tabloid and local print and online newspaper reporting.

Figure 9.1 is a visual representation of the timeline of events from December 2012 to October 2013 and indicates the months in which Meadows is discussed in the corpus. As the figure shows, events were reported simultaneously: for example, articles discussing the media response, remembrance events, the inquest into her death and news stories about other trans women were published in May.

However, Lucy Meadows' death was mentioned in other contexts and was used to launch other news stories. This included criticism of some newspapers and columnists by other newspapers and columnists, defences of previous reporting and metacommentary discussing the roles and responsibility of the press in covering sensitive stories. Finally, Lucy Meadows is discussed when reporting on other transgender women, primarily Chelsea Manning.

	Dec	Jan	Feb	Mar	Apr	May	Jun	Jul	Aug	Sept	Oct
Meadows' transition	■			■							
Meadows' death				■							
Media response				■	■	■	■				
Remembrance						■					
Other trans women					■	■	■		■	■	■
Inquest						■					
Coroner's rebuke									■		

Figure 9.1 Timeline of events in reporting of Lucy Meadows, December 2012 – October 2013

Keywords

In corpus linguistics, keywords are words that occur more frequently than expected in a target corpus than in a reference corpus. They are generated by calculating the actual occurrences of words in a target corpus, calculating the actual occurrences of the same words in a reference corpus, then calculating the expected frequency of those words in the target corpus based on the reference corpus. Keywords can be both positive (more frequent in the target corpus than expected) and negative (less frequent in the target corpus than expected).

A list of the words in a corpus ranked by frequency will usually contain function words in the top 50 words; typically, *the, and, a* and *to* are in the top five. Keywords, however, indicate what is different about a target corpus from the reference corpus and instantly offer an insight into the 'aboutness' of the target corpus. Reference corpora, therefore, have to be carefully chosen to highlight meaningful differences. For this reason, the reference corpus was built using the same criteria as the Lucy Meadows corpus, but without the focus on Meadows. In this particular piece of research, the target corpus is the small Lucy Meadows corpus (166 texts, 108,643 words) and the reference corpus is the corpus of general news texts (7000 texts, 3,954,808 words). A corpus tool, WordSmith 6 (Scott, 2012) was used to calculate keywords.

The most frequent key words tend to be concrete words and tend to be nouns. They are often proper names: *Meadows, Lucy, Upton, Accrington, Littlejohn* (Littlejohn is the author of a particularly transphobic commentary; I discuss this text later in this chapter). Some describe job titles, such as *teacher, teachers* and *coroner*. Others describe her place of work: *school, primary* and *Magdalen's*. Some describe gender, such as *transgender, gender* and *trans*. Some describe the manner and aftermath of her death: *suicide, press* and *inquest*. A small number of words are associated with the online platforms on which her transition, death and its aftermath were reported such as *http, Twitter* and *com*. Finally, there are two pronouns, *her* and *she*. It is these pronouns that I examine in greater detail.

Lucy Meadows' pronouns before and after her death

In the Lucy Meadows corpus, there are 2,515 third person singular gendered pronouns, of which 1,512 are used to describe Lucy herself. Significantly, gendered pronoun use shows a very clear trend, as indicated in Table 9.1. These are presented as raw figures in order to better represent the volume of coverage of Meadows before and after her death.

While the total number of the feminine pronouns *she* and *her* are most frequent overall, they were rarely used to describe Meadows before her death. Instead, there is a striking tendency for the masculine pronouns *he, him* and *his* to be used to describe Meadows while she was alive. These masculine pronouns continue to be used after her death, albeit less frequently; I explore the reasons for this in the next section.

Table 9.1 Frequency of gendered pronouns before and after Meadows' death

Pronoun	Total frequency	Frequency used before death	Frequency used after death
her	670	6	664
she	471	20	451
he	162	121	39
his	156	90	63
him	53	50	3
Total	1512	287	1220

Of the 670 occurrences of *her* used to describe Meadows in the corpus, only six occurrences (0.9%) were used to describe her before her death. In contrast, 664 (99.1%) of the occurrences of *her* when used to describe Meadows were used after her death.

Similarly, of the 471 occurrences of *she* used to describe Meadows in the corpus, only 20 (4.2%) were used to describe her before her death. However, 451 (95.8%) occurrences were used to describe Meadows after her death. What this quantitative evidence demonstrates is that while she was alive, Meadows was overwhelmingly described, through pronoun use, as male. Before her death, the corpus evidence shows that the pronouns used to describe her reflected her female identity a mere 26 times; instead, pronoun use represents her as male a total of 261 times. It is only after her death that Meadows is typically described, through pronouns, as female. These shifts in pronoun choice demonstrate a striking change in the way Lucy Meadows was represented in the press.

Accounting for masculine pronoun use

Here I account for newspapers' use of masculine pronouns to describe Meadows. As illustrated in Table 9.1, the frequency of *she* and *her* differ dramatically in frequency before and after Meadows' death. However, the masculine pronouns *he, him* and *his* tend not to exhibit the dramatic reversal in frequency seen in *she* and *her* and continue to be used to describe Meadows after her death. A variety of strategies are employed when using masculine pronouns; particularly significant is the use of direct and indirect quotations and journalists' repetition of quotations.

Tabloid misgendering

Tabloid misgendering is one of the four strategies identified by Trans Media Watch and is defined as 'using inappropriate pronouns'; these are understood as pronouns that do not reflect an individual's stated gender identity. Here I focus on pronoun use when paraphrasing Meadows, for example, in 'he told staff and parents he was changing sex'. In this sentence, *he* appears to reflect the journalist's reporting of Meadows' gender.

The use of *he was* and *he will* in the corpus is particularly revealing. These are different tenses of the same verb (*to be*) and are particularly significant in the context of gender transition; *was* describes a past state of being while *will* describes future intentions and possibilities. In the corpus, *he was* and *he will* are used to paraphrase Meadows' explanations to her pupils, the school's announcement and explanation to parents and some speculation about her future medical treatment; these uses indicate something about how the newspaper conceptualised Meadows' identity in the process of explaining her shifting gender presentation.

Concordance 1: occurrences of *he was*

1. CHER who told staff and parents he was changing sex and coming ba
2. e Church of England school that he was born 'with a girl's brain
3. ws. He explained to pupils that he was 'born with a girl's brai
4. Upton, 32, says he always knew he was born into the wrong sex. Y
5. ws. He explained to pupils that he was 'born with a girl's brain
6. who told parents and colleagues he was changing sex and coming ba
7. who told parents and colleagues he was changing sex and coming ba
8. er, 32, who announced to pupils he was changing sex is found dead
9. er, 32, who announced to pupils he was changing sex is found dead
10. Upton, 32, says he always knew he was born into the wrong sex. Y
11. Upton, 32, says he always knew he was born into the wrong sex. Y

Concordance 2: occurrences of *he will*

1. school teacher has told pupils he will return after the Christma
2. nuing sex change. It is thought he will undergo hormone therapy a
3. school teacher has told parents he will come back next term as a
4. s a sex change op at Christmas. He will return to the primary sch
5. nuing sex change. It is thought he will undergo hormone therapy a
6. school teacher has told pupils he will return after the Christma

Significantly, the notice in the school newsletter quoted by some newspapers (and which largely accounts for the 20 occurrences of *she* before the reporting of Meadows' death) reads, 'Mr Upton has recently made a significant change in his life and will be transitioning to live as a woman. After the Christmas break, she will return to work as Miss Meadows'. While this statement uses both masculine and feminine pronouns, it elegantly shifts between them to indicate that the masculine pronoun 'his' refers to Meadows' life before her transition and that feminine pronouns are to be used from then on. If the newspaper reporting followed this usage, we might expect *he was* – indicating Meadows' previous presentation as male – and *she will*, indicating her future intentions, potential and possibilities.[3] Instead, there are six occurrences of *he will*, indicating a male future for Meadows and a lack of recognition of her trans future.

Selective quoting

A second significant choice in newspaper reporting is deciding who to quote, and, in doing so, deciding whose point of view to reproduce to a wider audience. As Table 9.2 indicates, quotes accounted for a significant percentage of uses – a minimum of 42.6% in the case of *he* and a maximum of 70% in the case of *him*.

The people quoted include parents of Meadows' pupils, Meadows' former wife's parents and Meadows' pupils themselves. It is important to note here that use of masculine pronouns does not necessarily indicate an insult: for example, some uses are from Meadows' former father-in-law. Meadows' father-in-law, Mr Smith, is quoted extensively in the *Daily Mail* on 19 December 2012; this is one of the first articles to be published reporting Meadows' transition. In it, he says:

> He is a lovely person as well and we will support him no matter what [. . .] If he was a rubbish teacher then they would not have stood by him. All the time he has been teaching as a he or she, everybody has said what a good teacher he is. When we first heard it was a shock, yes, but we are going to stand by him.

This quote clearly affirms Smith's high regard for Meadows, and in its use of 'he or she' acknowledge that Meadows has been presenting as a gender other than male. However, this quote also reveals one of the issues in using quotes from people who know the person transitioning: that they sometimes have not adjusted to using pronouns which accurately reflect the transitioning person's gender identity. Similarly, a 10-year-old pupil is quoted in several newspapers:

> He spoke to us and said he's going to be changing into a woman and wearing women's clothes after Christmas. We were all a bit shocked.

Table 9.2 Frequency of masculine pronouns in direct and indirect quotes relating to Lucy Meadows

Pronoun	Direct quotes	Indirect quotes	Percentage accounted for by quotes
he	60	9	42.6%
his	71	20	58.3%
him	27	10	70%

Again, this quote is more likely to indicate the child's current understanding of their teacher's gender rather than any hostility on their part. A grandmother voices approval for Meadows' transition, describing Meadows as 'brave' but uses masculine pronouns:

> A grandmother, collecting her seven-year-old granddaughter from the school, said, 'It has been handled very sensitively by the school and I think it's a very brave thing for him to do'.

A mother of a child attending the school also uses masculine pronouns to describe Meadows but does so in a context of normalising Meadows' transition as something that has been done before and describing her children as 'happy', possibly responding to claims that Meadows' transition would upset and confuse children:

> One mother was quoted by the Mail as saying, 'My children are happy. I don't see anything wrong with it. He's not the first and he won't be the last'.

The four quotes just discussed so far appear to reflect a naïve usage of masculine pronouns: it is unlikely that Mr Smith, the school pupil, the parent or grandparent would expect their words to be used to attack or undermine Meadows. However, there are also usages in the corpus which reflect a more hostile response to Meadows' transition. The four following quotes from Wayne Cowie appeared more than once in the corpus:

> Wayne Cowie, whose ten-year-old son has been taught by Mr Upton for three years, said his children were worried and confused. 'My middle boy thinks that he might wake up with a girl's brain because he was told that Mr Upton, as he got older, got a girl's brains'.

> Dad-of-three Wayne Cowie said: 'I didn't think I'd need the birds and the bees talk with my sons until they were at high school, and now they are coming home asking about transsexuals. My lad is very confused and upset about it. He should have taken a couple of years off to sort himself out'.

> Wayne Cowie, 35, a father of three who has a child at the school, said: 'I have not forced my way of life on to him so why is he forcing his on to my kids? He went for the job as a man. The kids are all going to be laughing and giggling at him. He is still Mr Upton but in a dress. He should start a new life in a new place and at a new school'.

> Talking about Mr Upton, Mr Cowie said: 'I have not forced my way of life on to him so why is he forcing his on to my kids? We all knew what he was. My partner saw him dressed as a woman. This has been forced upon us. I can't fault the school but I'd like to see how it's doing in a year'.

In these quotes, Cowie rejects Meadows' identity: he explicitly identifies her in terms of her past male identity but 'in a dress', as an object of mockery in her workplace, as a man and, significantly, consistently uses masculine pronouns. While Cowie's is one of the most quoted parental responses and therefore has more presence in the corpus, other parents also undermine Meadows' gender identity as something that could be confined to her private life and from which children needed to be shielded:

> A mum said: 'It's his life, but he can dress as a woman in his own time. It's just going to confuse the children'. And another said he should have changed schools. She said: 'I think he should have left St Mary's and joined another school with his new name for a fresh start'.

While there are examples of naïve use of masculine pronouns to describe Meadows, these uses of masculine pronouns combine with transmisogynist tropes invoking the figure of trans women as 'men in dresses' to undermine Meadows' professionalism, the seriousness of her need to transition and her female gender identity.

As I have already discussed, a significant number of occurrences of masculine pronouns can be accounted for by quotes, thus enabling journalists to use masculine pronouns and position Meadows as male in the guise of reporting opinions. By examining these quotes in more detail it becomes apparent that some speakers are supportive of Meadows; however, the cumulative effect of such quotes is that Meadows is only recognised as female in pronoun use after her death. It is very much worth considering who gets quoted and why.

Repetition

The third strand in accounting for newspapers' use of masculine pronouns to describe Meadows is the use of repetition. As I discussed earlier, a particular strength of corpus linguistic analysis is identifying repeated patterns; pronoun use is one such pattern. Quotes are also recycled extensively which means that a quote misgendering Meadows as male may be repeated across different newspapers, on different days, and be resurrected at a later date.

One 10-year-old pupil's comment, 'He spoke to us and said he's going to be changing', was found five times in the corpus. This comment was initially printed in the *Lancashire Telegraph* on 19 Dec 2012, before being reproduced in the *Daily Mail* (20 December 2012), *Irish Daily Mail* (20 December 2012) and *MailOnline* (20 December 2012 and 12 March 2013), thus establishing its spread across different regions, news platforms and time.

Similarly, Cowie's statement of 'My middle boy thinks that he might wake up with a girl's brain because he was told that Mr Upton, as he got older, got a girl's brains' was found six times in the corpus. This statement was repeated twice in the *MailOnline* on 20 December 2012 – once in a report attributed to James

Tozer and Nazia Parveen and once in Richard Littlejohn's commentary before being used in the *Daily Mail* (20 December 2012), *MailOnline* (21 December 2012), *Daily Mail* (21 December 2012) and *Daily Mail* (12 March 2013). Again, this shows that the statement was reproduced across a number of days – even months – later, across both print and online platforms and in both news reports and commentary.

The most repeated set of words in the corpus was the title of Richard Littlejohn's commentary, 'He's not in the wrong body . . . he's in the wrong job'. Twenty-three occurrences of this phrase were found in the corpus. Littlejohn's commentary was published on 20 December 2012 on *MailOnline* before being printed by the *Daily Mail* on 21 December 2012. It was subsequently quoted in the immediate aftermath of Meadows' death: the first occurrence after her death was on the website Liberal Conspiracy on 21 March 2013 in a piece titled, 'Lucy Meadows, and the tabloids that harassed her'. The *Independent* quoted Littlejohn's title in an article on 22 March 2013. The *Guardian* also quoted it in two articles also published on 22 March 2013, one reporting Meadows' death and one reporting on the petition to fire Littlejohn for his comments. On 23 March 2013, the *Independent*, the *Independent's* online coverage, the *Huffington Post* and the *Guardian* quote the phrase in reports on 'intrusive press coverage' (the *Independent*) and that Meadows 'was "monstered" by media after transition became public' (the *Guardian*), thus contextualising her death and this quote within emerging concerns about press ethics. Finally, this line is quoted during the coroner's inquest into Meadows's death. The *Huffington Post* quotes it on 29 May 2013 in a report on the inquest, and the *Guardian* uses it in an article published on the same day reporting that the '*Daily Mail* [was] singled out over "ridicule and humiliation"'. The line is also quoted by Rod Liddle in the *Sun* on 30 May 2013, arguing that the coroner was the one guilty of bigotry rather than the press.

It is clear from the context that the line is often quoted in order to critique it. Littlejohn is described as 'a polemicist' with a 'prurient interest in transsexual people as far as asking how they take a pee' going 'on the offensive' who 'accused' Meadows of not caring about the children she taught. The *Daily Mail* is described as 'showing little contrition' but as having removed the commentary after Meadows' suicide. However, in critiquing the article, news organisations also reproduce the text they condemn. Repetition, therefore, poses a problem. As the data show, particularly in combination with selective quoting, use of misgendering pronouns can be widely disseminated across different newspapers, platforms, regions and time periods and perhaps even more widely than they would otherwise. This is particularly striking in the case of Littlejohn's comments which were reproduced in May 2013, almost exactly six months after they were first published. Reproduction of such obvious transphobic comments, even if to condemn them, risks legitimising them and may serve as a reminder that Meadows' gender was subject to hostility and rejection.

Conclusion

By examining the language used to describe transgender identities by the mainstream UK press, I am able to investigate issues of minority representation, press tactics of negative representation and the interactions among press, public, reporters and reported. I demonstrate that the use of the wrong pronouns, while a key part of negative media portrayal used to dismiss trans peoples' gender identities, is more complex than the hostile use of quote marks identified by Trans Media Watch.

Through repetition of selected direct quotes, the press is able to reinforce some voices and not others. In doing so, reporters are able to evade direct responsibility for misgendering while continuing to produce the effect of undermining a trans person's gender identity. This was particularly noticeable in journalistic quotation of Wayne Cowie, a parent of a child attending Meadows' school. Cowie strongly rejected Meadows' transition and female gender identity, describing her as 'Mr Upton but in a dress' and stating that 'He [Meadows] should start a new life in a new place and at a new school'. By quoting from Cowie so extensively, newspapers are able to voice transphobic attitudes without being directly responsible for their expression. Several of the people quoted – including those close to Meadows – use masculine pronouns. While they often express support and praise Meadows' teaching ability and bravery, their use of masculine pronouns contributes to the startling lack of realisation of Meadows' female identity through pronoun use seen before her death.

It is crucial to recognise that the reporting of Meadows' transition, death and its aftermath took place shortly after the Leveson Inquiry; by December 2012, Lord Leveson had already published the first part of the report. Trans Media Watch had submitted both written and oral evidence to the Inquiry identifying press strategies for misgendering trans people. As discussed, use of pronouns in quote marks was a tactic singled out by Trans Media Watch as particularly widespread and used to undermine trans people's stated genders. This tactic was not found in texts discussing Lucy Meadows; instead, the writing about her could be just as hostile but expressed through different, non-journalist voices and with an elision of journalistic responsibility. From this study it is clear that there are emerging strategies for the production and reproduction of transphobia in news texts. As transgender experiences and voices become more widely discussed, the expression (and mechanics for expression) of transphobia also has new possibilities of which we must be aware.

This article was previously published in the journal Sexualities.

Notes

1 I include the parentheses because not all discourse analysts work within a critical discourse framework; however, much of the work I cite does explicitly examine inequalities in power and how power is expressed, maintained and challenged in texts.
2 See, for instance, Baker's (2005) examinations of House of Lords reform on the age of consent and British tabloid representation of gay men.
3 See Pearce (2018) for a detailed analysis of trans time, and specifically transfuturity.

References

Antony, L. (2014). *AntConc* (Version 3.4.3). Tokyo, Japan: Waseda University.

Baker, P. (2005). *Public Discourses of Gay Men*. London: Routledge.

Baker, P. (2006). *Using Corpora in Discourse Analysis*. London: Continuum.

Baker, P. (2008). *Sexed Texts*. Sheffield: Equinox.

Baker, P. (2014). *Using Corpora to Analyze Gender*. London: Bloomsbury.

Baker, P., Gabrielatos, C., Khosravinik, M., Krzyzanowski, M., McEnery, T., & Wodak, R. (2008). A useful methodological synergy? Combining critical discourse analysis and corpus linguistics to examine discourses of refugees and asylum seekers in the UK press. *Discourse and Society*, **19**(3), 273–306.

Baker, P., Gabrielatos, C., & McEnery, T. (2013a). *Discourse Analysis and Media Attitudes: The representation of Islam in the British press*. Cambridge: Cambridge University Press.

Baker, P., Gabrielatos, C., & McEnery, T. (2013b). Sketching Muslims: A corpus-driven analysis of representation around the word "Muslim" in the British press, 1998–2009. *Applied Linguistics*, **34**(3), 255–278.

Barker-Plummer, B. (2013). Fixing Gwen. *Feminist Media Studies*, **13**(4), 710–724.

Billard, T. (2016). Writing in the margins: Mainstream news media representations of transgenderism. *International Journal of Communication*, **10**(2016), 4193–4218.

Capuzza, J. C. (2015). What's in a name? Transgender identity, metareporting and the misgendering of Chelsea Manning. In L. Spencer & J. Capuzza (Eds.) *Transgender Communication Studies: Histories, Trends, and Trajectories* (pp. 173–186). London: Lexington Books.

Fairclough, N. (1992). *Discourse and Social Change*. Cambridge: Polity Press.

Fairclough, N. (2000). *New Labour, New Language*. London: Routledge.

Fairclough, N. (2001). *Language and Power* (2nd ed.). Harlow: Longman.

Gabrielatos, C. (2016). *Bibliography: Corpus Approaches to Discourse Studies*. Available at: www.edgehill.ac.uk/english/dr-costas-gabrielatos/?tab=bibliography-corpusapproaches-to-discourse-studies (accessed 1 November 2017).

Gabrielatos, C., & Baker, P. (2008). Fleeing, sneaking, flooding: A corpus analysis of discursive constructions of refugees and Asylum seekers in the UK Press, 1996–2005. *Journal of English Linguistics*, **36**(5), 5–38.

Gupta, K. (2015) *Representation of the British Suffrage Movement*. London and New York: Bloomsbury.

Hunston, S. (2002). *Corpora in Applied Linguistics*. Cambridge: Cambridge University Press.

Jaworska, S., & Krishnamurthy, R. (2012). On the F word: A corpus-based analysis of the media representation of feminism in British and German press discourse, 1990–2009. *Discourse & Society*, **23**(4), 401–431.

Leveson, B. (2012). *An Inquiry into the Culture, Practices and Ethics of the Press*. Available at: www.gov.uk/government/publications/leveson-inquiry-report-into-the-culture-practices-and-ethics-of-the-press.

Mautner, G. (2009). Corpora and critical discourse analysis. In P. Baker (Eds.) *Contemporary Corpus Linguistics*. London and New York: Bloomsbury.

McNeil, J., Bailey, L., Ellis, S., et al. (2012). *Trans Mental Health Study 2012*. Available at: http://www.scottishtrans.org/our-work/completed-work/research-publications/ (accessed 6 June 2013).

Pearce, R. (2018). *Understanding Trans Health: Discourse, Power and Possibility*. Bristol: Policy Press.

Reisigl, M., & Wodak, R. (2009). The discourse-historical approach (DHA). In R. Wodak & M. Meyer (Eds.) *Methods of Critical Discourse Analysis* (pp. 87–121). London: Sage Publications.

Schilt, K., & Westbrook, L. (2009). Doing gender, doing heteronormativity "gender normals," transgender people, and the social maintenance of heterosexuality. *Gender & Society*, **23**(4), 440–464.

Scott, M. (2012). *WordSmith Tools* (Version 6). Stroud: Lexical Analysis Software.

Squires, C., & Brouwer, D. (2002). In/discernible bodies: The politics of passing in dominant and marginal media. *Critical Studies in Media Communication*, **19**(3), 283–310.

Taylor, C. (2014). Investigating the representation of migrants in the UK and Italian press: A cross-linguistic corpus-assisted discourse analysis. *International Journal of Corpus Linguistics*, **19**(3), 368–400.

Tognini-Bonelli, E. (2004). Working with corpora: Issues and insights. In C. Coffin, A. Hewings, & K. O'Halloran (Eds.) *Applying English Grammar: Functional and Corpus Approaches* (pp. 11–24). London: Hodder Arnold.

Trans Media Watch. (2011). *The British Press and the Transgender Community: Submission to the Leveson Inquiry into the Culture, Practice and Ethics of the Press*. Available at: www.transmediawatch.org/Documents/Publishable%20Trans%20Media%20Watch%20Submission.pdf.

Trans Media Watch. (2012). *Trans Media Watch – Additional Submission to the Leveson Inquiry*. Available at: www.transmediawatch.org/Documents/Additional%20Trans%20Media%20Watch%20Submission%20-%20Public.pdf.

Wayne, Linda D. (2005). Neutral pronouns: A modest proposal whose time has come. *Canadian Woman Studies*, **24**(2), 85–91.

10 'Girl brain ... boy body'

Representations of trans characters in children's picture books

Clare Bartholomaeus and Damien W. Riggs

Introduction

An increasing number of people report a gender that differs from that norma-tively expected of their sex assigned at birth (referred to here collectively as trans people). While there is a growing body of academic, popular and educa-tional writing that speaks about the lives of trans people (e.g. Brill and Ken-ney, 2016; Brill and Pepper, 2008; Erickson-Schroth, 2014; Meyer and Pullen Sansfaçon, 2014; Serano, 2007; Stryker and Aizura, 2013), very little has been written which is accessible to children. Materials targeted towards children are important for at least three reasons: 1) to enable trans children to see themselves reflected in the world around them, 2) to help aid understanding amongst cis-gender children of trans parents and 3) to support cisgender children to under-stand the lives of trans people. For this chapter we use the term *cisgender* as a way of referring to people who are not trans, although we note the diversity of gender amongst all people. Despite issues with the term (e.g. see Enke, 2012), we have found this is the most strategically useful way to highlight that books and other resources about trans people are significant for *all* people, particularly to facilitate inclusion and embrace diversity.

Picture books are an effective way to discuss diversity with children, as well as to promote inclusion across a range of issues (e.g. DePalma, 2014; Naidoo, 2014; O'Neil, 2010). In the past 20 or so years this has included the publication of numerous picture books with gay and lesbian characters, particularly focus-ing on families (for analyses, see e.g. Riggs and Augoustinos, 2007; Sapp, 2010). However, picture books with trans characters have been slower to appear, and have only been in existence for around a decade. Naidoo argues that:

> [C]hildren's books and materials that feature positive portrayals of transgen-der characters are needed to support the positive identity development of transgender children. Unfortunately, children's picture books and chapter books that present transgender children in such a matter-of-fact manner are virtually invisible in contemporary classrooms and libraries. Only a few are available from small presses and they rarely make their way into class-rooms and onto library shelves.
>
> (Naidoo, 2012: 39)

Others have also recently commented on the dearth of picture books with trans characters (Chukhray, 2010; Epstein, 2012; Naidoo, 2012; Paterson, 2015). While there are still relatively few picture books with trans characters, there has been what might be called a recent 'turn' to picture books in this area, with several new books being published in the past five years. This may at least in part be due to the increased availability of self-publishing options (Naidoo, 2012: 45).

Perhaps because of the relatively recent publication of picture books featuring trans characters, to date there has been no comprehensive audit of such books. The existing sources most relevant are those that provide an audit of picture books with LGBTQ characters (Epstein, 2013; Naidoo, 2012; Toman, 2014), although these do not offer a comparative analysis of key patterns and themes across multiple books. Lester (2014) examined a small number of 'queer-themed' picture books, including three books with trans characters, arguing that they are gender normative, and have little diversity in terms of race and class. Skelton (2015) also examined a small sample of picture books with trans or gender independent protagonists, arguing that such books tend to focus on characters who are accepted because they do something exceptional (like saving a parent from death) or who are constantly bullied.

Given the fact that previous analyses have not focused specifically on picture books featuring trans characters, and given the recent increase in the number of books published featuring such characters, this chapter reports on a comprehensive audit of picture books portraying trans characters. In this chapter we argue that while the presence of picture books with trans characters is likely to be useful in some ways, currently many perpetuate normative discourses and display only narrow forms of acceptance.

Sample of books with trans characters

Extensive searches were conducted to identify all existing English-language picture books that include trans characters which had been published up until the end of 2015. This involved searches for books and reviews on Amazon and Goodreads (particularly drawing on user-compiled lists such as 'LGBTQ Children's Literature' and 'Transgender Friendly Young Children's Books'), Google searches (particularly following links for lists of books such as 'LGBT' book lists) and following up books mentioned in previous publications and audits. As others have found with the 'LGBT' acronym generally (e.g. Greytak, Kosciw and Boesen, 2013), many books on these lists focused solely on lesbian or gay characters, and hence failed to address trans (or bisexual) people.

Books were included if they had a character who either was explicitly or could be read as trans. Both authors decided on the criteria for selection and the inclusion/exclusion of each book. Books with trans characters were generally easy to identify, as the stories tended to include an explicit discussion of identification with a gender which was different to that normatively expected of their sex assigned at birth. While most of the books featured human characters, three used a species change as a metaphor for gender transition (one of which also includes gender transition). We excluded one book (*Red: A Crayon's Story*, Hall, 2015) which some have read as a story about a trans character because it is about a 'blue' crayon with a 'red' paper cover (e.g. on Amazon reviews), but in our reading of this book we felt it was too ambiguous. Another criterion was that books were published as picture books which could be read with children in a way that other picture books would. For this reason, we excluded five 'do-it-yourself' type books which were more like pamphlets or slideshows. Finally, we excluded *A Girl Like Any Other* (Labelle, 2013) as it is for a slightly older audience.

All books deemed to fit the criteria were included in the analysis, totalling 21 picture books (Table 10.1). Fifteen of these books were published between 2012 and 2015. Sixteen of the books focus on human trans characters where the key characters are trans girls (ten), trans boys (three), trans women (one) and trans men (two). In addition, one book (*The Gender Fairy*) includes a trans

Table 10.1 Books with trans characters featured in analysis (2004–2015)

Title	Author/Illustrator	Year	Publisher
10,000 Dresses	Ewert and Ray	2008	Seven Stories Press
About Chris	Benedetto	2015	CreateSpace
The Adventures of Tulip Birthday Wish Fairy	Bergman and Malik	2012	Flamingo Rampant
All I Want to Be Is Me	Rothblatt	2011	CreateSpace
Backwards Day	Bergman and Diamond	2012	Flamingo Rampant
Be Who You Are	Carr and Rumback	2010	AuthorHouse
But, I'm Not a Boy!	Leone and Pfeifer	2014	CreateSpace
The Gender Fairy	Hirst and Wirt	2015	Oban Road Publishing
Goblinheart: A Fairy Tale	Axel and Bidlspacher	2012	East Waterfront Press
I Am Jazz	Herthel, Jennings and McNicholas	2014	Penguin
Muffy Was Fluffy	DuBois and Grenier	2012	PublishAmerica
My Favorite Color Is Pink	Benedetto	2015	CreateSpace
My New Daddy	Mossiano and Mossiano	2012a	Spun Silver Productions
My New Mommy	Mossiano and Mossiano	2012b	Spun Silver Productions
Pearl's Christmas Present	Wurst	2004	Pearl and Dotty
A Princess of Great Daring!	Hill-Meyer and Toczynski	2015	Flamingo Rampant
Rough, Tough Charley	Kay and Gustavson	2007	Tricycle Press
The Royal Heart	McGoon	2015	Avid Readers
When Kathy Is Keith	Wong	2011	Xlibris
When Kayla Was Kyle	Fabrikant and Levine	2013	Avid Readers
When Leonard Lost His Spots: A Trans Parent Tail	Costa and Shupik	2012	My Family!

boy and a trans girl, and another book (*All I Want to Be Is Me*) features multiple characters, with one page about a trans boy. The species change books focused on transitions from fairy to goblin, kitten to puppy and leopard to lioness (i.e. species and gender change). All of the books originate from the US, apart from *When Kathy Is Keith* and *Muffy Was Fluffy* which are both from Canada and *The Gender Fairy* which is from Australia. Hard copies of each book were purchased for analysis via Amazon, the Book Depository or the publisher's website.

We note that in addition to books featuring trans characters, we also identified more than a dozen additional books that featured gender diverse characters. We decided not to include these in this analysis so as to resist the conflation of trans and gender diverse experiences. Instead, we plan to explore the books featuring gender diverse characters in a separate publication.

Analysis

A thematic analysis of the 21 books was conducted. The authors read each book and made notes independently concerning the main themes in each book. These were then collated and mutually agreed-upon key themes were identified. In this chapter we analyse the three key themes: 1) adherence to a binary model of gender, 2) 'appropriate' gendered clothing, behaviours and interests and 3) the reliance on professionals for diagnosis.

Adherence to a binary model of gender

A key theme in many of the books (n = 18) was the reliance on a gender binary, where there were only two gender options discussed. In other words, the gender identity of trans characters was largely discussed as within the binary categories of either male or female. Given our focus in this chapter is solely on books featuring trans characters (i.e. not gender diverse characters), a focus on gender as a binary category may to a degree be understandable. However, a gender binary was reified as though it was 'natural' rather than a particular social construction. This framing of gender as a naturalised binary impacted on how being trans was explained to readers; for example:

> I have a girl brain but a boy body.
>   This is called transgender.
>   I was born this way!
>
> (*I Am Jazz* n.p.)

> The Wish Captain explained that sometimes, someone was born looking like a boy, but had the heart and mind and soul of a girl inside. Or they might be the reverse: the body of a girl, with the spirit and thoughts and feelings of a boy.
>
> (*The Adventures of Tulip Birthday Wish Fairy* n.p.)

In these two extracts, boys and girls are treated as paired opposites. Indeed, in the second extract the language of 'reverse' is used to depict males and females as naturally occurring opposites.

One consequence of the binary pairing of boys and girls was that the books were then left to account for why someone would be on the 'wrong' side of the binary. In many of the books this meant that the language of pathology was introduced, such as:

> As time passed, most of her friends and family understood that feeling like a girl wasn't Hope's choice at all.
> It was just who she was.
> She didn't choose to be born in the wrong body.
>
> (*Be Who You Are* p. 27)

> My mommy sat down with me and explained to me that nature made a mistake and she should have been born a boy like me.
>
> (*My New Daddy* n.p.)

In these extracts, the language of 'wrong' and 'mistake', while seemingly intended to provide readers with an account of being trans that promotes inclusion (i.e. if 'nature made a mistake', then the individual cannot be blamed), they nonetheless serve to construct being trans as a problem, and specifically that trans bodies are wrong. Trans people themselves have explored the ways in which this language of 'wrong bodies' impacts upon how they see themselves, suggesting that it may contribute to unhappiness for some trans people who feel that they should 'correct' the 'mistake', but that in some cases and contexts this is not a readily available option (Erickson-Schroth, 2014).

Our findings presented within this theme confirm Lester's similar argument in her analysis of three of the books we have analysed (*10,000 Dresses*, *Be Who You Are* and *When Kathy Was Keith*):

> [C]hildren's books that feature transgender children as main characters also maintain normative, binarist ideas about gender. These stories present the idea of two opposite genders and no other options. The dominant narrative is that of a girl trapped in a boy's body or, less commonly, vice versa.
>
> (2014: 251)

Along with the construction of a binary gender identity for characters, many of the books focused on 'appropriate' gendered clothing, behaviours and interests, a topic we take up in the following theme.

'*Appropriate*' *gendered clothing, behaviours and interests*

Clothing, behaviours and interests were similarly often framed in the books in terms of gender 'appropriateness' (n = 18), again reinforcing gender binary categories, a point that has been noted in relation to feminist picture books more broadly (Davies, 2003). Books in the sample frequently drew upon the idea of 'boys' things' and 'girls' things', either explicitly or implicitly.

Clothing was a key area in which this occurred in the sample of books. This was especially the case with regard to trans girls, where dresses featured strongly as key signifiers of what being a girl means. Dresses were sometimes explicitly contrasted with 'boy clothes' and sometimes, for trans girls, as clothing which is only initially allowed by parents at home, which seems to imply the need to transition before wearing such clothes in public:

> Sometimes my parents let me wear my sister's dresses around the house. But whenever we went out, I had to put on my boy clothes again. This made me mad!
>
> (*I Am Jazz* n.p.)

> Every day after school Nick came home and put on what he liked. He had all kinds of dresses, but he liked the ones with ruffles the best.
>
> (*Be Who You Are* p. 12)

> Over the next few months, Kayla's family and friends dropped off dresses, skirts and shoes for her. Kayla's mom took her to get a new hairstyle and manicure at the beauty salon. Kayla couldn't stop looking in the mirror and smiling!
>
> (*When Kayla Was Kyle* p. 4)

> She didn't want to wear a hat and vest and boots. She wanted to wear a pretty dress and stockings and a tiara. She didn't want to be a cowboy; she wanted to be a princess.
>
> (*But, I'm Not a Boy!* n.p.)

Similarly, a book which includes a character who is a trans boy emphasised the importance of clothing:

> I'm the kid who's great at soccer,
> For Christmas I got cleats,
> When Grandma tried to get me in a dress,
> I told her my new name is Pete.
> (*All I Want to Be Is Me* n.p.)

Importantly, in critiquing these books for their emphasis upon trans children wearing gender normative clothing, we are not intending to undermine the autonomy of trans people wearing clothes that they feel comfortable in, and which reflect social norms about their gender. Rather, our point is that most of the books depicted only trans young people who wore (or desired to wear) gender normative clothing. For readers for whom this is not their desire, the books may be experienced as exclusionary or not representative.

The significance of clothing in regard to gender also featured in the few books about trans adults, such as in the following example:

> After our talk, my mommy started buying men's clothes, and dressing like a daddy. She also started going by a new name, and I started calling her daddy.
>
> (*My New Daddy* n.p.)

In addition to clothing, behaviours and interests were also frequently divided by normative gendered behaviours, with stereotypically male and female behaviours contrasted:

> As I got a little older, I hardly ever played with trucks or tools or superheroes. Only princesses and mermaid costumes.
> My brothers told me this was girl stuff. I went right on playing.
>
> (*I Am Jazz* n.p.)

> Sarah didn't like playing war. She hated fighting more.
> She wished she could play with other girls. Where they could all play dress up and take care of their dolls together. Then she'd be happy as well.
>
> (*But, I'm Not a Boy!* n.p.)

> Her old boy's ice skates had been replaced by pretty figure skates, and her soccer uniform was for the girls' team.
>
> (*The Adventures of Tulip Birthday Wish Fairy* n.p.)

> Chris loved trucks, cars, Legos, mud and art, and cowboy boots.
>
> (*About Chris* n.p.)

> Andrea loved to be a boy on backwards day. She wanted to be a boy everyday [sic]. She kept her hair cut short and always wore dirty sneakers or cowboy boots. She loved fishing and exploring and playing baseball, and almost all of her friends were boys.
>
> (*Backwards Day* p. 23)

It is notable that this type of binary thinking about what properly constitutes behaviours for boys and girls would otherwise be challenged as reductive. In the context of trans children, however, and as we noted previously with regard to clothing, it may be important for trans children to engage in stereotypical behaviour precisely because it affirms their gender. This is a dilemma discussed by a mother of a young trans girl who was criticised by her friend for giving her daughter Barbies to play with. She asks:

> Do I wear my trans-ally hat and agree to the Barbie doll in order to validate her heartbreakingly fragile sense of entitlement to membership in the girl

club? . . . Or, do I don my feminist hat and say *no* to Barbie, thereby limiting
the possible negative effects on her self-esteem and body image?

(gendermom, 2013, emphasis in original)

Again as with regard to clothing, our concern is not to police what should be
'acceptable' behaviours for trans children. Rather, it is to suggest that the narrow range of behaviours depicted in the books may not always be intelligible or
applicable for all readers. This is notable given the fact that it reflects the ways
in which some trans adults have reported experiencing pressure to frame their
childhoods in order to validate their gender. For example, Michael Young, a
trans★ man, discusses this in relation to his own life:

> Many of us boast about hating dresses from an early age, or about wanting
> to be Spiderman for Halloween like that somehow validates our masculin-
> ity. Like we have to dress up our childhood as a stereotypical boyhood in
> order to be real, or to be taken seriously.
>
> (Young, 2013)

Given the injunction to present a normative gendered narrative to secure
support for gender-affirming hormones and surgery (Speer and McPhillips, 2013), this is perhaps unsurprising. Nonetheless, we would suggest that
normative gendered expectations potentially limit how some trans people
are able to express or feel affirmed in their gender, even if for some trans
young people (for whom a binary model is their experience) it may be
affirming.

Importantly, this critique of gender normative and binary representations
of trans characters is not limited to trans characters in the books. Illustra-
tions of the protagonists' friends, classmates and families were typically of,
for example, cisgender girls with long hair wearing skirts or dresses, and cisgender boys with short hair. This type of representation, we would suggest,
reinforces the naturalisation of social and cultural ideas about what girls and
boys should look like.

Reliance on professionals for diagnosis

In this final theme we explore the reliance on professionals for diagnosis, a
common trope that appeared across eight of the books. For the most part, these
professionals were referred to vaguely as 'doctors', who in some cases appeared
to be therapists, in others surgeons. In some books, professionals were more
creatively termed, such as a 'backwardsologist' (*Backwards Day*) and a 'Wish
Captain' (*The Adventures of Tulip Birthday Wish Fairy*).

Professionals were framed as significant in terms of gender transition
(or in some cases species transition), both in terms of understanding and

learning about gender. In other words, in many cases professionals were framed as necessary to affirm the protagonist's gender and as a required step in transitioning:

Mom and Dad took me to meet a new doctor who asked me lots and lots of questions. Afterward, the doctor spoke to my parents and I heard the word 'transgender' for the very first time.

(*I Am Jazz* n.p.)

Mom and Dad had a great idea. His family went to see a friend who was easy to talk with. Dr. Bee was a special person who talked with kids who felt like they were born in the wrong body.

She liked to play games, color pictures and help when kids had problems. Nick liked playing with Dr. Bee.

(*Be Who You Are* p. 10)

Kathy's parents speak to several doctors and other parents about Kathy wanting to be a boy. They are surprised to find out that they are not alone. There are other children who feel exactly like Kathy does.

(*When Kathy Is Keith* p. 24)

Andy's parents said: 'But what shall we do? How do we get Andy to turn back into Andrea?'

The backwardsologist looked at them like they were very confusing. He replied, 'What do you mean? It's been done! The miracle of backwards day strikes again. There's no going back. Now you have this wonderful son! Travel safely home.'

(*Backwards Day* p. 6)

'So David is a girl inside,' said Tulip. The Wish Captain nodded yes and said, 'And we're going to help her. We start by calling her by the name she chose, Daniela. It shows we like her and believe in her. And then, as Wish Fairy, here is what you can do: [a lengthy list of instructions follows]'.

(*The Adventures of Tulip Birthday Wish Fairy* n.p.)

Professionals were also discussed in terms of medical intervention and surgery, although notably in none of the books with children as protagonists:

My daddy went to go see Doctor Voltaire, so that he could start looking more and more like a daddy and less like a mommy.

After some time, my new daddy went to the [sic] see Doctor Voltaire again. He needed to have an operation to make him become a boy like me.

(*My New Daddy* n.p.)

So with the help of her owner, she went to a special pet doctor.

The doctor worked on her face. They made her nose longer and adjusted the way her eyes are.

They fixed her tail, so that she could wag it, and they gave her pills so that her fur will become thick like that of a dog.

Then she saw a voice doctor who taught her how to bark.

(*Muffy Was Fluffy* n.p.)

What is particularly clear is the linking of professionals with pronoun changes in five of the books. The overall sequence of this was often a declaration by the protagonist to their family about their gender, a visit to a professional and then a change of pronoun to reflect the protagonist's asserted gender. Changes in presentation and clothing usually occurred around the same time as the pronoun change. For example, in *My New Mommy* and *My New Daddy* (which are essentially the same story), the child narrator tells of their parent's change in presentation in relation to hair, the parent talks to the child about their gender, there is a change in clothing and a gendered parent name change (Mommy/ Daddy) on the same page and then the pronoun is changed when seeing the doctor for the first time (which is just before a depiction of 'the operation').

Again, as was the case with regard to our previously mentioned point about the expectation of gender normative presentations on the part of professionals, it is realistic that the books portray professionals as having a key role to play in the lives of trans people (Speer and Parsons, 2006). At the same time, however, we would emphasise that many trans people challenge the requirement of diagnosis, and the role of gatekeeping by professionals in terms of accessing services (Burke, 2011; Whittle et al., 2008). As such, that the books reify this role potentially instructs trans young people and their families to accept as a given that this will occur.

Discussion

As we noted in the introduction, there has been little analysis of picture books featuring trans characters. This chapter has identified three key themes in the 21 books we found with trans characters: 1) adherence to a binary model of gender, 2) 'appropriate' gendered clothing, behaviours and interests and 3) the reliance on professionals for diagnosis. We have argued that books which use ideas about having a girl brain in a boy body (i.e., *I Am Jazz*) and being 'born in the wrong body' (e.g. *Be Who You Are*) are particularly problematic, as are those which position a professional's affirmation of gender as central to the storyline. However, it is important to note that the themes in the books we examined are similar to current broader cultural representations and understandings of trans people, such as in documentaries which utilise the language of 'wrong body' (for a critique see e.g. McConnell, 2015). Our point is not to reify such representations, but rather to suggest that the books we examined reflect (as well as reinforce) such representations, and that to a degree this is understandable.

Given our concerns about the books, there is clearly a need for a more diverse range of stories to be published and for these to be readily available to children in places such as schools and public libraries. Certainly there was a degree of diversity in the books we examined. For example, books like *My New Daddy* and *My New Mommy* are potentially useful to support children who have a parent who is transitioning, just as books that focus on bullying are useful for children who have similar experiences. Books such as *When Kayla Was Kyle*, which depicts a very sad story about loneliness, bullying and a fear of her father, however, may perhaps be too negative for some children, even if representative of the experiences of some young people. Yet despite this relative diversity in terms of stories, there was little diversity in terms of characters, with all of the characters in some way conforming to the representations of trans people outlined previously. However, it should be noted that some of the more recent books, such as *The Gender Fairy* (Hirst and Wirt, 2015), provide more complex pictures of what it means to be trans.

It was also evident that there was little diversity in the books more broadly. In nearly all of the books the human protagonists were depicted with white skin. The only exceptions were Pete in *All I Want to Be Is Me* who may be viewed as African American and the characters in *Backwards Day* who are depicted as different colours (e.g. the protagonist is purple); however, the drawings in *Backwards Day* still appear to reflect largely white characters. This lack of diversity is particularly notable in *I Am Jazz* where the character of Jazz in the book has a much lighter skin colour than Jazz Jennings herself. Books with trans characters reflect findings about the dominance of white characters in picture books more broadly (e.g. Bradford, 2007; Joshua, 2002), as well as in picture books with LGBT characters where there is often a clear 'whitewashing' (e.g. Lester, 2014). In addition, in our analysis of picture books featuring trans characters, all of the child protagonists shown with parents had a mother and a father (with the notable exception of *A Princess of Great Daring* where Jamie has two mothers who appear on one page) and all of the characters were depicted as able-bodied. As Epstein critiques:

> Children's books do not seem to recognise that it is possible to have multiple identities and, in particular, to have multiple minority identities, i.e. that many people live at the intersections of identities. Characters may be lesbian, gay, bisexual, or transgender, but they seemingly cannot be both that and also, for example, Muslim and/or Chinese and/or dyslexic and/or working-class. It is as though children's books can only handle one deviation from the supposed norm at a time.
>
> (Epstein, 2013: 132)

While we have identified a number of issues with the books, it is important to note that there is anecdotal evidence that some trans young people and the family members of trans people find them useful. A book released after our audit titled *Introducing Teddy: A Story about Being Yourself* (Walton and MacPherson,

2016), for example, was written by the cisgender daughter of a trans woman for her young son because of the limited availability of books with trans parents and characters. In a news media report about the family, picture books featuring trans characters are depicted as an important resource for children (ABC, 2015). Furthermore, an Australian television documentary included a segment featuring a 7-year-old trans girl reading the book *Be Who You Are*, where she reiterates the title message to articulate her own experiences (SBS, 2013). Similarly, an episode of the reality docu-series *I Am Jazz* shows a 27-year-old trans man thanking Jazz for writing her book because it makes it easier for him to discuss being trans with other people. He says 'having your book back when I was 5, 6, or 7 would've changed it for me and maybe could've helped someone like my mom understand' (*I Am Jazz*, 2015, Episode 5, original US airdate 29 July 2015).

As such, we believe it is important to go beyond our own interpretation and analysis of these books. In particular, we are interested in how such books may be potentially useful sources for exploring trans issues and characters with cisgender children, particularly as a way of creating inclusive school cultures. As others have found in relation to feminist picture books more broadly, children have diverse understandings of messages in books which to adults may seem self-evident (e.g. Bartholomaeus, 2016; Davies, 2003). There are currently only a small number of publications exploring (cisgender) children's understandings of picture books with trans characters. The two publications we have found include mention of *10,000 Dresses* (Paterson, 2015; Ryan, Patraw and Bednar, 2013). Ryan, Patraw and Bednar (2013) found that picture books with trans characters (as well as other texts) were useful for teaching a class of third- and fourth-grade elementary school students in the US about gender diversity and trans experiences (see also Martino and Cumming-Potvin, 2014). They argue that:

> [C]hildren in this study made deep and lasting connections with the characters they read about. Especially in the absence of a teacher's personal lived experience with gender diversity, these texts do an excellent job of assuring the topic is connecting to children's lives.
>
> (Ryan, Patraw and Bednar, 2013: 102)

In 2006–2008, the *No Outsiders* project in the UK used picture books with themes about gender and sexuality diversity to promote equality (e.g. DePalma, 2014), emphasising the importance placed on this medium. Primary school teachers were given resource packs of 27 picture books which they chose from to read with their students. While some of the books explored gender diversity, no books with trans characters were included because the project preceded the publication of picture books featuring trans characters, except for *Pearl's Christmas Present*. Thus, following our audit, the next step in our research was to conduct book reading sessions to see how a class of Reception and Grade 1 children understood the books, and to explore how they might be useful for teaching about trans people's lives. These sessions suggested that the books were useful for encouraging discussion and exploration of trans people's lives, and that the children had a growing sense of understanding over the sessions. However, in some ways the children reiterated the framings of the books we have critiqued here in terms of the constructions of binaries (girl/boy) and gender-typed clothing and hair length (for findings, see Bartholomaeus, Riggs and Andrew, 2016).

Finally, following Chapman (2007, 2013), and despite our concerns about some of the books examined in this chapter, it is important to promote the inclusion of books featuring trans characters in schools and public libraries (see also Lukoff, 2015; Naidoo, 2012). In her research in the UK, Chapman (2007, 2013) found that of the public libraries she examined, only one had holdings of books featuring trans characters, and this library only had one such book. While, as we have argued in this chapter, some of the representations of trans people in children's picture books currently available may be problematic, it is nonetheless vital that trans young people in particular see themselves reflected in the world around them. This suggests to us both the importance of increasing library holdings that feature trans characters, but also the need for the continued production of children's books that include a more diverse range of representations of trans people and which engender alternative ways of representing trans issues to young people in general.

References

ABC (2015) Meet the family who lost their father but gained so much more. Original Australian airdate 28 October 2015. Available at: www.abc.net.au/7.30/content/2015/s4341049.htm (accessed 29 October 2015).

Bartholomaeus C (2016) 'Girls can like boy toys': Junior primary school children's understandings of feminist picture books. *Gender and Education*, 28(7): 935–950.

Bartholomaeus C, Riggs DW and Andrew Y (2016) *Exploring trans and gender diverse issues in primary education in South Australia.* Adelaide: Flinders University.

Bradford C (2007) *Unsettling narratives: Postcolonial readings of children's literature.* Waterloo, Ontario: Wilfrid Laurier University Press.

Brill S and Kenney L (2016) *The transgender teen: A handbook for parents and professionals supporting transgender and non-binary teens.* San Francisco: Cleis Press.

Brill S and Pepper R (2008) *The transgender child: A handbook for families and professionals.* San Francisco: Cleis Press.

Burke MC (2011) Resisting pathology: GID and the contested terrain of diagnosis in the transgender rights movement. In: McGann PJ and Hutson DJ (eds) *Sociology of diagnosis (Advances in medical sociology, volume 12).* Bingley: Emerald Group Publishing Limited, pp. 183–210.

Chapman EL (2007) *Provision of LGBT-related fiction to children and young people in public libraries.* Master's Thesis, University of Sheffield, Sheffield.

Chapman EL (2013) No more controversial than a gardening display? Provision of LGBT-related fiction to children and young people in U.K. public libraries. *Library Trends*, 61(3): 542–568.

Chukhray I (2010) *Analysis of children's literary criticism: How scholars examine gender, race/ethnicity, and sexuality in picture books.* Master of Arts Thesis, San Diego State University, San Diego.

Davies B (2003) *Frogs and snails and feminist tales: Preschool children and gender* (Revised ed.). Cresskill, NJ: Hampton Press.

DePalma R (2016) Gay penguins, sissy ducklings . . . and beyond? Exploring gender and sexuality diversity through children's literature. *Discourse: Studies in the Cultural Politics of Education*, 37(6): 828–845.

Enke AF (2012) The education of little cis: Cisgender and the discipline of opposing bodies. In: Enke AF (ed) *Transfeminist perspectives in and beyond transgender and gender studies*. Philadelphia: Temple University Press, pp. 60–77.

Epstein BJ (2012) We're here, we're (not?) queer: GLBTQ characters in children's books. *Journal of GLBT Family Studies*, 8(3): 287–300.

Epstein BJ (2013) *Are the kids all right? Representations of LGBTQ characters in children's and young adult literature paperback*. Bristol: HammerOn Press.

Erickson-Schroth L (ed) (2014) *Trans bodies, trans selves: A resource for the transgender community*. Oxford: Oxford University Press.

gendermom (2013) Dang! I forgot about feminism! In: gendermom. Available at: gendermom.wordpress.com/2013/08/14/dang-i-forgot-about-feminism/ (accessed 30 June 2015).

Greytak EA, Kosciw JG, and Boesen MJ (2013) Putting the 'T' in 'resource': The benefits of LGBT-related school resources for transgender youth. *Journal of LGBT Youth*, 10(1–2): 45–63.

Hall M (2015) *Red: A crayon's story*. New York, NY: Greenwillow Books.

Hirst J and Wirt L (2015) *The gender fairy*. Balaclava, Victoria: Oban Road Publishing.

I Am Jazz (2015) Episode 5. Original US airdate 29 July 2015. Executive producer A James, TLC.

Joshua MB (2002) Inside picture books: Where are the children of color? *Educational Horizons*, 80(3): 125–132.

Labelle S-G (2013) *A girl like any other*. Montreal: Editions SGL.

Lester JZ (2014) Homonormativity in children's literature: An intersectional analysis of queer-themed picture books. *Journal of LGBT Youth*, 11(3): 244–275.

Lukoff K (2015) Evaluating transgender picture books; calling for better ones. *School Library Journal website*, 8 May. Available at: www.slj.com/2015/05/diversity/evaluating-transgender-picture-books-requesting-better-ones/ (accessed 22 October 2015).

Martino W and Cumming-Potvin W (2016) Teaching about sexual minorities and 'princess boys': A queer and trans-infused approach to investigating LGBTQ-themed texts in the elementary school classroom. *Discourse: Studies in the Cultural Politics of Education*, 37(6): 807–827.

McConnell F (2015). Channel 4's obsession with genitalia and surgery demeans trans people. *The Guardian*, 15 October. Available at: www.theguardian.com/commentisfree/2015/oct/14/channel-4-genitalia-surgery-trans-people-girls-to-men?CMP=fb_gu (accessed 30 October 2015).

Meyer EJ and Pullen Sansfaçon A (eds) (2014) *Supporting transgender & gender creative youth: Schools, families, and communities in action*. New York, NY: Peter Lang Publishing.

Naidoo JC (2012) *Rainbow family collections: Selecting and using children's books with lesbian, gay, bisexual, transgender, and queer content*. Santa Barbara, CA: Libraries Unlimited.

Naidoo JC (2014) *The importance of diversity in library programs and material collections for children*. Chicago, IL: Association for Library Service to Children.

O'Neil K (2010) Once upon today: Teaching for social justice with postmodern picturebooks. *Children's Literature in Education*, 41(1): 40–51.

Paterson K (2015) *'They're trying to trick us!': Making sense of anti-oppressive children's literature in the elementary school classroom.* Master's Thesis, Brock University, Canada.

Riggs DW and Augoustinos M (2007) Learning difference: Representations of diversity in storybooks for children of lesbian and gay parents. *Journal of GLBT Family Studies*, 3(2/3): 133–156.

Ryan CL, Patraw JM and Bednar M (2013) Discussing princess boys and pregnant men: Teaching about gender diversity and transgender experiences within an elementary school curriculum. *Journal of LGBT Youth*, 10(1–2): 83–105.

Sapp J (2010) A review of gay and lesbian themed early childhood children's literature. *Australasian Journal of Early Childhood*, 35(1): 32–40.

SBS (2013) Crossover Kids. Producer G McNab. Original Australian airdate 30 April 2013. Available at: www.sbs.com.au/news/dateline/story/crossover-kids (accessed 30 October 2015).

Serano J (2007) *Whipping girl: A transsexual woman on sexism and the scapegoating of femininity.* Emeryville, CA: Seal Press.

Skelton JW (2015) Not exceptional or punished: A review of five picture books that celebrate gender diversity. *TSQ: Transgender Studies Quarterly*, 2(3): 495–499.

Speer SA and McPhillips R (2013) Patients' perspectives on psychiatric consultations in the gender identity clinic. *Patient Education and Counseling*, 91(3): 385–391.

Speer SA and Parsons C (2006) Gatekeeping gender: Some features of the use of hypothetical questions in the psychiatric assessment of transsexual patients. *Discourse & Society*, 17(6): 785–812.

Stryker S and Aizura AZ (eds) (2013) *The transgender studies reader 2.* New York, NY: Routledge.

Toman LA (2014) *Queering the ABCs: LGBTQ characters in children's books.* Master of Arts Thesis, East Tennessee State University, Johnson.

Walton J and MacPherson D (2016) *Introducing teddy: A story about being yourself.* London: Bloomsbury.

Whittle S, Turner L, Combs R and Rhodes S (2008) *Transgender EuroStudy: legal survey and focus on the transgender experience of health care.* Brussels and Berlin: The European Region of the International Lesbian and Gay Association and TransGender Europe.

Young M (2013) Trans* men and the erasure of childhood femininity. In: The Rainbow Hub. Available at: www.therainbowhub.com/trans-men-and-the-erasure-of-childhood-femininity/ (accessed 22 February 2015)

Part IV

Trans epistemologies

Foreword

Epistemology 'deals with the study of the nature, scope, and sources of knowledge, as well as its conditions of production, structure, and validation' (Radi, 2019: 43). Epistemologists are concerned with questions around how knowledge might be produced, how it is possible to produce knowledge and, by extension, *who* can produce knowledge.

As previous chapters of this book have explored, the knowledge that emerges about trans people is so often produced by *non*-trans people, sometimes in ways that work to actively erase trans people's own ideas and accounts of lived experience. Moreover, knowledge produced by trans people can have its limits, especially if the diversity of possible trans experiences regarding factors such as gender, geographical location, personal interests and intersecting forms of marginalisation are not taken into account. It is for this reason that trans philosopher Blas Radi (2019) emphasises the importance of a trans epistemology that retains both theoretical precision and a practical commitment to improving the life conditions of trans people, while retaining a sensitivity to trans diversity in all its forms, as well as the limits of knowledge itself.

The contributors to this final section explore questions of knowledge production from a range of perspectives (and in more than one medium): visual, methodological, philosophical. Two key elements are present throughout this diverse collection of reflections. The first of these is a focus on the importance of knowledge produced *by* trans people, *for* trans people. The second is an acknowledgement of the importance of collaboration, a space for trans knowledge and understanding to emerge from and be shaped by a multiplicity of voices. Here, we see the promise of an idea explored in the introduction to this volume play out: the promise of the many-voiced monster.

Chapter 11 offers perhaps the most radical departure from traditional notions of academic knowledge production. Rami Yasir offers theory without words in a comic strip that explores themes of ignorance, awareness, epiphany and becoming. This is a story without an explicitly 'trans' character, a story that is in a sense *without gender*. Yet, it offers a profound reflection upon how we might negotiate normativity and realise the possible from an undeniably 'trans' perspective, with the central character (re)making themselves as they break through seemingly impenetrable boundaries. Notably, this change in embodiment and the character's relationship to the world does not follow only from their personal explorations and subsequent breakdown; it is very much facilitated by a supportive ally (and who knows what kind of journey this individual might have previously made in turn?)

Themes of allyship are also central to Chapter 12, in which Rhi Humphrey, Bróna Nic Giolla Easpaig and Rachael Fox provide an account of ethical processes in empirical research with trans populations. The authors outline two case studies involving research with trans people (in the UK and Australia, respectively) and reflect on research design, participation and the emergence of knowledge when working with a population that might be regarded as 'at risk'. They emphasise the importance of flexibility and the continual re-assessment of values and methods in research with trans people, to co-construct knowledge *with* trans research participants. These are topics of importance to all researchers doing empirical work – trans and cis alike.

In Chapter 13, Mijke van der Drift seeks to articulate an ethics that creates space for nonnormative, indeterminate becoming, drawing very deliberately on the productive parallels present in the otherwise seemingly contrasting ideas of Aristotle and Gloria Anzaldúa. This is an ethics of personal responsibility towards the self, of (continual) self-emergence; yet it remains bound to others. This is not to say that van der Drift argues for any kind of surrender to norms; rather, the chapter makes a case for the generation of indeterminate forms in a manner that is sensitive to the inequalities and injustices of the world, and rejects individualism.

Finally, in Chapter 14 we close with a genealogy of genealogies. Igi Moon provides an account of the 2012–2014 *Emergence of Trans* seminar series that inspired this book. They describe the themes present in those events, as well as the ideas and questions raised in turn by speakers and seminar attendees. While we hope this book provides a number of fulfilling concepts for readers hungry for answers regarding trans emergence, we intentionally close this book by sharing a series of open questions. Trans knowledges have not 'stopped' emerging. We cannot provide any kind of neat conclusion through some closure for trans possibility; nor, to follow van der Drift, would we want to.

Reference

Radi, B. (2019) 'On Trans* Epistemology: Critiques, Contributions, and Challenges', *TSQ: Transgender Studies Quarterly*, 6(1): 43–63.

11 Make yourself

Rami Yasir

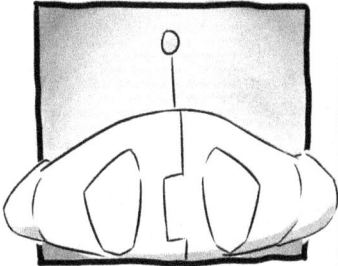

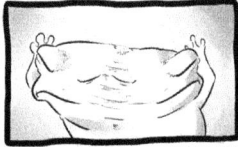

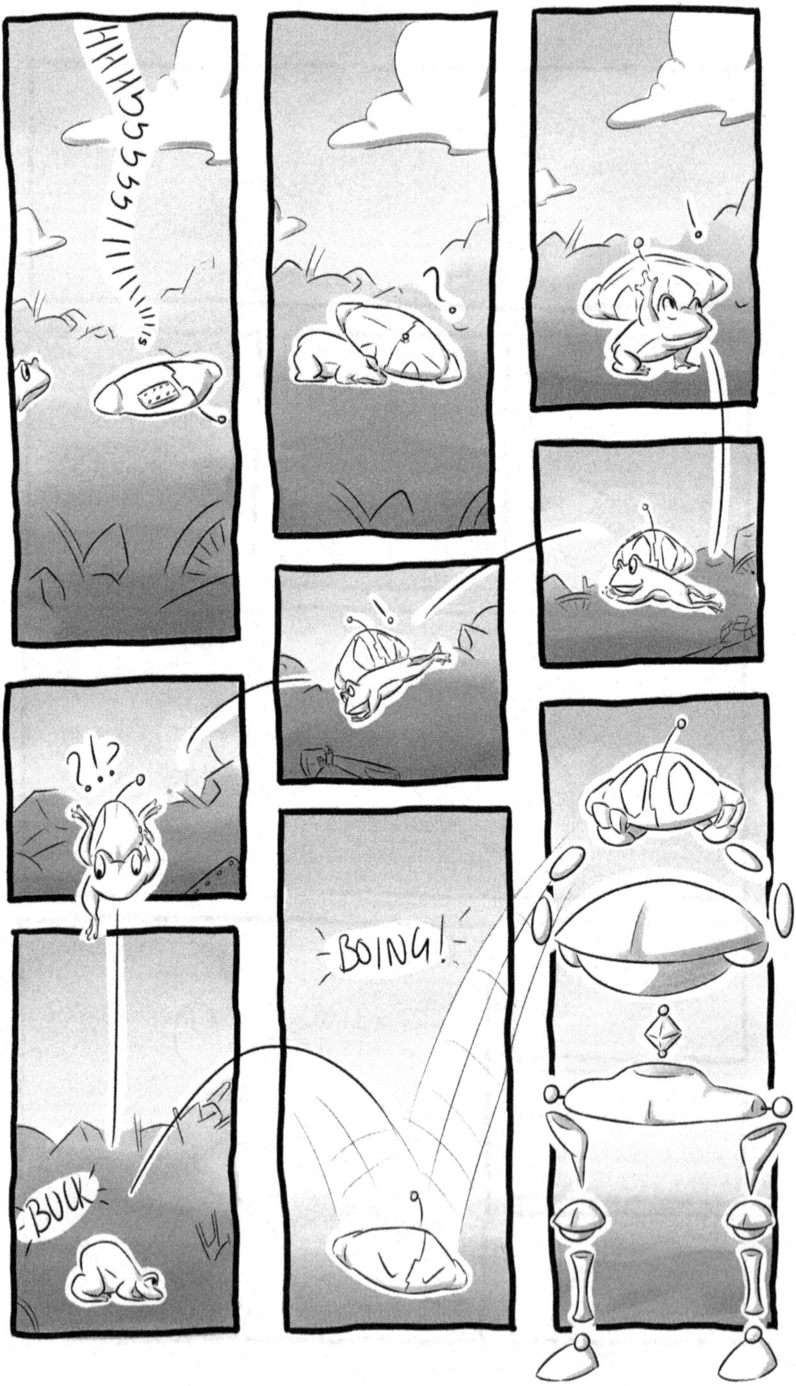

SSSSGGGGGGGGGGGHHHH
?
!
?!?
BUCK
BOING!

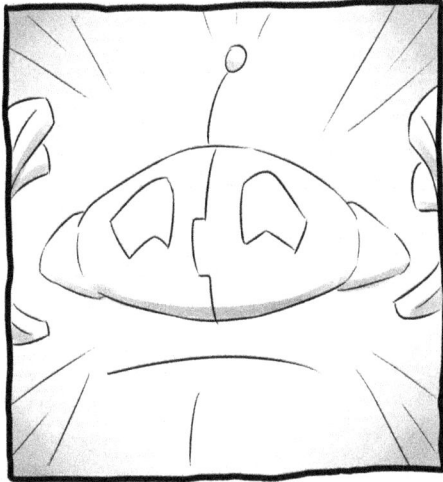

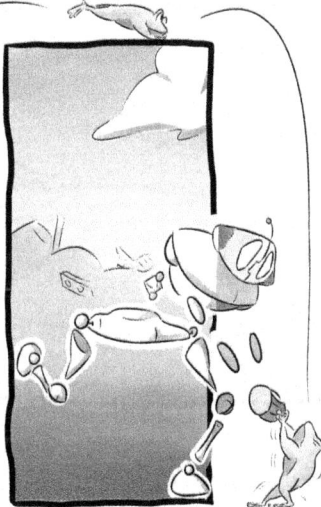

FLING!

CRACK!

THE END

12 Co-producing trans ethical research

Rhi Humphrey, Bróna Nic Giolla Easpaig and Rachael Fox

This chapter engages with the way in which the emergence of trans discourses challenge conceptualisations and practices encountered within ethical processes in research. Advancing progressive research merits critical reflection and a productive rethinking in sexuality and gender studies. Our engagement with ethical issues here is oriented towards addressing questions of how trans subjectivities challenge and develop understandings of gender and sexuality expressed within research settings, and the extent to which research practices are fit for engaging trans subjects.

Our understandings of trans have been formed through participant engagement within research, such as in that outlined in the case studies in this chapter. We specifically understand trans to include non-binary, genderqueer and genderfluid people as a result of these engagements.

We begin by outlining concepts, practices and procedures in ethical approaches in a brief summary of scholarship in this area. Following this, we present projects undertaken in UK and Australian contexts to draw out specific issues. Specifically, we discuss: conceptualisation of participants/co-researchers in ethical practices that pose barriers to participation; ethical considerations in relation to space, place and time for online methods; and community or co-researcher collaboration to enhance accountability and participant engagement. This piece does not offer an exhaustive ethical review or proposed guidelines, but instead reflects upon how challenges emerged in our practice and were negotiated, with the intent of contributing to an existing dialogue about creating ethical contexts for engagement.

There are multiple reasons for the focus of the chapter. First, all research requires approval from ethical committees, and we argue that it is crucial to develop a better understanding of the facilitating and constraining roles of formal processes in research practices with this community. Furthermore, ethical practices should be continuously evaluated and engaged with by researchers, including co-developing with community partners, ethical accountabilities and practices, to best serve the interests of the communities and individuals involved in or impacted by research. It is important to locate this endeavour within emerging developments in relation to theoretical frameworks (e.g. Hale, 2009;

Rooke, 2010), guidelines for practice (e.g. APS, 2013) and new methodologies (e.g. Adler and Zarchin, 2002).

Background literature

Ethical concepts, guidelines and practices as they relate to research are understood here to be informed by cultural and societal representations of morality, responsibility, risk, harm and benefit and as such are located within specific socio-historical, cultural and geopolitical contexts (Parker, 2005; Taylor, 2008). Conventional ethical notions and discourses are wide ranging, and this chapter concerns ethical frameworks produced through national research body frameworks and guidelines (Research Councils United Kingdom, 2013; National Health and Medical Research Council, 2015), professional codes of practice (Australian Psychological Society, 2007), research conventions such as qualitative ideas about morality and the individual responsibility of the researcher, and decision-making in institutional ethical committees. Engagement within these frameworks is facilitated and sometimes complicated by the specific ethical principles that underpin the individual research investigation, including the theoretical framework, research approach and the involvement of communities impacted by the project. Within the broad domain of ethics we focus on a commitment to critiquing and developing meaningful forms of engagement with individuals and communities involved in and impacted by the research activity. As scholars existing both inside and outside of the research communities we work with, there are ethical implications for our research projects and our understanding of ourselves as researchers.

Our conceptualisation of ethical issues is aided by the concept of 'cisgenderism' – a systemic, ideological and structural violence, often reflected in discourses pertaining to legitimacy (Ansara and Hegarty, 2012). Distinctions are often made between people classified as 'normal' and trans people, with trans people requiring explanation (Ansara, 2010); the cisgenderism framework enables an interrogation of this ideology. Cisgenderism alerts us to obligations to question problematic assumptions that may be embedded and enacted through 'standard' research practices. For instance, psychology scholarship has a long history of pathologisation, misgendering or exclusion based on problematic assumptions about gender (Ansara and Hegarty, 2012, 2014).

A few issues have been raised in the literature that assist thinking through the contemporary research context. Often in research terminology is used which ignores or excludes particular identities, or which offers a limited set of ways of describing identities that tend to hold more social currency and are better known (e.g. LGBTIQ). Additionally there are well-noted issues with obtaining representative samples in research; there is a particular concern that findings may over-represent views and experiences of people who are more 'visible' or face fewer barriers to research participation (Hines, 2013; McDermott, Roen and Piela, 2013). Furthermore, Morgan and Taylor (2016) have discussed the differences between trans-specific and trans-inclusive research, with the inclusion of stakeholders helping to achieve meaningful rather than tokenistic engagement. Reflection upon this issue highlights the limitations of understanding experiences more broadly and the necessity of careful consideration regarding what we can assume about community members' experiences and what we can claim to know based on research.

Moreover, pertinent ethical concepts merit contextualised consideration. For example, in thinking about the notion of risk, we must also consider that risk may be something which is negotiated through daily experience in discriminatory societies (Taylor, 2008). Acknowledging this prompts a critical consideration of associated ideas such as 'vulnerability'. Conventional ethics is bound up in notions that participants are vulnerable and that the 'professional' researcher has knowledge and power. When the British Psychological Society's Code of Ethics and Conduct first mentions an imbalance of power, it is to reinforce rather than challenge this notion: 'ethics is related to the control of power. Clearly, not all clients are powerless but many are disadvantaged by lack of knowledge and certainty compared to the psychologist whose judgement they require' (BPS, 2009: 5). Boyle (2003: 27) describes society's tendencies towards a discourse of vulnerability as a 'social category applied . . . only to those groups who are already socially and economically subordinate'. Boyle (2003: 28) argues that describing groups as vulnerable can imply 'a set of behaviours associated with passivity, and possibly gratitude, [being perceived as] seemingly reasonable . . . [and] just as important, the opposite behaviours [being perceived as seemingly] unreasonable'. Structures in society, discourses and lack of power are positioned as creating vulnerability more profound than individualising, pathologising and disabling views of biological factors. The notion of 'vulnerability' within this chapter is therefore contextualised to consider structural and social means of disempowerment and marginalisation that result in detrimental impacts on well-being.

The literature reviewed highlights many of the challenges encountered in fieldwork and contextualises the contemporary conditions in which the research in our case studies is undertaken. We now move on to describe two studies; one in the UK and one in Australia.

Study 1: Trans representation in the UK media, UK

The UK study aimed to analyse the effects that trans representation in UK newspapers have on trans audiences. The impact of this coverage was investigated through online interviews and focus groups with trans people; trans participants were selected because they are the most familiar with the ways in which newspaper reporting and surrounding discourses affect their lives, and because they could offer reflections from lived experience. The questions for interviews were influenced by an analysis of trans newspaper coverage over one year to consider emerging patterns. The articles were published during the final operating year of the Press Complaints Commission (which has since been replaced with the Independent Press Standards Organisation) and the first year of new guidance for reporting and researching stories involving trans people. The focus on newspaper content was influenced by the work of Trans Media Watch and their research from 2009–2010. The interviews conducted within this case study are considered in the context of literature on trans studies, the media and gender theory (Humphrey, 2016).

Study 2: Collaboration with young LGBTIQ people on survey design, Australia

The Australian study involved collaboration with young LGBTIQ people on survey design. Current research indicates that members of this community negotiate intersecting forms of disadvantage that contribute to poorer health and wellbeing. The project partner, Headspace, is a national Australian youth mental health foundation and community service provider (www.headspace.org.au/). The Headspace centre in a semi-rural town in New South Wales recently completed a two-year project titled, 'Training for Change – Improving the Mental Health Outcomes for LGBTIQ Youth (Lesbian, Gay, Bisexual, Transgender, Intersex and Queer/Questioning)'. This examined health issues for young people who identify with a diverse range of gender and sexual identities, in order to develop training programs for service providers with the aim of improving service provision to this community. Two of the authors (Fox and Nic Giolla Easpaig) provided support with the research components of this project. Community psychology methodology informed the approach. Young people who identified as genderqueer, non-binary and trans made valuable contributions and provided important insights for service providers through steering group collaboration as well as conventional data collection (see Nic Giolla Easpaig and Fox, 2017 for findings).

One of the first stages of research involved gathering information from young people, and this was done through an online survey and focus groups. The use of a survey measure in the research allowed a larger number of young people to contribute, and to do so anonymously. However, survey measures can also be problematic with particular regard to the way in which data concerning sexual and gender identities and practice are collected, an issue raised by the young people who participated in the project (as we discuss later in this chapter). To improve the survey, a steering group of young LGBTIQ people collaborated with the researchers in designing a more appropriate format and set of questions. This collaboration continued through the life of the project and has endured, but this chapter focuses primarily on the valuable insights gained in this initial work on the survey.

Ellisa, Bailey and McNeil (2015) highlight that there has been a problematic tendency for trans peoples' experiences to be subsumed within the more general category of 'LGBT' experiences, which fails to engage with the specific and distinct complexities of trans peoples' experiences. When drawing upon the example presented in this chapter, it is important for us to acknowledge that project involvement was not limited to young people who identified as trans, and that this may have indirect implications for processes that we examine.

Ethical issues for engagement

'Risky subjects'

We now outline issues that have arisen in our research in regard to inclusion, the characterisation of risk and vulnerability within ethical application processes, and the potential for re-researching. Research findings are implicated in the practice of constructing knowledge about subjectivities and identities for groups such as trans communities. Given those findings are in turn based upon methodological assumptions, it is important to engage with conventions about the way participants and researchers are positioned and conceptualised within ethical practices.

Limits of inclusion

In Study 2, the ethical positioning of 'risky subjects' was twofold, located firstly in working with young people and secondly in the specific intersections of youth, sexuality and gender identity. Participants in research on sexuality and gender are positioned as 'vulnerable' and 'risky' by ethics committees, and research with youth compounds this issue.

The steering group of young LGBTIQ people in the project quickly identified a desire to include younger teenagers and simultaneously identified the need for participants to give consent themselves (as opposed to a parent or guardian giving consent on their behalf). The very serious possibility of *creating* risk and vulnerability by requiring parental consent for young people who are not 'out' to their parents was identified by these young people, as has been documented in research elsewhere (Taylor, 2008). If research does require parental consent, young people who are not 'out' to their parents are effectively excluded.

The first crucial stage in this study therefore was to convincingly argue to the relevant ethics committee that parental consent could be waived. This was done using the National Statement on Ethical Conduct in Human Research, which allows for waiver where 'the risk of research participation is no more than discomfort, the aim is to benefit young people, and there are additional good reasons not to involve parents' (NHMRC, 2007: 56). This was achieved successfully for young people down to the age of 16 in this study, but regrettably not below.

Possibility of re-researching

Study 1 was informed by Trans Media Watch's trans audience research (Kermode and Trans Media Watch, 2010) in which several participants were featured in UK media articles, a finding echoed here. As Trans Media Watch assisted with participant recruitment, there was a possibility that some participants had engaged with similar research before. Re-researching participants may put anonymity at risk, especially for those who live stealth or within smaller-population demographics within trans communities such as non-binary, genderqueer and genderfluid people (Humphrey, 2016). In this study, demographic information such as race and class was removed to reduce this risk. However, this approach does risk homogenising trans people by rendering invisible intersectional lived experiences. This problem has been acknowledged by Roen (2001:262) who finds 'perspectives of whiteness echo, largely unacknowledged, through transgender (and queer) theorising' and calls for more research on 'racialised aspects of transgender bodies'. This issue was not overcome in Study 1 and remains something which intersectional researchers need to find practical solutions for.

Reformulating consent-giving

Within Study 1, participants were given three ways to indicate informed consent: signing by hand or electronically typing names on a consent form; replying yes or similar wording that indicated consent in an online interview or pre-interview email; or by logging in and attending the online focus group on the understanding that to click the link and participate was to indicate informed consent to the research. Previous research finds that signatures are hard to obtain online and that participants are unlikely to print, sign and scan a consent form because of the time and hardware requirements (Keller and Lee, 2003). It is notable that only one participant provided a signed consent form; this participant requested forms in alternative formats, so this signature option could be due to an undisclosed disability.

While there are legitimate concerns about being unable to speak to participants face to face before they indicate consent (Varnhagen et al., 2005; Gill and Baillie, 2018), including risks of not reading or skimming the consent documents and the lack of indication of research access issues, there are ways to alleviate this through communication about consent in interactions with participants, including focus groups and interviews. McDermott and Roen (2012) argue that issues with obtaining informed consent are not unique to online research. For example, Pawa et al. (2013: 3) reveal that 'transgender people in Pattaya would be unwilling to provide signatures or written consent due to concerns about stigma and safety of identifying information'. Trans people who are non-binary or multigendered may have specific barriers relating to signatures and the name or names they use day to day. These considerations are further complicated by emerging non-binary recognition in certain countries. For example, locating the research online may mean that some participants are in geographical locations in which they are unable to legally change names and rely on using signatures attached to names they do not use day to day. Furthermore, if the research will involve multiple sessions, then genderfluid individuals may feel that being asked for just one signature is a barrier to participation. Challenging cisgenderist assumptions inherent in research requires attentions to the limits and implications of consent-giving practices.

Space, place and time for facilitating safe research

This section focuses on the ethical implications of decisions we make in research in relation to space, place and time, with a focus on online methods. For Seymour (2001: 159) '"giving a voice" means more than providing the researched with an opportunity to speak: it involves creating the appropriate means and communication context for research participants'. Online methods can provide such opportunities. Online research can offer inclusion for harder-to-reach individuals (Adler and Zarchin, 2002). However, online methods are not accessible to everyone. They require internet access and a device through which to connect.

In Study 1, participants were offered different ways to participate online: either a focus group, or interview using their choice of instant messenger (IM) software. Kazmer and Xie (2008: 273) advocate participant choice over the research means of participation to 'increase retention and rapport'. For trans subjects, these options for participation may not be a simple matter of choice, but the only way they can participate. For instance, stealth participants may require a certain level of anonymity that is not afforded within focus groups.

Decision-making about communication

Synchronous communication methods were used for the online interviews and focus groups: this allows communication to occur in 'real time', with conversational benefits that are useful to semi-structured interviews. Although only one online focus group software was offered, interview participants could choose the IM software. Participants were also given opportunities to choose their pseudonym and an avatar. Participants were asked not to use a name or avatar with which they were known elsewhere online because these could be identifiable, as Buchanan (2011) notes. This is of particular note for the focus groups in Study 1; participant recruitment was achieved through a number of trans organisations and online community groups, as well as snowball sampling, so there was a risk that participants in focus groups could realise they knew one another because of familiar avatars or usernames.

Dodd's (2009) reflections on ethical LGBTQ research advocate that researchers discuss the possibility of 'nonstudy interaction' between participants or between the researcher and participants beyond the parameters of the research project. This is particularly relevant for Study 1 because the researcher recruited from trans groups and LGBTIQ groups of which they were also a member, adding further complexity to the shifting power relations researchers negotiate as community 'insiders' (Dodd, 2009: 482).

Finding safe spaces

With online research, individuals can participate from the physical space in which they feel most comfortable to discuss the issues so long as that space has internet access. However, there are limits to what can be known about the location from which participants respond and it is not necessarily safe. Stieger and Göritz (2006) note that IM and online focus group research offer no clues as to the distractions present. For online trans research there may be issues if what was thought to be a safe space with internet access becomes unsafe quickly because of the changing environment of public spaces. Making participants aware of the expected length of the focus group or interview, as well as scheduling a time that suits them, can alleviate some scenarios but in certain instances participants may log off for their own safety. Safety is particularly important for 'stealth' participants who might not have participated in an offline environment.

The internet itself is not always a safe space for trans individuals and it may be associated with experiences of transphobia, especially in relation to online newspaper article comments. Atkinson and DePalma's (2008) research on gender and sexuality with young people suggested that online environments could reproduce inequalities. The focus groups in Study 1 attempted to offer an environment in which to challenge these inequalities without reproducing other inequalities, so private messaging facilities within the focus group software were used to ensure all members felt included. For instance, disabled participants felt able to provide details about ableism in media articles within private messages, a topic that was not discussed in the group conversation. The one-to-one interviews faced less of a problem in this regard because the interviewee and the researcher could communicate more directly; however, there is no way of knowing what other activities participants could be engaged in and how this affected their participation in their interview and/ or the focus group.

Seymour (2001) suggests that online research might not necessarily be more accessible to participants than face-to-face research because some barriers to participation may not be apparent or be less obvious. Locating research online allows participants greater control over information disclosure but it does not remove participants from their bodies, genders or other lived experiences, so comparable contexts and research experiences should not be presumed on the basis that each participant was able to access the research setting. Locating research online may allow for safer spaces for some trans subjects, but these settings must be continually critiqued and scrutinised to best serve the needs of trans participants as a research method.

Promoting participation and working collaboratively

For us, serving the needs of participants includes participant engagement with how the research is undertaken, to what ends and by whom. This allows for more insightful information and constructs progressive research processes that can be of benefit to those affected by it. We address the following areas for ethical consideration: collaboration to foster expertise; explicating the research rationale and purpose; and validation of research accounts produced.

Collaboration to foster expertise

In Study 2 a broad community psychology approach was taken in relation to the project. Here a steering group was formed, composed of young people who identified with a range of sexual and/or gender identities, the researcher and the project manager. The researcher and project manager consulted and received feedback from the young people belonging to the steering group in the design of the research, specifically with regard to the survey design. Working closely with the young people revealed a range of practices that from a research perspective tend to be assumed as 'standard', but which are problematic and may create barriers to participation.

For example, when advising on the questions within the online survey, the young people's steering group discussed the problems that standard demographic questions pose. The demographic section represented the most significant site for issues and suggestions of change. The first suggestion was to put that section of the survey at the end rather than the start: for the young people it always felt like it was the first thing they had to do in many situations and the most problematic. On the advice of the young people, survey respondents were also invited to include their own description in relation to both gender and sexuality status. The inclusion of the young people's own terms and descriptions allowed them to challenge the othering typically associated with the cisgenderism inherent within the categorisation of trans identities, and enabled them to articulate their identities in a way that was relevant for them. In a shift away from a limited range of set options, this could include multiple terms and combinations of terms. To represent the responses to this question in the research report, a word cloud (based on word frequency) was used to ensure that, while more frequently used descriptors were highlighted as such, the full array of identities was also acknowledged. This range of terms used by young people to describe their gender identity was helpful in the training that was developed for health professionals to improve service provision to young people (based on the survey as well as focus groups conducted with service providers).

Explicating rationale and communicating purpose/benefits

When grounding Study 2 in a broad community psychological methodology, there was a desire to work transparently with participants and contributors, communicating purpose and desired outcomes. There was also a desire to consider participant benefits in a more meaningful fashion. Significantly, two issues were also raised by the young people's steering group, particularly when designing the survey. The young people were in favour of much more description for participants to read at the start of the survey. This description included reasons for conducting the survey, a careful explanation of who was conducting the survey and what the survey results would be used for. It was also important not to overstate the benefits of participation. The following text was therefore inserted into the survey: 'There are no direct medical benefits or significant risks for participating in this study, but your participation is likely to help us find out more about how to improve health services for LGBTIQ young people'. This may seem a simple and basic action to take, but both the researchers and the young people felt information like this is often absent; the inclusion of such information helps to construct a safer survey space where participants feel comfortable to share their information.

Transparent reasoning and communication of value was further woven into various sections and questions of the survey. For the demographic section, the following introduction was inserted:

> We are sure that you get asked these all the time and it's OK if you don't want to answer them, but we would like it if you could. This information will help us understand a little bit more about the issues facing young LGBTIQ Australians. It will help us to know for example where there are bigger gaps or problems in services or where young people face greater difficulties, and help us to tailor our program to address these issues. To do this, we need to understand a little bit about you.

Here the steering group felt it was important to communicate that the researchers were aware of the sensitive nature of demographic questions, and to explain why we had still chosen to ask them. Sensitive questions were also contextualised, as in the following example: 'Please write the postcode/town in which you live (this helps us to know for example which areas might have more or fewer services)'. These alterations to the language in the survey were undertaken for a community who sometimes find that information about their gender and/ or sexuality is used against them, not least by researchers. This improvement in communication with participants is therefore an example of how collaborative work at margins can improve research, with wide-reaching consequences for our understandings of methodology.

Participant validation of research accounts produced

As previously noted, it is crucial to engage critically with the representation of trans individuals, communities and accounts in research. As researchers, power differentials arise in our role of reporting on findings, analysing accounts and representing participants within written statements. In this sense ethical considerations arise from ensuring the promotion of an accurate participant 'voice' and from attending to the power differentials that are deeply embedded within the traditional role and practice of research reporting. One approach taken in Study 1 was to include validation which, while of broader use in qualitative research (Namaste, 2000), we regard to be of particular importance when working collaboratively with trans participants and LGBTIQ participants who have historically had their bodies written on largely for the benefit of medical discourse (Oosterhuis, 2000).

The definition of validation we have adopted is taken from disability research in which Barnes (2009: 467) highlights that 'taking fieldwork data back to respondents for verification is generally regarded as a key criterion'. For Namaste (2000: 266), 'validating the interpretation of research data remains a crucial component of any reflexive sociological practice' (which also adjusts the power imbalance between researcher and researched at the analysis stage). Namaste adds that:

> Transsexuals and transgendered people must be actively involved in the construction of academic knowledge about our bodies and our lives: anything less advocates a position wherein knowledge is produced, in the first and last instance, for the institution of the university.

> (2000: 267)

To avoid the use of trans lives to benefit only academic discourse, this research was also shared with a number of trans organisations that may benefit from it. Many of the organisations that wished to see a results summary were also active in seeking participants, so ensuring participants could not be identified from the research was of great importance. The validation request asked that participants check that they did not feel misrepresented and that they had not revealed anything they no longer wished to or had given responses that they thought were unique enough to identify them to the organisations that may see the results. Three participations offered this validation via email to say they felt accurately represented by the findings. One further IM discussion was conducted, resulting in rewording to reflect participants' feedback. This IM discussion was the most in-depth of the validations received and allowed for a conversation to occur that resulted in repeated checking of that participant's views. For online research, there is a benefit in seeking validation via synchronous communication rather than asynchronous communication so a conversation can develop about the analysis.

Conclusion

The case studies present contextualised, imperfect work which is problematic in a number of ways; however, we hope they capture some of the complexities negotiated when working in the fieldwork. In seeking to contribute to what Seymour (2001) discusses as *creating conditions for ethical engagement*, we found the following elements to be useful in our research practice, and propose these may form starting points for the practice conditions we aspire to. We argue that it is crucial to reform knowledge-making processes in research, especially methodological components such as rethinking design in Study 2, in order to better align the aims of gender and sexuality studies research to the tools adopted. We propose that examinations and critique of methods should not only share theoretical and epistemic orientations but should also actively resist cisgenderism. Within these case studies, research methods that positioned knowledge-making *about* trans lives were considered secondary to knowledge-making *with* trans individuals. Active participation includes a say in how the research is undertaken, to what ends and by whom. These are important considerations, not only for producing 'accurate' or insightful information, but also for ensuring progressive research processes that are of benefit to those impacted by them. In gender and sexuality research, ethical concepts and practices used to engage with frameworks such as institutional committees can be contextualised through critiquing and developing meaningful forms of engagement with the individuals and communities involved in and impacted by the research activity. Moreover, we believe that the challenges presented to ethics in research by trans communities and with trans individuals offer ways to strengthen and improve research practice more widely.

Funding acknowledgements

The researchers provided research support in the 'Training for Change: Improving the Mental Health Outcomes for LGBTIQ Youth' project for Headspace in NSW (Headspace is a national youth mental health foundation and community service provider in Australia) on their Service Innovation Grant (Department of Health and Aging).

References

Adler, C & Zarchin, Y (2002) 'The "Virtual Focus Group": Using the internet to reach pregnant women on home bed rest', *Journal of Obstetric, Gynecologic and Neonatal Nursing*, vol. 31, no. 4, pp. 418–427.

Ansara, YG (2010) 'Beyond cisgenderism: Counselling people with non-assigned gender identities', in L Moon (ed.), *Counselling Ideologies: Queer Challenges to Heteronormativity*. Ashgate, Aldershot.

Ansara, YG & Hegarty, P (2012) 'Cisgenderism in psychology: Pathologising and misgendering children from 1999 to 2008', *Psychology & Sexuality*, vol. 3, pp. 1–24. doi:10.1080/19 419899.2011.576696.

Ansara, YG & Hegarty, P (2014) 'Methodologies of misgendering: Recommendations for reducing cisgenderism in psychological research', *Feminism & Psychology*, vol. 24, pp. 259–270.

Atkinson, E & DePalma, R (2008) 'Dangerous spaces: Constructing and contesting sexual identities in an online discussion forum', *Gender and Education*, vol. 20, no. 2, pp. 183–194.

Australian Psychological Society (2007) *Australian Psychological Society Code of Ethics*. Retrieved from: www.psychology.org.au/about/ethics/#s1.

Australian Psychological Society (2013) *Ethical Guidelines for Working with Sex and/or Gender Diverse Clients*. APS, Melbourne, Vic.

Barnes, C (2009) 'An ethical agenda in disability research: Rhetoric or reality?' in D Mertens & P Ginsberg (eds.), *The Handbook of Social Research Ethics*, Sage, London.

Boyle, M (2003) 'The dangers of vulnerability', *Clinical Psychology*, vol. 24, pp. 27–30.

British Psychological Society (2009) *Code of Ethics and Conduct: Guidance Published by the Ethics Committee of the British Psychological Society*. BPS, Leicester. Retrieved from: www. bps.org.uk/what-we-do/ethics-standards/ethics-standards.

Buchanan, E (2011) 'Internet research ethics: Past, present, and future' in M Consalvo & C Ess (eds.), *The Handbook of Internet Studies*. Blackwell, Chichester.

Dodd, SJ (2009) 'LGBTQ: Protecting vulnerable subjects in *all* studies', in D Mertens & P Ginsberg (eds.), *The Handbook of Social Research Ethics*. Sage, London.

Ellisa, SJ, Bailey, L, & McNeil, J (2015) 'Trans people's experiences of mental health and gender identity services: A UK study', *Journal of Gay & Lesbian Mental Health*, vol. 19, no. 1, pp. 4–20. doi:10.1080/19359705.2014.960990.

Gill, P & Baillie, J (2018) 'Interviews and focus groups in qualitative research: An update for the digital age', *British Dental Journal*, vol. 225, no. 7, pp. 668–672.

Hale, J (2009) 'Suggested rules for non-transsexuals writing about transsexuals, transsexuality, transsexualism, or trans_', *www.sandystone.com*. Retrieved from: www.sandystone.com/hale.rules.html.

Hines, S. (2013) *Gender Diversity, Recognition and Citizenship*. Macmillan, London.

Humphrey, R. (2016) '"I think journalists sometimes forget that we're just people": Analysing the Effects of UK Trans Media Representation on Trans Audiences', *Gender Forum*, vol. 56, pp. 23–43.

Kazmer, M & Xie, B (2008) 'Qualitative interviewing in internet studies: Playing with the media, playing with the method', *Communication & Society*, vol. 11, no. 2, pp. 257–278.

Keller, H & Lee, S (2003) 'Ethical issues surrounding human participants research using the internet', *Ethics & Behavior*, vol. 13, no. 3, pp. 211–219.

Kermode, J & Trans Media Watch (2010) 'How transgender people experience the media: Conclusions from research November 2009-February 2010', *Trans Media Watch*, viewed 3 June 2014. Retrieved from: www.transmediawatch.org/evidence.html.

McDermott, E & Roen, K (2012) 'Youth on the virtual edge: Researching marginalized sexualities and genders online', *Qualitative Health Research*, vol. 22, no. 4, pp. 560–570.

McDermott, E, Roen, K, & Piela, A (2013) 'Hard-to-reach youth online: Methodological advances in self-harm research', *Sexuality Research and Social Policy*, vol. 10, pp. 125–134.

Morgan, E & Taylor, Y (2016) 'TransForming research practice: Collaborative foundations in trans and non-binary inclusive research', Retrieved from: www.scottishtrans.org www.scottishtrans.org/wp-content/uploads/2016/06/TransForming-Research-Practice-Collaborative-Foundations.pdf, pp. 1–14.

Namaste, VK (2000) *Invisible Lives: The Erasure of Transsexual and Transgendered People*. University of Chicago Press, Chicago.

National Health & Medical Research Council (2007) *National Statement on Ethical Conduct in Human Research*. NHMRC, Canberra. Retrieved from: www.nhmrc.gov.au/guidelines-publications/e72.

National Health & Medical Research Council (2015) *Australian Health Ethics Committee*. NHMRC, Canberra. Retrieved from: www.nhmrc.gov.au/about/nhmrc-committees/australian-health-ethics-committee-ahec.

Nic Giolla Easpaig, B & Fox, R (2017) 'Young people's experiences of negotiating healthcare services in relation to sexual and gender identities: A community-based approach to service improvement', *Psychology of Sexualities Review*, vol. 8, no. 1, pp. 39–52.

Oosterhuis, H (2000) *Stepchildren of Nature: Krafft-Ebing, Psychiatry, and the Making of Sexual Identity*. University of Chicago Press, Chicago.

Parker, I (2005) *Qualitative Psychology: Introducing Radical Research*. Open University, Berkshire.

Pawa, D, Firestone, R, Ratchasi, S, Dowling, O, Jittakoat, Y, Duke, A, & Mundy, G (2013) 'Reducing HIV risk among transgender women in Thailand: A quasi-experimental evaluation of the Sisters Program', *PloS One*, vol. 8, no. 10. doi:10.1371/journal.pone.0077113.

Research Councils United Kingdom (2013) *RCUK Policy and Guidelines on Governance of Good Research Conduct*, RCUK. Retrieved from: www.rcuk.ac.uk/documents/reviews/grc/rcukpolicyguidelinesgovernancegoodresearchconduct-pdf/.

Roen, K (2001) 'Transgender theory and embodiment: The risk of racial marginalisation', *Journal of Gender Studies*, vol. 10, no. 3, pp. 253–263.

Rooke, A (2010) 'Telling trans stories: (Un)doing the science of sex', in S Hines & T Sanger (eds.), *Transgender Identities: Towards a Social Analysis of Gender Diversity*. Routledge, Oxon.

Seymour, W (2001) 'In the flesh or online? Exploring qualitative research methodologies', *Qualitative Research*, vol. 1, no. 2, pp. 147–168.

Stieger, S & Göritz, A (2006) 'Using instant messaging for internet-based interviews', *Cyberpsychology & Behavior*, vol. 9, no. 5, pp. 552–559.

Taylor, C (2008) 'Counterproductive effects of parental consent in research involving LGBT-TIQ youth: International research ethics and a study of a transgender and two-spirit community in Canada', *Journal of LGBT Youth*, vol. 5, no. 3, pp. 34–56.

Varnhagen, CK, Gushta, M, Daniels, J, Peters, TC, Parmar, N, Law, D, Hirsch, R, Sadler Takach, B, & Johnson, T (2005) 'How informed is online informed consent?', *Ethics & Behavior*, vol. 5, no. 1, pp. 37–48.

13 Nonnormative ethics

The ensouled formation of trans

Mijke van der Drift

Introduction

This chapter explores a conceptualisation of trans practice through an engagement with Aristotelian ethical formation. This exploration aims to offer a grounding for a nonnormative ethics that centralises the body, while retaining space for the emergence of new forms of life. In recent years this discussion has played out around the concept of *somatechnics*. While somatechnical conceptions of ethical and political practice make space for the role of the body, the discussion seems hesitant about exploring emergent forms of life. I propose a conceptualisation of the body as propelling emergence in order to explore this potential. While Aristotelian ethics might be considered rather normative, it provides a platform for engagement with the work of Gloria Anzaldúa to show how Aristotelian understandings can be envisioned to operate within emergent nonnormative lives. Trans as ethical formation in this conceptualisation does not need to conform to current relational or classificatory codes, and enables generative understanding of emergent and indeterminate forms of life.

Somatechnics and indeterminate formation

Susan Stryker (2008) conceptualises trans as the activity of moving out of the normative confinements of gender. Consequently, A. Finn Enke emphasises trans is a politicised identity describing 'individuals by what they do' (Enke, 2012: 63), which indicates a focus on actions, rather than an epistemic account. This suggests that trans can be understood as a process of indeterminate activity, which would shift the emphasis from an epistemic angle onto a question concerning the possibility of indeterminate ethics. This trans activity has been conceived as 'the mutually generative relation between bodies of flesh, bodies and knowledge, and bodies politic – or, in short, as *somatechnics*' (Stryker and Sullivan, 2009: 50). Somatechnics is the contraction of *soma*, meaning body, and *techne*, which can be understood as skill, or craft, and is used to discuss modes of relation, for instance, in Aristotle and Plato. Somatechnical becoming can be understood as a contextual navigation of the body in action, knowledge about what a body is and how it can live, and the political tensions upon bodies. This would seem to keep the body confined to existing forms of life.

Elaine Laforteza argues that somatechnical bodily practices can constitute a colonial governmentality, while *techne* is conceptualised as a mode of inscription of imageries and norms on the body, to 'shape the body in accordance with [their] self-image' (Laforteza, 2015: 51). These methods 'simultaneously limit and constitute the potential to break normative boundaries', while possibilities surface to 'reconceptualise this attention on the other to concentrate instead on oneself', in ways that 'does not always induce resistant strategies but can counter relations of power' (Laforteza, 2015: 52). Marquis Bey emphasises such a movement by conceptualising trans as fugitivity. This places trans beyond known patterns, because 'hegemonic patterns disallow the very possibility of trans[gender]' (Bey, 2017: 277). Bey proposes trans as the 'undoing of stasis, of being-as-such, tied to a known and knowable fixed identity' (Bey, 2017: 287), and claims conceptual lineage to Heraclitus and Aristotle. Connecting with Aristotle opens trans up as an anti-static bodily practice signifying an 'ethic of genders' (Preciado, 2013: 322). I make the case that a nonnormative reading of Aristotelian ethical agency centralises the body without restricting agents to existing forms of life.

Aristotelian theory offers an ethics of self-constituting actions. Resonating with somatechnical theorising of the body, I propose conceptualising trans practice using an Aristotelian approach in order to unpack emerging forms of life from a generative body. Aristotle suggests the practice of ethics neither functions as 'inscription' (Sullivan, 2005), where inscription carries a passive connotation, nor as 'somatophobic practice' (Murray and Sullivan, 2012: 1), but as actions generative of a form of life. Furthermore, the Aristotelian concept of *logos* – the principle of organisation of the Soul – can be fruitfully redeployed to provide a generative space for indeterminate becoming, and suggests the possibility for an articulation of somatechnic relationality that goes beyond current patterns of domination and exploitation.

Formation logic: technes and logos

In Aristotelian ethics, the agent is conceptualised as an *ensouled* body navigating a normative and social environment. These navigations constitute the ensouled body through the formation of dispositions. Dispositions are action generating, and influence perception and practical reflection. By structuring perceptions and suggesting courses of action, dispositions make the world appear in a certain way in accordance with navigated patterns. This is summarised as *logos* – the form of a being. In Aristotelian ethical theory, these agential navigations are aimed at fitting in the form of life of the *polis*, the ancient city state Athens. These normative patterns of perception, reflection and action are known as virtues. However, the structure of action is not confined to the *polis*. And Aristotle's argument that patterns of action, *technes*, are not determinate like crafts,[1] leaves space for emergent relations and forms of life. I argue that this insight can extend the current conception of somatechnics, where there seems insufficient space for indeterminate emergence.

In the current articulation of somatechnics, *techne* functions a central element in the constitution of relations:

> [T]echnés [. . .] are techniques and/or orientations (ways of seeing, know-ing, feeling, moving, being, acting and so on) which are learned within a particular tradition or ontological context (are, in other words, situated), and function (often tacitly) to craft (un)becoming-with in very specific ways. Perception, then, is both the vehicle and effect of a particular situated somatechnics, an orientation to the world in which the I/eye is always-already co-implicated, co-indebted, co-responsible.
>
> (Sullivan, 2012: 302)

Nikki Sullivan explains *techne* as craft that functions to instil certain behav-iours, leading to specific modes of relation. *Techne* can be envisioned to func-tion comparatively similar to virtues: as recognisable patterns of interaction and social knowledge stored in dispositions. Contrasting a generative modus, Dinesh Wadiwel (2009) articulates how *techne* may be deployed against the functioning of the soul. This is illustrated by a discussion on the whipping of indigenous bodies as *techne*, which inscribes patterns of racialisation by contracting the soul to a bare state of functioning, and in permanent question. Whipping of white bodies does not function in a similar fashion, by coming with different demands on relation. In these conceptions, relations recoil as inscriptions upon bodies. However, for a conceptualisation of nonnormative genders, as well as non-normative ethics, it is important to explore an open content of *techne* to allow emergence of new forms.

Stryker's conceptualisation of trans as negation of normative patterns sug-gests an attendant first-person-authority, which Bettcher (2009) claims is a kind of ethical agency. This indicates for an ethical functioning the negation of present relations, while situating agential activity as central to trans becoming. Indeed, Paul Preciado argues for a negation of current modes of relationality in combination with an affirmative trans practice of shifting relational codes, *technes*, to new possibilities. Preciado's plea for an ethical practice suggests a somatechnics of indeterminate generation. Ethical generation beyond negation aligns with the transformation of *logos*. Here I propose *logos* to make space for trans as emergent becoming, which utilises a *techne* of negation, while retaining space for indeterminate directions of agency. This conceptualisation allows trans as an anti-static and continually emergent form.

Logos is the driving form of an interwoven tripartite soul, made up from nutrition, affects, imaginations, perceptions and reason.[2] This *ensouled* body nav-igates the environment through *dunamis*: the active powers of the soul (Charl-ton, 1987; Lee-Lampshire, 1992). Exercising one's *dunamis* results in dispositions. This conception of *dunamis* departs from a reading that centres faculties as pas-sive (Preciado, 2013). Conceptualising a body through active *dunamis* suggests the body is able to constitute itself in relation to the environment, and thus allowing mutual interaction (Lee-Lampshire, 1992). Changes in the operations of *dunamis* can be seen as the changes in the *ensouled* body. Reading the body as active is a preamble to conceptualising trans bodies as generative of forms of life, rather than disciplined by inscriptions.

The *logos* of the ensouled body is a constellation of dispositions. A disposition is a decision, reflection and perception-generating state of the soul.[3] Dispositions are formed upon already present capacities and sensibilities. These capacities indicate we are susceptible to certain things, like smells, are more introvert, or extrovert to a certain extent, see suffering faster or slower, and come with tendencies to respond in certain ways (Aristotle, 2002: 1105b20–1105b28). Dispositions form and direct some of those capacities: direct sensitivity in one direction or another, without subsuming all agents to the same possibilities. Dispositions taken together form a *logos:* an ensemble of affective, intuitive and perceptive structures supporting an agent-dependent practical truth. Changing *logos* means changing both the formation of the body as well as its mode of relations. Sylvia Wynter suggests humans are hybridly *logos* and *bios* (McKittrick, 2015). Wynter conceptualises humans as locally situated, with body and social formation intermixed, in order to make space for creativity in the conception of beings in relation, and suggests the humans need to move beyond current limiting categorisations (Wynter, 2003). *Bios* can be understood as the particular contexts the agent is immersed in, which influences *logos* while simultaneously extending beyond the agent. *Bios* and *logos* are not reducible to each other, and while *bios* finds expression in *technes*, these do not capture *logos*.

Aristotle describes agential ethical action as a navigation of contexts. These actions lead to the contextual formation of an Aristotelian agent, which alters perception, action and evaluation. This conceptualisation of agency as navigation resulting in *logos* means that an agent is also constituted by relations, external influences and dependency on others. This in turn implies that Aristotelian agency should not be thought of as predominantly directed to the world, but equally directed towards changing the dynamic of the *ensouled* body. Hereby, an Aristotelian conception of agents provides a complication for the model of successful agency, as emerged in late modernity (Lugones, 2003). The Aristotelian agent is not a manager of frictionless action, the primary initiator of causal effects in the world (Lugones, 2003), but instead navigates their surroundings through actions emerging from their *logos*. This means that change and becoming are in relation to one's surroundings, even if it is a negation of these surroundings. These actions will partly be imprecise and require improvisation – as dispositional operation changes over time. Within nonnormative ethics there is no *telos* leading to a stable end point. The ensouled body keeps changing form, relative to agential action.

Intermediacy

Aristotle describes the process of becoming as focusing within the action on 'the intermediate', which is inconclusively articulated as the perceived middle course between two rejected extremes (Aristotle, 2002: 1109a25). This model has attracted criticism for incoherence and inconsistency, and is also not followed through by Aristotle themself (Williams, 1985). However, the attraction for a trans somatechnical conception of formation lies in its structure of a double negation, with a single course of indeterminate affirmed action. This structure allows the negation of existing patterns of social relation, without falling into what Jose Esteban Muñoz describes as 'counter-identification', which ties agents to the norm (Muñoz, 1997: 83). The structure of double negation functions as *techne* of departure of existing relations, while the generative body enables indeterminate affirmation, that is, unknown action. This results in a *logos* that is not predetermined within existing relational structures.

Aristotle describes a plane of action from the perspective of the agent, where the options for action exceed adaption to existing patterns. Aristotle formulates this as follows: 'by the intermediate "relative to us" I mean the sort of thing that neither goes to excess or is deficient – and this is not one thing, nor is it the same for all' (Aristotle, 2002: 1106a32–1106a33). The intermediate is thus agent relative in both perspective and action, and can be seen as personal modulations of accepted forms. However, caution remains necessary; both the idea of the intermediate, as well as what might count as outlying or extreme, should be approached with care. The intermediate is not moderation. Moderation would suggest a single principle applicable to all actions. However, if dispositions are to count as intelligent, and structure perception and action, it is unclear how moderation would be the evaluative standard usable in that formation. Moderation would suggest blandness as principle (Williams, 1985: 36). In contrast, aiming for the intermediate provides leeway for agent relativity in navigating contexts.

The second problem is Aristotle's suggestion of continuous and divisible planes of action. To negotiate actions through such visualisation retains a conception of action confined to the modulation of existing forms. Indeterminate action is retained within existing patterns. This allows agency in formation, but limits the courses of action. When the structure of double negation and single and indeterminate affirmation is taken more broadly, space for the emergence of nonnormative forms of life is generated, as I argue subsequently with reference to the work of Gloria Anzaldúa.

Aristotle explains that dispositions as such need not be virtuous (Aristotle, 2002: 1108a11), which consequently means they need not match the Athenian *polis* – the city state. For a nonnormative ethics, the process of becoming for the ensouled body leads away from dominant, and thus normative, forms of life. Such a process of agential change has been offered by Gloria Anzaldúa (1987), using a model of agential action that is conceptualised tantalisingly close to the Aristotelian frame. I will let Anzaldúa's articulation function as a critique and, importantly, as an extension of Aristotle's model. While Aristotle and Anzaldúa have parallel views on agential action, their ends are readily described as normative versus nonnormative.[4]

Gloria Anzaldúa's theorisation of intermediacy dismantles the idea that a coherent plane of action is necessary for agential ethics. Anzaldúa refigures actions as moving in-between two different and self-consistent dominant norms. Hereby, agential actions aim at the generation of a new form of life. This form emerges through the movement between contrasting demands, by uprooting dualistic thinking. Anzaldúa suggests the possibility of negating two separate clusters of norms. The resultant plane of action can thus be inconsistent and incoherent, turning actions into an expression of an agentially perceived intermediate, instead of a socially coherent, interlocking plane of action as in the Aristotelian model. In short, Anzaldúa offers the possibility of navigating away from a binary. This shifts the model of double negation and indeterminate affirmation towards emergent forms of life.

Anzaldúa portrays action as a navigation of multiple possibilities:

> [. . .] but it is not enough to stand on the opposite border [. . .] at some point on our way to a new consciousness, we will have to leave the opposite bank, [. . .] so that we are on both shores at once [. . .] or we decide to disengage with the dominant culture [. . .] and cross the border into a new and separate territory [. . .] or we might go another route. The possibilities are numerous once we decide to act and not react.
>
> (Anzaldúa, 1987: 100)

Within action the interstice can take many different forms and is not so clear-cut as Aristotle suggests, with the account of coherently interlocking forms of the good in the Athenian *polis*. Furthermore, Anzaldúa emphasises that actions are generative of outcomes beyond the negated normative clusters. It is important, however, not to see the metaphor of 'border crossing' as a new call for trans travel metaphors, nor evocative of imageries of invading nation states. Anzaldúa writes from a chicana experience of borderlands, which contrasts the automatically assumed connection between 'home' and 'travel' that can be found in transnormative accounts, which Nael Bhanji cogently critiques (2012). Migration is a common trans practice (Cotten, 2012), but that is not at stake in this reconceptualisation. Muñoz's concept of *disidentification* can be understood as comparative strategy, drawing on a double negation, but with a more limited scope: 'Disidentification [. . .] is a reformatting of self within the social, a third term that resists the binary of identification and counteridentification' (Muñoz, 1997: 83). Rather than proposing a new culture, Muñoz suggests disidentification remains within the social. The structure of action remains within a similar format, while a question to the extent of change lingers. Where Anzaldúa aims far and thus connects more easily to the Aristotelian scope, Muñoz keeps change closer to the immediate surroundings as, perhaps, a navigational tactic.

Anzaldúa's and Muñoz's theorisations thus negate the idea that pre-established normative patterns are determinants of action, and thereby offer an escape out of disciplinary formation. This implies that agents not only adapt or aspire to follow culture, and thereby inscribe norms, but that agents also *generate* forms. Importantly, this agential agency is conceived as a navigation of the *soma*: 'In our flesh, (r)evolution works out the clash of cultures' (Anzaldúa, 1987: 103).

This generation of a new form of life unfolds in Anzaldúa's work as the double negation of two dominant forms and the consequent movement in-between. Here the in-between is an indeterminate space, and not – as in Aristotle – a merely non-calculable space approachable through agential *techne*. Through the imagery Anzaldúa offers, *techne* can be conjured up to suit the possibilities and demands for action away from current forms of life.

Agential generation takes place over time – as the process of formation relies not only on the negation of dominant patterns, but also on formative change centred within the action: 'Awareness of our situation must come before inner changes, which must come before changes in society' (Anzaldúa, 1987: 109). Negation is therefore a situated activity, which connects the agent with their surroundings, and takes place over time. The negation of normative surroundings leads to new forms of life. Williams' conceptualisation of dispositional change explains this process: 'if the ethical life [...] is to be effectively criticized and changed, then it can only be so in ways that can be understood as appropriately modifying the dispositions that we have' (Williams, 2006: 75).

Since new forms of life are indeterminate, actions are not utopian-mimetic aspirations, but emergent within situated means, which will indicate ends. In this sense, the means determine the ends.[5] Nonnormative action-navigation constitutes *telos* (end) as an emergent vector, gesturing beyond the immediate action towards an imagined, imaginary or, as in Anzaldúa, a mythological end (1987: 101). Over time this vector shifts, suggesting new futures as a result of continued change. Nonnormative vectors remain emergent unfoldings in the present as they materialise within negations of coherent normative ends.

Aristotelian ethical theory therefore offers underlying principles of action that – when directed away from the *polis* – make a strong claim about the constitution and potential for change of bodies, and the attendant effects on perception, action initiation and practical reflection. Anzaldúa further enables the unfolding of Aristotelian theory towards a nonnormative reading. My argument has indicated how *ensouled* bodily change is constituted, suggesting a conceptualisation for reading trans as formation beyond binaries. I now extend arguments for a disruption of the social reproduction of normative forms of life. These forms are currently racist, colonialist and not trans friendly (Haritaworn, 2015; Bhanji, 2012; Raha, 2017; European Union Agency for Fundamental Rights, 2014). I outline another layer of agential change and discuss the shifting of practical truth as means to disrupt the hold of confining normativities.

Practical truth and ensouled action

New forms of life emerge with altered perspectives as theorised within the Anzaldúan-Aristotelian account of action. Sarah Broadie emphasises that within Aristotelian action theory there is truth expressed in a course of action:

> And it is important for [Aristotle] to speak of *truth* in this connection, not merely of the *good, right,* or *appropriate.*
>
> (Broadie, 1991: 224)[6]

Broadie's assertion creates space for an understanding of emergent practice that goes beyond defying normative standards. While normative patterns are expressed as evaluative standards, the added notion of practical truth can suggest a further critical approach. Recalling Anzaldúa, this means that agents' defiance of normativity proclaims a veridical state of the world. Nonnormative agents thus make a truth claim in their constitution of new forms of life.

This notion of practical truth signifies – in epistemic terms – the correctness of an assertion: that is, it signifies that the way that the world is *spoken about* is the way the world *is*. In ethical practice, this analogously indicates that the way the world is acted in, is the way the action *indicates how the world is true from my being active*.[7] This truth is a shift from 'know that' – the object-oriented approach and the categorical verity of states of affairs – to 'know how': the action-oriented verity of agents in flux.[8] The agents are in flux, because their perspective changes with the formation of their *logos*. Good, right and appropriate are contextual evaluations, which a word like 'truth' aims to overcome. Truth fixes flux, and introduces a grounding measure in a world that will otherwise be solely structured around agential vectors and multiplicities of ensouled formation. Practical truth can form the ground against the demands of logistics – the normative ordering of frictionless flow (Harney and Moten, 2013; Cowen, 2014).

While norms encapsulate actions in evaluations of goodness or appropriateness,[9] truth-values bypass the normative, expressing an evaluation stretching beyond the current state of affairs. Nonnormative truth stakes a para-ontological claim, disrupting contingent forms (Bey, 2017). Hereby, a notion of the good changes from a stable valuation of lives, or states of affairs, into a relative appraisal of changing circumstances with indetermined agents. The good as aspirational standard changes into an indicator of directedness of specific agents: as vector. Consequently, ethical goodness moves away from values to vectors, and forms lose stability within indeterminacy of lives. Nonnormative ethics is the formalisation of changing agential *logos*. This *logos* may be, as Bey argues, fugitive when approached as epistemic question (Bey, 2017).

The intermediate in transsomatechnical action is thus the expression of both vector and verity, of good and truth, two categories that lost their normative ontological stability and have instead gained status as a temporal assertion of limited scope. The practical truth claim thus defies the claim that the world is stable and that a single ordering principle can be brought to bear on all agents. Nonnormative ethics claims that agents live in different realities: realities shaped by perceptions structured in dispositions emerging from nonnormative courses of action. Instead of inscribing norms upon bodies, *transsomatechnical* change re-emerges as the formation of new *ensouled* truth, creating different forms of life. *Somatechnical* formation is thus not only a reshaping of the *ensouled body*, directing the energy towards different relationality, but also entails a strategy for overturning prevalent societal ethical codings (cf. Wynter, 2003; Williams, 2006). Nonnormative ethics indicates a strategy for understanding the emergence of new agential worlds (cf. Lugones, 2003, 2005).

The temporal *dunamic* unfoldings of agents as formative of situated *logos* destabilises ideas of linearity and normative ordering according to dominant patternings. Trans formation can thus be understood as an opening, unfolding, shifting situational practice, leading to new localised epistemologies. Agential *transomatechnical* practice aligns *dunamis* differently, leading to a changing *ensouled* body with different praxis. Agential navigation is not so much a travel metaphor standing in for 'transition', but an indicator about engaging with space that leads to shifting dynamics (Lugones, 2003: 216). Navigation is the daily activity of working against different forces pressing the agent in prescripted directions, demanding fragmentation, piecing and adaption (Puar, 2015; Raha, 2017).

Ethics and the possibility of futurity

Bodily change – as central to ethical and epistemic change – features strongly in Octavia Butler's work. Butler brilliantly offers imageries of the necessity of bodily change, in order to come to a renewed relation to the world (eg. Butler, 1987, 1988, 1989). Parallel to Anzaldúa's (1987) reading of the necessity of changing the body through the flesh, Butler unfolds these somatechnical developments as the generation of new worlds, through an oeuvre that suggests the simultaneity of apocalypse and new dawns enabled through bodily change (cf. van der Drift, 2018). Likewise, Anzaldúan-Aristotelian double negation in agential interaction is generative of newly ensouled forms of life, while not reproducing current dominant fields of power. Ending the world is as much part of shifting *logos* as the generation of new forms of life through dynamic bodily change.

Lisa Duggan likewise warns not to conflate *forming* oneself with *conforming* oneself:

> When I think about hope, I set it alongside happiness and optimism, which I immediately associate with race and class privilege, with imperial hubris, with gender and sexual conventions, with maldistributed forms of security both national and personal. They can operate as the affective reward for conformity, the privatized emotional bonus for the right kind of investments in the family, private property and the state.
>
> (Duggan and Muñoz, 2009: 276)

For nonnormative agents the idea of happiness and the possibility of normative futurity functions to confine and exclude (Ahmed, 2010). However, by refusing an ethic, new forms of life come to pass. Normative standards are expressive and constitutive of the exclusions that create nonnormativity in the first place.

A nonnormative ethic is consequently a form of life – a structure of shared agential *logos* – that exists outside of the dominant standard. Muñoz elaborates:

> Feeling revolutionary opens up the space to imagine a collective escape, an exodus, a "going-off script" together. [. . .] It is not about announcing the way things ought to be, but, instead, imagining what things could be.
>
> (Duggan and Muñoz, 2009: 278)

The space that is opened up by going off-script is more than imaginative, however. Ethical futurity as indeterminate bodily formation means that ending the world and generating new indeterminate forms go together. Nonnormative agents have already departed from the normative world, in a collective escape.

Conclusion

The nonnormative Anzaldúan-Aristotelian agent can be read in line with Stryker's definition of trans as 'the movement across a socially imposed boundary away from an unchosen starting place – rather than any particular destination or mode of transition' (Stryker, 2008: 1). This reading of agential formation does not posit unquestioned belonging to an overarching category, as it situates agents contextually. This in turn claims space to include a wider range of social forces, privileges and pressures, which enables an understanding of difference and overlaps between agents, without subsuming agents into a single form of being.

I have offered a reading of trans through the double negation and indeterminate affirmation in action as combined Anzaldúan-Aristotelian practice. This articulation of trans agency and formation does not make a claim to a perpetual and fetishistic fluidity (Ahmed, 2004: 151), but instead creates space for situatedness and a relation to existing forms of life as an anti-static ethics. By articulating the *ensouled* body as generative, space is created for reading the body as living through situated forms, which are beyond current social relations.

Furthermore, what my reading of trans doesn't try to achieve is an argument for the space in-between or interstice, as a zone of indeterminacy that figures either as hope or horror. My reading of Aristotle suggests an understanding of *techne* with wider implications than offered by Sullivan. I agree that somatechnics is the 'dynamic means in and through which corporealities are crafted' (Sullivan and Murray, 2011: vi); I have followed somatechnics as an attentive relationship of the ensouled body to its surroundings. This builds upon the insights of Pugliese and Stryker, who see somatechnics as a:

> Re-evaluation and reframing of ethics of the proper regard for the interrelationship between other, self, and world. It raises anew the hoary questions of agency and instrumental will, of freedom and determination.
>
> (Pugliese and Stryker, 2009: 2)

Crucially I have thus made the case that a nonnormative agent does not follow scripts of strict disciplinary formation and existing relation, but instead unfolds a form through open-ended aims, as a reframing of ethical possibility.

Intermediate spaces are where forms emerge from – in the Anzaldúan reading these are new cultures; in the Aristotelian reading they are agential actions that aim to match the going form of life of the *polis*. This is important, as not every emergence is new, radical or nonnormative, as Snorton and Haritaworn contend (2013). A liberal body politic might not mind difference, as long as the current order remains preserved. I have argued for an Anzaldúan-Aristotelian approach that suggests somatechnical strategy at the level of the agent, through actions consisting of a (minimally) double negation, implying a new indeterminate affirmation. This tripartite functioning of the agent enables a negation of the current social hierarchical ordering, ending the current order of the world to generate new futures.

Acknowledgements

I would like to express my gratitude to Deborah Lynn Steinberg for her belief in my work, and I wish we would have known each other better. A special thanks goes to Ruth Pearce for editorial patience and commitment. I would like to thank Igi Moon for the invitation to speak at the Warwick Seminars *The Emergence of Trans★*, an invitation made possible by Greygory Vass. Various anonymous peer reviewers have offered very helpful comments; many thanks too. Also I would like to thank Shamira A. Meghani and Sebastian De Line for comments on (very) early drafts of this chapter. Lastly, my thanks go to Chryssy Hunter and Nat Raha whose support, deep thinking and discussion have made great impact on my work.

Notes

1 Aristotle makes the argument that the clarity of ends in crafts makes it possible to evaluate them – for instance, if someone is a good lute player, convincing orator or bad builder. All these outcomes need practice. While virtues also need action, these actions do not come with the same level of clarity. Aristotle contrasts with Plato in this matter, who thought that *technes* of relation could be of a more scientific nature.
2 I choose to read *logos* as form, rather than principle, as form can both comprise functional and non-functional parts (cf. Aristotle and Hamlyn, 1968: 79 & 403a24).
3 *anima*: that what moves by itself
4 It might be worthwhile to recall here that Aristotle was an immigrant in Athens. Socrates (the mentor of Plato, who in turn taught of Aristotle) refused to go into exile after what was essentially a censorship trial, because as immigrant he would have even less power of speech (Plato, 2010). Aristotle can be conceived as not being able to speak outside the going norm, thus the principles of action that are put forth do not indicate a necessity of normative becoming.
5 Interestingly, this suggests that strategies change the way one views ends. This can function as an explanation for why certain collectives confuse disagreement over strategies with aiming at different ends.

6 The full argument is more complicated; I offer an examination of this elsewhere – as it is beyond the scope of this chapter.
7 I owe thanks here to Martin Stokhof, who set me on this path after a discussion at the University of Amsterdam. After giving a definition of 'know that', Martin looked pleasantly surprised when I asked to give a definition of 'know how' and admitted that they never thought about that.
8 Katherine McKitrrick recently made the case at Duke's Eleventh Annual Feminist Theory Workshop that 'know where' deserves further emphasis as well.
9 But do not forget the Wobbly and later surrealist T-Bone Slim's statement, 'wherever you find injustice the proper form of politeness is attack' (Roediger, 1994: 129), which gives an alternative reading of the notion of the appropriate, instead of a knee-jerk normativity.

References

Ahmed, Sara. (2004). *The Cultural Politics of Emotion*. Edinburgh: Edinburgh University Press.
Ahmed, Sara. (2010). *The Promise of Happiness*. Durham, NC: Duke University Press.
Anzaldúa, Gloria. (1987). *Borderlands/La Frontera*. San Francisco: Aunt Lute Books.
Aristotle. (2002). *Nicomachean Ethics*. Translated by Christopher Rowe. Oxford and New York: Oxford University Press.
Aristotle, and Hamlyn, D.W. (1968). *De Anima Books II, III*. Oxford: Oxford Clarenden Press.
Bey, Marquis. (2017). 'The Trans*-Ness of Blackness, the Blackness of Trans*-Ness'. *TSQ: Transgender Studies Quarterly* 4 (2): 275–295. https://doi.org/10.1215/23289252-3815069.
Bhanji, N. (2012). 'Trans/Scriptions. Homing Desires, (Trans) Sexual Citizenship and Racialized Bodies'. In *Transgender Migrations. The Bodies, Borders, and Politics of Transition*. New York y Londres: Routledge, 157–175.
Broadie, S. (1991). *Ethics With Aristotle*. Oxford: Oxford University Press.
Butler, O. (1987). *Dawn. Xenogenesis, I*. London: VGSF.
Butler, O. (1988). *Adulthood Rites. Xenogenesis, II*. London: VGSF.
Butler, O. (1989). *Imago. Xenogenesis, III*. London: VGSF.
Charlton, W. (1987). 'Aristotelian Powers'. *Phronesis* 32 (3): 277–289.
Cotten, T.T. (2012). *Transgender Migrations: The Bodies, Borders, and Politics of Transition*. New York and London: Routledge.
Cowen, D. (2014). *The Deadly Life of Logistics*. Minneapolis and London: University of Minnesota Press.
Drift, M.v.d. (2018). 'Radical Romanticism, Violent Cuteness, and the Destruction of the World'. *Journal of Aesthetics and Culture* 10 (3).
Duggan, L., and Muñoz, J.E. (2009). 'Hope and Hopelessness: A Dialogue'. *Women & Performance: A Journal of Feminist Theory* 19 (2): 275–283.
Enke, A.F. (2012). 'The Education of Little Cis'. In: Enke, A.F. (ed) *Transfeminist Perspectives in and beyond Transgender and Gender Studies*. Philadelphia: Temple University Press, 60–77.
European Union Agency for Fundamental Rights. (2014). 'Being Trans in the European Union'. https://fra.europa.eu/sites/default/files/fra-2014-being-trans-eu-comparative_en.pdf.
Haritaworn, J. (2015). *Queer Lovers and Hateful Others*. London: Pluto Press.
Harney, S., and Moten, F. (2013). *The Undercommons: Fugitive Planning and Black Study*. New York: Minor Compositions.
Laforteza, E.M.C. (2015). *The Somatechnics of Whiteness and Race: Colonialism and Mestiza Privilege*. Aldershot: Ashgate.
Lee-Lampshire, W. (1992). 'Telos and the Unity of Psychology: Aristotle's "de Anima" II 3–4'. *Apeiron* 25 (1): 27–48.

Lugones, M. (2003). *Pilgrimages/Peregrinajes: Theorizing Coalition against Multiple Oppressions*. Lanham, MD: Rowman & Littlefield Publishers.

Lugones, M. (2005). 'From within Germinative Stasis: Creating Active Subjectivity, Resistant Agency'. In *EntreMundos/AmongWorlds*. Berlin: Springer, 85–99.

McKittrick, K. (2015). *Sylvia Wynter: On Human Being as Praxis*. Durham, NC: Duke University Press.

Muñoz, J.E. (1997). '" The White to Be Angry": Vaginal Davis's Terrorist Drag'. *Social Text*, (52/53): 81–103.

Murray, S., and Sullivan, N. (2012). *Somatechnics: Queering the Technologisation of Bodies*. Farnham: Ashgate Publishing, Ltd.

Plato. (2010). *The Last Days of Socrates*. London, UK: Penguin.

Preciado, B. (2013). *Testo Junkie: Sex, Drugs and Biopolitics in the Pharmacopornographic Era*. New York: The Feminist Press Cuny.

Puar, J.K. (2015). 'Bodies with New Organs: Becoming Trans, Becoming Disabled'. *Social Text* 33 (3 124): 45–73.

Pugliese, J., and Stryker, S. (2009). 'The Somatechnics of Race and Whiteness'. *Social Semiotics* 19 (1): 1–8.

Raha, N. (2017). 'Transfeminine Brokenness, Radical Transfeminism'. *South Atlantic Quarterly* 116 (3).

Roediger, D.R. (1994). *Towards the Abolition of Whiteness: Essays on Race, Politics, and Working Class History*. London and New York: Verso.

Snorton, C.R., and Haritaworn, J. (2013). 'Trans Necropolitics: A Transnational Reflection on Violence, Death, and the Trans of Color Afterlife'. In: Stryker, S. and Aizura, A. (eds) *The Transgender Studies Reader 2*, 66–75.

Stryker, S. (2008). *Transgender History*. Berkeley, CA: Avalon Publishing Group.

Stryker, S., and Sullivan, N. (2009). 'King's Member, Queen's Body: Transsexual Surgery, Self-Demand Amputation and the Somatechnics of Sovereign Power'. In *Somatechnics: Queering the Technologisation of Bodies*. Farnham: Ashgate Publishing, Ltd.

Sullivan, N. (2005). 'Somatechnics, or, the Social Inscription of Bodies and Selves'. *Australian Feminist Studies* 20 (48): 363–366.

Sullivan, N. (2012). 'The Somatechnics of Perception and the Matter of the Non/Human: A Critical Response to the New Materialism'. *European Journal of Women's Studies* 19 (3): 299–313.

Sullivan, N. and Murray, S. (2011). 'Editorial'. *Somatechnics* 1 (1): v–vii.

Wadiwel, D.J. (2009) 'Thick hides: whipping, biopolitics and the white soul of power'. *Social Semiotics* 19 (1): 47–57.

Williams, B. (1985). *Ethics and the Limits of Philosophy*. London: Routledge.

Williams, B. (2006). *Philosophy as a Humanistic Discipline*. Princeton, NJ: Princeton University Press.

Wynter, S. (2003). 'Unsettling the Coloniality of Being/Power/Truth/Freedom: Towards the Human, after Man, Its Overrepresentation – An Argument'. *CR: The New Centennial Review* 3 (3): 257–337.

14 A genealogy of genealogies – retheorising gender and sexuality

The emergence of 'trans' (ESRC seminar series 2012–2014)

Igi Moon

In the autumn of 2011, Deborah Lynn Steinberg, Ruth Pearce and I worked through the night to submit a seminar series grant application to the Economic and Social Research Council (ESRC). We were thankful for the opportunity to offer the seminars once we heard we had been awarded the grant. We believed it was time to provide an opportunity for people to congregate in a safe(r) space (albeit a space that is institutional and prized for its pedagogy), where ideas about trans theory and practice could be shaped and re-shaped – perhaps even produce the starting point for a trans-positive epistemological framework.

We decided that this exploration of a trans-potential to broaden gender and sexuality studies could best be offered through a series of open events, with attendees invited from across the UK to join us in a cross-disciplinary discussion about the emergence of 'trans'. Months of preparation then took hold as we negotiated endless discussions around how to budget for and theme the seminars, how we would publicise them, where they would be held, how we could bring together activists, academics and lay people and how we might support them in feeling they could openly listen and talk to and with one another. The resulting four seminars each took a key thematic trajectory, focusing respectively on everyday lives, clinical and therapeutic contexts, popular discourse and gender and sexuality theory. The question of 'trans' provided both a focal point and locus for wider explorations of normative and alternative practices, identifications, body-ethical/bioethical understandings, health, rights, politics and welfare issues on the terrain of gender and sexuality.

We aimed to bring together clinical and psychotherapeutic practitioners and patient groups with educators, academic researchers and community groups and activists. The emphasis on cross-disciplinary conversation arose from a desire to do justice to the material realities of trans experience as well as implications for theory and therapeutic practice. A mix of determination, skill and logistics led us to think that between November 2012 and November 2014 we could draw people together to explore a range of social imaginaries, occupy gendered and sexual spaces, reveal social stories of gender plurality – maybe even re-cognise or literally trans-form personal and intimate stories of the self so that we may take these out into the wider world and let these ideas unfold and possibly democratise desire.

The series focused on a number of interlinked questions:

- To what degree does 'trans' reconfigure everyday lives or herald new normativities?
  - What is the meaning of normativity as shaped by and through cisgender discourse?
  - To what degree does 'trans' represent a 'post-closet' epistemology?
  - What and how will knowledge shape and be shaped by 'trans'?
  - How does the emergence of 'trans' challenge, develop or extend dominant understandings of gender and sexuality?
- What is the impact of 'trans' discourse on questions of rights, discrimination and citizenship, health and welfare, education and popular common sense?
- What challenges do 'trans' identities present for clinical and therapeutic practice, for gender and sexuality theory and for everyday articulations of identity and intersubjective and communal connection?

I have listed these questions as they appeared on the outline we disseminated to attendees because they offer food for thought. They help us begin the search to trans-form meanings about the body, psyche and affect, extending and expanding meanings. They ask us to drill down into the questions surrounding trans-ness as phenomenon, as a salient case study of wider shifts in gender and sexuality politics and discourse, and as a site of convergence and divergence, involving a spectrum of professional, academic and everyday experiences, stakeholders and practices.

Seminar structure

We decided that the following four seminars would address themes that we believed were emerging in the confines of everyday life, whether recognised or not. We chose these areas as sites of contestation and shifting paradigms, with implications for trans identities and repertoires of practice.

To discuss the topics, we held seminars in an open and engaging structure. A number of the seminars were filmed (thanks to the awesome Alex Drummond for her diligence and kind offer to film) and the seminars can be viewed at www.transseminars.com.

Each seminar lasted a full day, with various breaks and lunch provided. We arranged overnight accommodation for those travelling long distance, and travel bursaries for attendees on low incomes. For each event we recruited three to four speakers, with up to 50 attendees from across the UK. Each speaker was followed by a carousel-sharing experience – usually involving conversation at four to six large, circular tables, with up to eight attendees and a rapporteur per table. Reflections on the topic would be fed back to the larger group by each rapporteur after we had explored the issue for approximately 30 to 40 minutes. With this process taking place after each presentation, we had a range of excellent ideas and questions produced by everyone present in response to the speakers. Our final seminar also enabled a number of people to re-think how they presented publicly via the symbolic and imagined meanings of haircuts, and how this might reflect (quite literal) trust and negotiation. The fabulous Greygory and Felix from Open Barbers offered their beautiful skills, cutting hair throughout the day in a makeshift salon following a talk in the morning. We ended the evening with an arranged screening of the beautiful film *Tom/Trans/Thai* by Jai Arune Ravine; this was followed by an impromptu session in which attendees took turns using YouTube and Vimeo to share other films that they were aware of or had been involved in making.

This open, collaborative, discursive approach enables a trans imaginary of possible futures, in which ideas may be contested and negotiated. I discuss these ideas in more detail later in this chapter, but first outline the seminars, which provide some insight into the development of our thoughts and the emergence of this book's structure.

Seminar 1: 'Trans' genealogies: shifting paradigms and practice in clinical and therapeutic contexts

This seminar focused on the implications of 'trans' identifications and repertoires for two key arenas of professional practice: clinical and psychotherapeutic. The seminar aimed to promote a conversation among clinical, bioethical and cultural perspectives to consider a range of themes, including: narratives of 'authenticity' that guide clinical protocols, psychotherapeutic approaches and patient self-identifications; 'pathways of care' surrounding interventions and management of 'trans' bodies; professional discourses (educational, diagnostic) and clinical and practice protocols vis a vis patient or client experience; and 'alternative' therapeutic discourses and the 'trans' self-help context.

Speakers: **James Morton**, '"Help or harm"? Trans people's experiences of health services and the impact on their mental health'; **Y Gavriel Ansara**, 'From "affirmation" to liberation: The cisgenderism framework as a new model for clinical and psychotherapeutic practice'; **Alex Drummond**, 'Knowing the unknown: Therapeutic issues in working with queer identities'; **Michelle Bridgman**, 'From pathology to identity: The emergence of transgender and the meaning for clients'.

Seminar 2: 'Trans' as everyday culture: social networks, social movements, everyday lives and everyday repertoires

This seminar focused on the emergence of 'trans' social networks, social movements and citizenship struggles. It explored the impact of digital technology and web-based resources on gender and sexuality activism and new identifications. The seminar explored emergent communal, popular and 'everyday' repertoires of body, identity, feeling and experience heralded by (but not limited to) the emergence of 'trans' repertoires. Key themes included digital technology and social networking, transformations in everyday vernaculars of gender and sexuality, everyday lives and 'on the ground' experiences.

Speakers: **Surya Monro, '**Theorising gender diversity: Current trans, future directions'; **Natacha Kennedy,** 'Prisoners of lexicon:Young trans people and trans children:A social activity analysis'; **Ruth Pearce and Kirsty Lohman,** 'Trans music isn't: De/constructing DIY identities'; **Freiya Benson, '**Genderfork:True stories from the edge of gender identity'.

Seminar 3: 'Trans' in popular representation

This seminar explored the spectacular, social semiotic, aesthetic and visual repertoires of 'trans'. Focusing on 'trans' as a cross-media phenomenon involving traditional and new media from film and television to web-based media to photography to performance art, the seminar considered the popular and commonsense dimensions of 'trans'. It aimed to extend the question of 'technologies of the body' set out in the first seminar to consider the intersectionalities of medical, therapeutic and popular cultures.

Speakers: **Kat Gupta, '**Response and responsibility: Mainstream media and Lucy Meadows';**Lee Gale,'**Widening the depth of field:Trans★ lives behind the lens'; **Del LaGrace Volcano,** 'Trans★Inter★ bodies that queer: art as activism'.

Seminar 4: After Kinsey: (Re)theorising sexuality and gender in a 'post-closet' context

This concluding seminar considered the epistemic, intersubjective and affective implications of 'trans' culture, discourse and practice. It asked how, to what degree and in what terms the emergence of 'trans' might challenge conceptual norms across different cultural sites from professional to popular to everyday practice. What challenges do the epistemic underpinnings of 'trans' herald for sexuality and gender studies? Does 'trans' represent a 'post-closet' epistemology? Does it represent an emergent meta-narrative and, in its wake, a transformed 'post Kinsey' understanding of gender, sexuality, bodies and experience?

Speakers: **Zowie Davy, '**Kinsey's misused legacy: Moving on from continuums'; **Chryssy Hunter,** 'Sex and gender, sex/gender or sexgender: A politics of embodiment and identity in a neoliberal age'; **Kat Gupta,** '"Her only crime was to be different": Mainstream media and Lucy Meadows in a post-Leveson context'; **Mijke van der Drift,** 'Trans★as the pursuit of Eudaimonia'; **Greygory Vass, '**Open Barbers'.

Rapporteur feedback

For every seminar we had a group of rapporteurs, who included the seminar organisers as well as invited volunteers. Each rapporteur was asked to take notes as they listened to 'their' table, managing the interactions and exchanges and taking note of the core debates and concerns that arose. Sometimes these appeared controversial, but were often shown to be issues that people were grappling with because they had come along with little or no knowledge about specifically trans issues but did have familiarity with the wider topic area. On other occasions, people with plenty of everyday of experience of living transness and exceptional knowledge of trans social life wanted to share their ideas with non-trans attendees, and explore how their social knowledge and lived experiences might re-shape and reorganise spaces so that trans people could safely attend.

The extensive reflections and questions that follow next are representative of the generosity of ideas emergent from the group discussions, shared among activists, academics, practitioners and clinicians. The listed categories aggregate concepts, positions and viewpoints from across the seminar series. These are shared with you in turn, so that you may find inspiration to further develop trans research and theory, and empower trans perspectives and knowledge, so that together we may cultivate a trans epistemology.

The intelligibility of trans

There are differing ideas about the meaning(s) of 'trans', as well as related concepts such as 'transition'; this is relevant to practitioners as well as trans people. Ideas that were presented and that I am asking you to now think about, included:

- The limitations imposed upon bodies and how this is different for those named from birth as 'boy' or 'girl'. We considered the meanings of 'tomboy' for a child and how later these meanings might surface for an adult. How can these limitations and meanings be explored in relation to particular examples (e.g. space assigned to those named as tomboy), and if/how people named as such might legitimately organise their own space – as children and as adults?
- Acceptance by society. For example, how does the idea of 'actualisation' or 'gender self-determination' link to ideas of social acceptability and bodily acceptance?
- Notions of therapist (psychologist, psychotherapist, counsellor) as activist. How is this position negotiated if activists are 'pathologised' in some way – for example, positioned as inherently militant, as troublemakers – even in the confines of the workspace? How does this sit alongside the role and meaning of being a therapist?

- Does distress link to experiences of isolation and alienation for trans and non-binary people who are excluded from a paradigm of normativity? Does the confidence to self-define as trans and/or non-binary link to 'fitting' within a paradigm (e.g. transsexual, genderqueer)? How might this happen, and who shapes a paradigm?
- How do we negotiate meaning when the issue under discussion (trans and non-binary bodies, identities and experiences) is already problematised? How does language change with regard to cognition, semiotics and such forth, and what are the implications? What is the language of practitioners, researchers and medical practitioners within the arena of trans-ness?
- What is dysphoria? Can we talk separately about, for example, affective dysphoria, cognitive dysphoria, social dysphoria? How do these link? Is the emergence of the language of dysphoria part of a wider paradigmatic social shift linked to emergence of trans?

Knowledge within services

With patients, researchers, therapists and health-care practitioners from gender identity clinics in conversation, questions and ideas that emerged in relation to knowledge within therapeutic, clinical and support services included:

- What is meant by practitioner 'knowledge', and does this imply a 'privacy' of knowledge? How do practitioners shape knowledge about clients/patients who are trans and non-binary, and what do they edit for supervision? What happens in supervision sessions?
- Discussion of gender and sexual diversity in training courses is limited and there is often no response to questions asked about 'why' trans and non-binary issues are not recognised or included. What are the expectations and needs that guide clients in therapy compared with the provision for cis clients?
- The trans community is a marginal community, and therapists are not realising that they don't know about trans and non-binary issues – this has implications for the evaluation of health care.
- Trans knowledge is not encoded into training and therefore not into thinking.
- Therapists/practitioners are disequipped – for example, rape crisis centres may have little or no trans provision; discussions around gender and gendered violence are aimed primarily at cis women – what about trans women and trans bodies?
- Rape crisis centres are literally 'in transition' as they navigate the emergence of trans. This can impact on mental and physical health needs if people are referred elsewhere.
- Gender clinic 'pathways' oriented towards a notion that identity is ideally fixed (as male or female) are problematic – how is identity regulated in this way? And why?

- How is normality acceptable and accepted? Is normality honest? Is there a culture of ignorance in gender services about the broader meanings of 'trans'?
- There are issues about how theoretical assumptions are framed within services. If the body is positioned within a biological (rather than social) framework, how does this impact on service users and practitioners?

The imperatives of dysphoria

In this section, there is a focus on the imperatives at play with regard to how dysphoria intersects with power, negotiation and meaning. How is permission negotiated? If pathologising frameworks (i.e. trans as requiring a diagnosis for mental health in order to access hormones/surgery) are shaping meanings for dysphoria, then does this tell us more about the relationship to society rather than self? For example, if cosmetic surgery is considered an imperative that is not dysphoric, then why does trans have assigned to its status a 'dysphoric' imperative?

- Subjectivity vis a vis 'one body' as either 'male' or 'female' is normalised through cis-genderism. Are there many versions of subjectivity at play in trans/non-binary experiences, and what does this mean for the meaning of subjectivity? Self? Authenticity?
- Is there a cisgender experience of dysphoria? Questions regarding the body arise in relation to breast augmentation and chest reconstruction, as well as uses of hormone replacement therapy.
- Is there a social dysphoria as well as a body dysphoria? Do clinicians expect or desire an innate meaning rather than a social meaning? By using the voice of authority, do clinicians procure the trans body as demonstrating the authenticity of a 'real' cisgender body?
- Are feelings about the body mediated by social/cultural/discursive meanings, that is, the existence of social dysphoria? How does this align with notions of authenticity? What about trans-affective meanings, and can there be an affective dysphoria?
- The complexities of distinguishing between dysphoric (distressed by body) and dysmorphic (where a part of the body is understood as seriously flawed) experiences – do these operate separately or at one and the same time?

Cultural imperialism of intelligibility

How does cultural imperialism operate through 'trans' – how might we impose the meaning of a culture onto/into a body? How do these lead to particular forms of intelligibility about 'the body' and 'trans'-ness? Can different forms of intelligibility be reconciled? Productive and reproductive cultural power was recognised as operating through:

- Organisations, including universities, the voluntary sector, medical/NHS settings.
- Processes of medicalisation and pathologisation, including the imperatives of discourses around 'dysphoria'.
- Therapeutic interventions, particularly in distinctive contexts such as talking therapies.
- Training, such as within therapeutic contexts.

Open territories: academia and activism

A notion of 'open territories' was developed to explore how academic and activist 'territories' may productively come into contact. Participants asked if online and offline territories exist separately and/or together, and how conversations across these spaces might work productively and in unity. Initially we discussed the realities of activism with limited resources – considering how the seminars could bring together activism and academia – before moving to consider where new spaces of exploration might be located, and how we might utilise academic resources to expand community spaces.

- Who is present and not present within different spaces, and who *can* be present? People of colour attending the seminars noted the whiteness of the space, something that is common within both the academy and within many 'mainstream' trans communities.
- We discussed how terminologies of 'trans' have been rooted in both academia and activism – for example, Riki Wilkins helped to promote the term 'genderqueer' as an activist *and* an academic.
- Questions were raised regarding the circulation of academic practice within trans communities, and what would enable trans communities to coalesce within academic spaces. How can academic work circulate beyond academia? What is trans pedagogy? Where and how does it emerge?
- Participants discussed the idea of 'crossover', with academic and activist sites coming together via social media, blogs and conferences.
- It was suggested that 'online' communities can offer strength to people in their 'offline' lives – there is a complex context to how this happens, drawing from interaction/activism/community that comes into existence via the internet.
- Online communities offer new ways of shaping biography, whereas in the past this was only available offline. But what happens where communities cannot access the internet, or where the local trans community is small and socially isolated? While progressive spaces in urban centres may offer a plurality of meanings about gender, sexuality and race, and accommodating communities within communities both offline and online, it may not be the same for those communities who are isolated or cannot access resources because of class or financial inequalities.

- There were questions around the meaning of 'transition' – in the past, did this mean 'blending' with the gender you were trying to acquire? The 1990s and the coming together of social activism and social media offered new challenges – the emergence of 'virtual worlds' and the existence of digital spaces such as Second Life where one can construct a new 'autobiographical' life.
- The culture of 'trans' has changed over time and the stories have altered: we no longer isolate stories of 'the transvestite' or 'the transsexual'. Rather, these have become expanded categories with people themselves offering new forms of self-definition.
- Are some stories 'normalised' – are certain stories reproduced more than others? Why? How? Who or what is invested in reproducing or retelling these stories? Are norms then reproduced via these stories? For example, documentaries on 'transition' are often written by cis journalists and offer very few interesting alternatives. The genderqueer story offers an alternative narrative that breaks with cis journalism.
- Who shapes the narratives and establishes normativity – and how does this sit alongside meanings for power of the trans-voice?
- Media narratives are difficult to reshape – what do these represent? What is being reported about trans lives and why? What happens to those left unrecorded?
- Is transition only attractive according to a heteronormative standard of beauty – what happens to other people? Mainstream visibility can be both useful and problematic – planning activity in this arena is difficult.
- Websites such as Genderfork offer diversity of identities and narratives that may reform and reshape biographies of the self. While one may have an 'offline' identity, by accessing Genderfork, a new identity may be lived/ narrated 'online'. This identity may eventually become a new 'offline' identity – can this be understood as a new form of 'transitioning' (biographical transitioning)?
- Narratives for young people are changing. This challenges the way children may be viewing themselves and how they are viewed by others. The experiences of trans and non-binary children and young people question how and where gender is being 'imposed'. How would gender be understood if self-imposed? How might we move away from pathologisation and investment in notions of childhood 'normality'?

Language and semiotics

Event participants discussed issues of language and semiotics. We explored how and when meanings become essentialised, regarding terminologies such as 'trans' and 'cis' as well as wider questions about gender and growing up:

- What does 'cis' mean and does it simply provide another social label, thereby limiting discussion? Does cis/trans mark a new binary?

- How do 'cis' experiences retain privilege to the extent that this can legitimate misgendering, pathologising and even torment?
- The death of trans teacher Lucy Meadows followed her deliberate and calculated misgendering by the press. Words are used to shape meaning – when trans lives and deaths are reported using the language of hate, anger and intolerance, what does this communicate to a wider cis audience?
- Media discourses can link trans people to notions of danger, particularly with regard to children. With Meadows being a school teacher, implications of trans-as-danger were used to inspire fear and mistrust in parents who might have children being taught by a trans person.
- Children's worlds are becoming open to trans meanings – are children 'very clearly' cis or trans at a young age? Is gender fixed at a young age?
- How do trans and cisgender children differ?
- Childhood may be understood as the beginning of an 'experiential dissonance', where meanings for embodying the social and understanding of 'self-hood' lend themselves to an experiential sense of gendered difference.
- Fantasy is important for enabling movement away from 'fixture', enabling self-reflection (sometimes facilitated through social media, for instance through the use of gendered avatars). Ideas of 'being' and 'becoming' may overlap, causing distortions of meaning that unsettle ideas of childhood and gender imposed by adults.
- What are the physical and social oppressions faced by children and do these underpin the way gender is configured as 'either' male or female? How does the child/adult binary reflect upon the meaning of male and/ or female? How is this narrated and imposed? This idea was linked to how clothing gives a 'felt sense' of gender and age – for example, clothing can lead to psychological distress if it does not align with a felt sense of identity, making social limitations evident.
- There is a colonisation of gender – a solidification of meanings about how gender should be presented and performed as a function of ethnocentricity.
- How do we think we are a gender? How might we not have a gender? At what point does gender 'become' fixed?
- There are normative pressures in everyday interactions. Emotions act as 'social values' and reflect norms that may be challenged by trans interactions and actions. For example, young children may not be displaying the emotions expected of their gender – what does this mean for the way gender is understood?

Queer theory, gender diversity and materiality

A series of questions were posed and attendees worked in groups to share a range of answers:

1. How useful is queer theory and politics for understanding gender diversity in your field or practice?

- There is a need to separate queer politics from queer theory in order to conduct social research. Ideas of 'category hostility' limit exploration. How do we construct identity categories and what do these mean?
- Queer activism and queer theory emerged via different routes but merged at some point – arguably reflecting the (limited) perspectives of white gay male activists within the HIV/AIDS arena and white female academics within North American English and Philosophy departments.
- 'Radical' queer logics move beyond binaries, but this agenda is not necessarily representative of all trans people.
- Queer may be understood as 'vanguardist': there is consequently a danger to how it might be seen by those unfamiliar with its ideas.

2. What does considering gender diversity in Southern contexts mean for UK-based thinking and practice?

- Research is conducted and questions are asked in ways that often rely on a Western framework of understanding.
- We may be imposing meanings for gender 'diversity' (including 'trans' language) in ways that need to be re-evaluated in light of global challenges.
- The categories in social circulation are there as part of the project of colonialism. How these are clustered together can impact on the way meaning is interpreted – this is especially relevant to research.
- A productive aim would now be to try and unfix or unsettle binaries that have previously been the objective of colonialism.

3. How do materialist approaches 'speak to' your work as academics, practitioners, policy makers?

- How are 'materialist' approaches translated? There was concern that the interpretations of everyday lived experience is translated through academic discourse and misses the voices of those 'speaking' about everyday life.
- How do researchers and practitioners understand people's everyday experiences, and is this understanding helpful?
- Is it accurate to say that queer theory ignores material reality – especially as it has moved on from original conceptualisations?
- How is a trans materiality subject to interpretation – how are meanings expanded? What theoretical forms are developing?
- What would a trans-citizenship look like in relation to human rights or a right to work? We need new approaches to understanding relational citizenships.
- Should there be more focus on small groups or larger contingencies in relation to research? Are sexual and gender minorities really being researched and interpreted and what meaning do their voices have for

the wider landscape of gender and sexual minority research, practice and policy?

Stand-alone ideas

These are simply ideas selected by rapporteurs for us to consider, asking us to question what may emerge from questioning in a form of Socratic pursuit:

- Is 'trans' an ideology? What type of ideological form might it take with input from different fields such as sociology, neurology, psychology and/or philosophy?
- Why are assumptions made within medical and professional circles about trans and non-binary experience not scrutinised, even as these professionals have the power to scrutinise trans and non-binary socialisation, everyday life, pasts and futures.
- How does therapy understand what is meant by gendered authenticity or inauthenticity if teaching around gender is not incorporated into training?
- What exactly is the Real Life Experience and why should anyone be subject to this? How might activists retaliate?
- What is body autonomy? Does this exist for trans and non-binary people?
- Is there agency within medical and therapeutic settings?
- Is body re-alignment of any form 'trans-ness'? How might this link to notions of dysphoria?
- Who shapes the meaning for an ethics of the body?

Conclusion

The seminar series was intense, fun and productive. The foregoing ideas and questions raised in our discussions show how we gradually navigated complexity of 'trans' discourse in the seminars, and grateful for the explorations of meaning that circulated at each event.

To follow up on the success of the seminar series, we were invited to produce a special issue of the journal *Sexualities*; the resulting articles were pre-published in January 2018, with a hard copy of the issue formally released in February 2019. In the process of assembling this issue – which could only feature a very limited number of articles – we were informed there had been an unprecedented number of submissions to the journal. Many of these were of a very high quality, and we did not want to see them rejected out of hand. We therefore decided to supplement that special issue with this edited text, which represents and explores in greater detail some, but not all, of the ideas listed in this chapter.

We hope in turn that you find the energy to pick up these ideas and make them your own – through forming groups to discuss them, inviting speakers, holding salons, going for a haircut at Open Barbers, and chatting with your friends, family and colleagues about gender, bodies, feelings and citizenship. We hope that you, too, might work to legitimise, validate, question, challenge and build on these concepts and hypotheses.

The seminar series, journal issue and book are also a testimony to our dear friend, Deborah Lynn Steinberg, who died in February 2017. She gave her life to generously offering ideas and words that we might transform the world we share. We miss you Deborah. xx

Index

ethnography; focus groups; interviews; Social Activity Method
misgendering 65, 103, 120–122, 130–132, 166, 201; in tabloid newspapers 126–128
Money, John 24–25
monsters 3–10, 14, 60–61, 151; 'monstered' 131; monstrosity 4–6, 20, 72
Mumsnet 117
Muñoz, Jose Esteban 183–184, 188

newspaper 53, 120, 122–124, 126–128, 130–132, 167–168, 172; *see also* media
non-binary 25–26, 50, 52, 64, 72, 81, 103–114, 165, 170
normative: categories 25; clothing 140; discourses of gender 2, 7, 103–104, 107, 110, 136, 139, 141–142, 144; defying normativity 2, 181, 186–188; ethics 179–180; heterosexuality 25; intimate labour 94; *vs.* nonnormative 183–185, 192; pressures 201; *see also* cisnormativity; transnormativity
North Carolina House Bill 2 114
Not Right 69, 71, 79
nourishment 8–10

online *see* internet

parenthood 25–30; *see also* reproduction; sterilisation
parents 104, 109, 117–118, 128–130, 135, 140, 143–146, 169, 201
partners 39, 63–64, 85–101, 111–112; heterosexual 85–101; lesbian 92, 99; queer 112; same-sex 66
pathologisation 1, 7, 29, 54–56, 166–167, 196, 198–201; of femininity 21; of lesbians 22
pathology 19–20, 139; psychopathology 19, 28
performance (artistic) 63, 69, 71, 82
performativity 14, 34–35, 37, 40–41, 43–44, 82, 87, 89–90, 95
picture books 135–137, 140, 144–147
possibility 1–4, 6–8, 13–14, 52, 63, 68, 72–75, 81–83, 103–104, 113, 119, 127–128, 151–152, 179–189; monstrous possibility 4, 6–8, 10
possibility models 1–3
power 7, 22, 36, 42, 56, 87, 88, 91, 108, 113, 118, 132n1, 167, 171, 174–175, 180–181, 187, 198; of monstrosity 5–6, 61

Pride: Nottinghamshire Pride 63, 65–66, 68, 78–83; Trans Pride 82
prisons 18, 22, 23, 29n4
pronouns 6, 98, 119–121, 125–126, 144; feminine 39, 125, 127; masculine 126–132; non-gendered 119
Proust, Marcel 20
psychiatry 1, 21, 23–26, 54

queer 1, 6, 28, 65–66, 68, 72, 81, 82, 111–112, 136, 201–202
Queer Fest 82
queer theory 201–202

race 4, 20–21, 28, 69, 79, 136, 170, 187
racialisation 170, 181
racism 5, 21, 185; *see also* anti-Semitism; eugenics; whiteness
Raymond, Janice 3
reassignment *see* health care; medicine; sex; surgeries
recognition 4; legal 3, 17, 24–26, 29, 97, 99; as non-binary 75, 113, 170; of partners 85–87, 94; social 35, 37, 40–41, 44, 64, 89, 113; as a woman 34–35, 43; *see also* gender labour; gender recognition (legal); women, recognition of being a
relationship: with family of origin 109; to others 72; to social norms 73, 198
relationship to partners *see* partners
reproduction 3, 17–20, 23, 26–29, 42; *see also* parenthood; sterilisation
reproductive justice 26–29
risk 5, 152, 166–171; *see also* vulnerability

safe(r) spaces 77, 80, 171–172
schools 18, 118, 122–123, 127, 129–130, 145–147
science fiction and fantasy 5–6, 72
sex 1–3, 7, 14, 20, 24, 34–36, 37, 43–44, 71–72, 114; 'sex change' 22, 24–26, 29, 42, 127; sex reassignment 27, 35, 40, 42–43; *see also* gender; sexuality
sexology 1, 20, 22–25, 37
sexuality 20–21, 27, 52, 86–88, 90, 92, 100, 146, 193; *see also* heterosexual, lesbian
sex work 20
Social Activity Method 45; *see also* methodology
social interactions 40, 64, 103–106, 113
somatechnics 179–183, 186–189
space 63–64, 69, 77, 171, 179–189, 199–200; binary 106; heterosexual 85,